The primary group

The primary group
a handbook for analysis and field research

Dexter C. Dunphy

University of New South Wales

with the collaboration of
David Fraser, Eric Neilsen, & Rev. Ricardo Zuniga, S.J.

APPLETON-CENTURY-CROFTS
EDUCATIONAL DIVISION
New York MEREDITH CORPORATION

Preface

It is always hard to specify where one's interest in a particular area of study began. My interest in groups was certainly kindled, however, by a youth club I formed and directed for some years while I was an undergraduate at Sydney University. It was in this group that I first became aware of group processes which seemed independent of, or at least not reducible to, the individual characteristics of group members. I was puzzled by the problem and so, when the opportunity presented itself through my courses in education, I moved fairly naturally into an interest in group dynamics. It was Bill Connell, Head of the Department of Education at Sydney University, who actually suggested that I study adolescent groups for my M.Ed. thesis. I remember going to him with a grandiose proposal to synthesize all existing research findings on small groups. I came away having agreed to carry out a field study of some adolescent groups.

While I was involved in carrying out the study, I couldn't rid myself of the idea that *someone* must have written a handbook for the guidance of field researchers involved in this kind of work. No amount of library research unearthed such a book. I was convinced from that time that such a book was needed and that it should outline the main variables a researcher could consider and show him how to measure the variables in terms sufficiently precise to make comparative work possible.

After finishing my M.Ed. thesis, I headed for the Department of Social Relations at Harvard to work with Freed Bales. Reading in the small groups area had left me convinced that most of the creative and quantitative research in small groups stemmed from Freed or his students, and that what I needed was an apprenticeship with him. I have never regretted my choice. Six years of working with Freed, first as a student and later as a colleague, has left me with an enduring admiration for his sensitivity and insight into group processes and a profound gratitude for his disciplined approach to group observation and analysis. This book owes much to his influence and his thinking.

After completing my Ph.D. dissertation, I began work on this book. I had by then accumulated many hours of systematic observation and research on a range of groups, and was even more convinced of the importance of moving laboratory techniques out of the laboratory and into the field. And so I decided this should be the kind of handbook I had once wanted and which could be put into the hands of those with intellectual and practical interests in studying primary groups.

I could not have finished the book without the enthusiasm and hard work of three very competent graduate research assistants at Harvard. Ricardo Zuniga, my giant Chilean friend and student, was involved in the first stages and contributed a great deal to the formulation of the model. Some of his writing survives in condensed form in chapter 3. David Fraser and Eric Neilsen followed Ricardo, and my indebtedness to them in terms of ideas, library research, and the actual writing of drafts of some parts of the book is great indeed. I have tried to indicate in the text where they contributed most. However, there is hardly an idea in the book which we did not debate at some time and even now, while 12,000 miles apart, we continue to exchange ideas. Although I am indebted to all these people, I take responsibility for the book as it stands for I have not hesitated to rework, revise, or scrap any suggestions or ideas that came my way.

The book would have been finished earlier but for my family and friends, and particularly my wife. There were many times when they jointly or individually undermined my devotion to writing about primary groups and, by recreating primary bonds, provided the kinds of direct and immediate satisfaction that make a man human. And that, after all, is what primary groups are about.

D. D.

Contents

basic standards or do they include all specific preferences and standards? Values and the Primary Group: *the relation of group values to the social environment.* Charting Group Values by Content Analysis. Non-functional Values and Primary Group Interests. Group Resources and Resource Processing: *the nature of resources; types of resource processing; the analysis of resource processing.*

The primary group

part I

TOWARD A
PRIMARY GROUP MODEL

associations formed w/in a group

chapter 1

The study of primary groups: An historical view

Introduction

Over our lifetime we spend much of our time in small groups. We are born into a family. As we grow older we venture out from our family into the play groups of childhood and later into the cliques and crowds of adolescence. We marry and establish a new family group of our own and participate in the work groups and leisure groups of adulthood. Out of the associations formed in these groups, we fashion and have fashioned in us a changing and developing conception of self; we learn ways of behaving appropriate to varied social situations, and we acquire a set of social values and attitudes that allow us to respond to the structure and pressures of the larger society about us.

harmony

This book deals with small personal groups of the kinds described above, with the ways in which they operate to shape the emerging personality of the individual, with the forms that they can take, and with the dynamic processes that operate in them. Most of all it focuses on ways to conceptualize and study such groups so that more may be learned about them.

For reasons which we will examine below, social scientists have devoted relatively little effort to a close and detailed study of such groups even though these groups play a vital part in creating human personality and maintaining the integration of the secondary structures of society. We use the term *primary group* to describe groups of this kind. The term was first introduced into social science by Charles Horton Cooley in 1909. At that time Cooley wrote in his book *Social Organization:*

Basis for your study on small groups

By primary groups I mean those characterized by intimate face-to-face association and cooperation. They are primary in several senses, but chiefly in that they are fundamental in forming the social nature and ideas of the individual. The result of intimate association, psychologically, is a certain fusion of individualities in a common whole, so that one's very self, for many purposes at least, is the common life and purpose of the group. Perhaps the simplest way of describing this wholeness is by saying that it is a "we," it involves the sort of sympathy and mutual identification for which "we" is the natural expression.[1]

In Cooley's definition, the word primary is used mainly in reference to the fundamental effect such groups have on the formation of the individual personalities of their members. Cooley makes this even clearer when he goes on to state: "The view here maintained is that human nature is not something existing separately in the individual, but a *group-nature or primary phase of society,* a relatively simple and general condition of the social mind." [2] Thus the term primary refers to the fact that such groups are the earliest kind of human association experienced by the maturing individual and also that the primary, or basic, human qualities are learned in them. Cooley's definition also makes it clear that the effect of such groups on the personalities of members derives from the internalization by them of a psychological representation or image of the group, and that such an identification is indicated by a strong emotional involvement with the group and its members.

In *Introductory Sociology,* written with Angell and Carr, Cooley specified five basic characteristics of primary groups:
1. Face-to-face association;
2. the unspecialized character of the association;
3. relative permanence;
4. the small number of persons involved;
5. the relative intimacy prevailing among the participants.[3]
Cooley himself did not designate larger, more formally organized groups as *secondary groups* but the latter term is now widely used and the two kinds of groups are frequently contrasted.

Later writers dealing specifically with the concept have attempted to modify it in various ways. For instance, Shils gave explicit and thoughtful attention to Cooley's criteria in his important work on the effects of primary group membership in the army in World War II[4] and in his more recent review of primary group research.[5] Shils argues that the existence of an implicit set of group norms is another necessary aspect of the primary group:

By 'primary group' we mean a group characterized by a high degree of solidarity, informality in the code of rules which regulate the behavior of its members and autonomy in the creation of these rules.[6]

Thus, although the primary group is a "small group" in the sense in which that term is used in the social sciences, it is a particular kind of small group. Small groups vary all the way from ad hoc collections of students assembled for a single experimental hour to long-term, emotionally involving, highly institutionalized groups such as families. It is the latter rather than the former kind of small group to which the term primary group refers.

However, the concept of a primary group is better thought of as a variable than as categorical. A group is primary insofar as it is based on and sustains spontaneous participation, particularly emotional involvement and expression. It also provides intrinsic personal satisfaction, that is, personal relationships in the primary group are considered valuable in themselves and not only as means to other ends. This element of intrinsic value is often lacking in formal secondary relations which are explicitly designed to be instrumental.

We define a primary group therefore as *a small group which persists long enough to develop strong emotional attachments between members, at least a set of rudimentary, functionally differentiated roles, and a subculture of its own which includes both an image of the group as an entity and an informal normative system which controls group-relevant action of members.* For Cooley, the important general categories of such groups in our society were "groups of the family, the playground, and the neighborhood." [7] We feel it is necessary to include other kinds of groups which meet our definition but which Cooley did not recognize. As we see it, the following general classes of groups are properly referred to as primary groups:

1. Families;
2. Free association peer groups of childhood, adolescence, and adulthood. This category would include delinquent gangs and some small, cohesive political elites ("cabals");
3. Informal groups existing in organizational settings such as classroom groups, factory work groups, small military units, and "house churches;"
4. Resocialization groups such as therapy groups, rehabilitation groups, and self-analytic groups.

This chapter reviews literature relevant to the study of these groups, treating it in a historical perspective. In the process, we hope to make clear what has been learned about the functions of primary groups, both for society and for the individual, and to suggest the major areas of knowledge, relating to primary groups, that are still unexplored.

The primary group in nineteenth-century social thought

Although the *term* primary group originated with Cooley, primary groups were given some attention in the writings of the early social thinkers of the nineteenth century, and nineteenth-century thought on the subject strongly influenced twentieth-century theory and empirical research. In nineteenth-century thought, the primary group was generally regarded as a vestigial remnant of traditional society and one that was being steadily eradicated by the massive social changes of the industrial revolution. Nineteenth-century European thought was generally more concerned with macroscopic structures of society and especially with the movement from status to contract, from Gemeinschaft to Gesellschaft, from mechanical solidarity to organic solidarity. The terms used differed from one theorist to another, but all were concerned with the disintegration of a traditional society characterized by intimate, cohesive, communal associations and its replacement by an impersonal, individualistic, and rationally oriented society characterized by a multitude of secondary organizations.

In his *Gemeinschaft und Gesellschaft* (1887), for instance, Toennies was concerned with describing and explaining the qualitatively different characteristics of social relationships in traditional and industrialized societies. Writing of positive social relationships, he distinguished two different types :

. . . the relationship itself, and also the resulting association, is conceived of either as real and organic life—this is the essential characteristic of Gemeinschaft (community)—or as imaginary and mechanical structure—this is the concept of Gesellschaft (society).[8]

As Toennies develops and contrasts these concepts it becomes clear that Gemeinschaft society is society based upon primary relations. "All intimate, private, and exclusive living together is understood as life in Gemeinschaft." [9] Family life is the prototype of Gemeinschaft society for the family is characterized by concrete face-to-face relationships and a common life marked by mutual understanding and concord. Traditional rural society was dominated by kinship relations and hence traditional society is seen as generally communal in character.

On the other hand, Gesellschaft society is directly associated with the development of urban centers and exists particularly in the realms of business, travel, and the sciences where relationships are more transitory and superficial. Gesellschaft society is individualistic, competitive, and contractual. Thus in Toennies' view the sphere of social activities marked by primary group relations was rapidly diminishing and being replaced by secondary relations of the kind found in economic organizations. Toennies' analysis is somewhat evaluative for he sees Gemeinschaft society as more "lasting and genuine," more "real and organic," while Gesellschaft society is seen as more "transitory and superficial," more "imaginary and mechanical." Thus Toennies' point of view was similar to that now held by contemporary critics of "mass society."

Simmel was another great German social thinker who contrasted small town life with metropolitan life. He portrayed small town life as engendering more deeply felt emotional relationships and metropolitan life as fostering a heightened awareness and intellectuality. Simmel's analysis is similar to Toennies' in that the relationships of small town life are seen as personal, while those of metropolitan life are seen as highly impersonal. The life of the small town is corporate life, firmly based on the personal relationships of primary groups, while life in the metropolis is marked by individualism.

Thus in Simmel's view the metropolis is essentially a collection of individuals :

. . . the individual has become a mere cog in an enormous organization of things and powers which tear from his hands all progress, spirituality, and value in order to transform them from their subjective form into the form of a purely objective life.[10]

Simmel was the only nineteenth-century theorist to present a systematically worked out set of hypotheses concerning the internal dynamics of primary groups. He held that the absolute numbers in a group fundamentally affect the character of relationships within the group. He went on, therefore, to examine in detail the significance of numbers in group life, paying some attention to the family and small religious sects, but concentrating on some of the ephemeral social groups such as transient teams engaged in games and brief social gatherings where interpersonal games such as coquetry prevailed.

Weber built upon Toennies' distinction between Gemeinschaft and Gesellschaft and the terms used were very similar : that is, Vergemeinschaftung or communal, affectual traditional society and Vergesellschaftung or associative, rationally motivated, voluntary association based on self-interest.[11] In characterizing the latter, Weber used the example of free market exchange. Communal society, as Weber described it, is a much wider concept than the primary group, but, nevertheless, Weber emphasized the associative base for most communal relationships, in particular "association in the same military unit, in the same school class, in the same workshop or office." [12] The essential character of a communal relationship involves "a common feeling" about a common situation and its consequences, "a feeling of belonging together," a "mutual relationship within the group as well as with the environment." Thus Weber, like Cooley, was most impressed by the feeling of mutual identification exhibited by members of primary groups.

Weber's analysis of particular kinds of primary groups was limited to the family which he analyzed within the framework of Wirtschaft and Gesellschaft so that he was primarily concerned with its economic functions. He defined the household community as "the most widespread economic group" and pointed out that it "involves a continuous and intensive communal action." He was particularly interested in the separation of economic functions from the family, which occurs with urbanization, but, because he was primarily interested in these functions, he did not specifically analyze the remaining functions performed by the family. While Weber's thought is less evaluative than that of the other theorists discussed so far, he accepted the basic idea that communal relationships were becoming more restricted in modern urban society.

It can be seen that the German theorists reviewed so far were in mutual agreement about the fact that developing urban life was becoming independent of primary group relationships and that these were being replaced by the more self-interested and detached relationships characteristic of economic life. This was not a uniquely German view but was widely shared by other social theorists of the time. The French thinker LePlay, for instance, was concerned with the significance of primary groups and particularly the extended family, in the maintenance of the social structure. LePlay's first work, in 1855, was a collection of monographs on the material and moral life of forty-five families—one of the first major empirical studies of concrete primary groups.[13] LePlay studied two kinds of families: those which were highly stable, traditional, and offered a basic security to the individual; and those which were disorganized, secular, and individualistic.

As a result of his study, LePlay distinguished three types of family. The unstable family type he saw as most likely to develop when traditions are overthrown (his examples were drawn mainly from postrevolutionary France). There were, however, two clear types of stable families. One type was patriarchal and was to be found in areas, such as the steppes, where economic and political conditions make such a family system extremely functional. The other stable type was the stem family where children leave home and start branch families. The characteristic of the traditional stem family is that the family home is maintained and those children who leave may return for security if necessary. It was LePlay's view that the stem family combined some of the best features of the patriarchal family with some of the freedom of movement and flexibility of adaptation shown by families in postrevolutionary France. But LePlay, like the other theorists we have reviewed, identified primarily with the old order and viewed the character of emergent urban society with considerable anxiety. LePlay viewed the patriarchal family as the basis of moral order and advocated that it be preserved, as far as possible, against erosion by contemporary forces.

Against this background, the social theories of Emile Durkheim, another great French thinker, stand in considerable contrast. Durkheim is unusual, not in his analysis of the evolution of primary group structures, but in his attitude towards this evolution. For unlike other theorists of the time, Durkheim identified with the emergent urban order. This is reflected even in the terms he used to characterize the familiar dichotomy of traditional and modern society. Here, by some strange irony of circumstance, he chose virtually the same terms as Toennies—*organic* and *mechanical*— but applied them in reverse. Thus for Toennies traditional society is organic while for Durkheim it is mechanical, for Toennies modern society is mechanical, while for Durkheim it is organic! Durkheim explained his use of these terms in the following way :

We call it that [mechanical] only by analogy to the cohesion which unites the elements of an inanimate body, as opposed to that which makes a unity out of the elements of a living body. What justifies this term is that the link which thus unites the individual to society is wholly analogous to that which attaches a thing to a person. The individual conscience, considered in this light, is a simple dependent upon the collective type and follows all of its movements, as the possessed object follows those of its owner. In societies where this type of solidarity is strongly developed, the individual does not appear.[14]

In his *Division of Labor in Society*,[15] Durkheim pursued the theme that the increasing differentiation of work roles and functions produces greater human individuality. He likened this process to the specialization of function in the higher animal species and hence labeled urban, specialized society as more "organic." He claimed that the "organic solidarity" of modern society was more human because more rational and more free because social rules reflect the interests of individuals and are subject to change to meet individual needs.

In his work on *Suicide* (1894),[16] Durkheim stressed the central importance of primary groups in maintaining the stability of the human personality. He carefully analyzed the causes of suicide and viewed it mainly as a result of the disruption of primary group relations. Stable group relations provide an individual with values and symbols transcending his own activity. When his primary groups disintegrate the individual becomes bereft of reasons for existence. The incidence of suicide in society, Durkheim declared, varies inversely with the degrees of integration of the social groups of which the individual forms a part.

However by his own analysis, the increasing division of labor was leading to a society characterized by secondary rather than primary associations. Consequently, Durkheim was faced with the problem of reconciling his positive attitude to contemporary society with his discovery of the importance of primary groups—in the process of dissipating—for social and personal cohesion. In the *Division of Labor in Society* (1833),[17] he first vigorously attacked the then current view of modern society, deriving from the work of many previous social theorists, concerned with the disintegration of primary group relationships. A "veritable sociological monstrosity" he calls the idea of "a society·composed of an infinite number of unorganized individuals that a hypertrophied state is forced to oppress and contain." He points out that a nation can only be maintained if, between the state and the individual, there is interposed a whole series of secondary groups with which individuals can identify and which link the individual to the central functions of social life. In his view, occupational groups would increasingly fill this role. Many of the functions previously performed by the family would be taken over by the "corporation of the future," for a corporation is not only a moral authority dominating the life of its members, but also a source of life which destroys individual egotisms and creates a solidarity based on interdependence. Thus Durkheim was positive in his attitude toward emerging secondary structures and secondary relationships and, unlike other social thinkers, did not identify with and idealize rural life. However, Durkheim did accept the basic analysis of emerging urban society as one characterized by a lack of primary groups and primary group relationships. Since he correctly perceived that the basis of social order was not force alone, but a moral solidarity stemming from membership in cohesive primary groups, he sought another source of social solidarity in the emergent secondary structures of the corporation. He stressed the fact that a new type of secondary structure was needed that could be suffused with some of the qualities of the primary group. He did not, however, seem aware of the fact that the primary group might continue to exist in new forms within secondary organizations and so provide the necessary source of social and personal integration. The rediscovery of the primary group in new forms within secondary structures and in the communal life of the new urban centers was to be the result of empirical investigations of the twentieth century.

Durkheim deliberately excluded a consideration of psychology from his sociological analysis; but with his central emphasis on the importance of internalized moral norms as the basis of the social order, it was inevitable that he should have given consideration to psychological issues. It was Durkheim's view that a psychology of a special type must be established, taking into account the actions and reactions which individual consciousnesses exercise on one another and the syntheses which are produced when consciousnesses are united. It was Sigmund Freud who, though virtually unaware of the theorists whom we have discussed, laid down the basis for just such a psychology.

In his analysis of the individual personality, Freud was driven to the view that the family into which the individual is born is responsible for the basic structure of the individual's personality. It is not our intention at this point to review psychoanalytic theory but it is interesting to note that Freud made significant attempts to understand the psychology of group processes as well as individual processes. In his *Group Psychology and the Analysis of the Ego*,[18] Freud focused on the relation of individual personality to the group. He found the key to group integration in the mutual identification of members with the group leader. In making this observation, Freud laid the basis for the future, more detailed work on social cohesion in both psychology and sociology. It is interesting to observe, however, that Freud used two secondary organizations, the army and the church, as his major examples in this work and does not indicate that he recognized or placed any great importance on primary groups as intermediate between the individual and these larger corporate structures. Despite this, as we shall show later, Freud's work has been a fruitful source of hypotheses for subsequent theory and research concerning primary groups, particularly for the family and the therapy group.

The study of primary groups in the twentieth century

In the twentieth century, the locus of social theory and research shifted from Europe to the United States. The pragmatic character of American thought led to a greater emphasis on research, although much of the research was guided by a theoretical standpoint derived from European thought. Many of the early American social theorists received their training in Europe and so they adopted current European ideas. At the same time, they were also influenced by the more pragmatic character of American culture and more prone to put their ideas to the test.

The discovery of new primary groups in urban community

The first school of sociology in the United States was founded in 1892 at the University of Chicago, and, from the inception of the school, thought and research pointed up the importance of primary groups. At Chicago, those involved in developing social theories were strongly influenced by pragmatism which emphasized the social nature of the self and the significance of others in personality development. John Dewey had a major impact on philosophy and education by emphasizing that meaning is developed in social groups through interaction with others. In sociology, G. H. Mead developed the theme that the individual is an active organism who, in taking on or acting the roles of others with emotional significance for him, develops a view of a "generalized other." This generalized other becomes the basis of the individual self and is the means by which the individual incorporates external reality into his own developing pattern of behavior. Thus, in Mead's view, the personality derives largely from primary group relationships, particularly the family.

As discussed earlier in this chapter, Cooley's view of the development of the self was basically congruent with this but he was much more explicit about the role of primary groups:

Human nature is developed and expressed in those simple, face-to-face groups that are somehow alike in all societies: groups of the family, the playground, and the neighborhood. In the essential similarity of these is to be found the basis, in experience, for similar ideas and sentiments in the human mind. In these, every-where human nature comes into existence. Man does not have it at birth; he cannot acquire it except through fellowship and it decays in isolation.[19]

Cooley even went so far as to pose the question: "What else can human nature be than a trait of primary groups?"

The Chicago school had a rich background of social theory suggesting the importance of the primary group, but from the first it had also a strong empirical emphasis in this direction. A year after the department was founded, the first head, A. W. Small, was joined by W. I. Thomas, principal author of *The Polish Peasant in Europe and America*.[20] This study was a massive investigation of Polish migration in Europe and America, which identified the disintegration of primary groups consequent upon migration and pointed out the resulting disorganization in the personal behavior of the migrants. Thomas's work was directly influenced by Mead and Cooley and also by the European analysis of the impact of urbanization on primary group relationships.

Robert Park, who joined the department about 1915, reinforced and structured this early emphasis on field work. Park was a student of Simmel's with a passionate concern for the analysis of urban life. It was Park who formulated a program for continued research into the urban life and culture of Chicago. Park argued that "the city [is] a laboratory or clinic in which human nature and social processes may be conveniently and profitably studied." [21] Park's interest was a direct outgrowth of European theoretical analysis for, in his words, "the growth of cities has been accompanied by the substitution of indirect, 'secondary,' for direct, face-to-face, 'primary' relations in the associations of individuals in the community." [22] He continues to explicate this point of view further by stating:

Touch and sight, physical contact, are the basis for the first and most elementary human relationships. Mother and child, husband and wife, father and son, master and servant, kinsman and neighbor, minister, physician, and teacher, these are the most intimate and real relationships of life, and in the small community they are practically inclusive. . . . In a great city, where the population is unstable, where parents and children are employed out of the house and often in different parts of the city, where thousands of people live side by side for years without so much as a bowing acquaintance, these intimate relationships of the primary group are weakened and the moral order which rested upon them is gradually dissolved.[23]

As a result of Park's inspiration, a continuing program of research into the ecology of Chicago was instituted and carried out, resulting in many published studies of different aspects of the city's life. These studies clearly documented the disorganizing effect of urbanization on the traditional family, but they also resulted in the discovery of a relatively new kind of primary group which seemed to have taken over many of the functions of the family. This group was the gang.

The lower class gang: The first major study of gangs was carried out by Thrasher, one of Park's students. Thrasher located and studied over 1,000 boys' gangs in Chicago and presented his findings in a classic volume *The Gang*.[24] Thrasher defined the gang as "an interstitial group originally formed spontaneously and then integrated through conflict." Gangs are clearly primary groups for, according to Thrasher, they develop "a tradition, unreflective internal structure, esprit de corps, solidarity, morale, group awareness, and attachment to a local territory." Thrasher was able to delineate clearly the influence of membership in these primary groups on the facilitation of delinquent actions. Clearly these groups were socializing their members into delinquency.

Thrasher's work was continued by others—in particular by Furfey, Landesco, Shaw, McKay, and Tannenbaum. Shaw and McKay,[25] for instance, showed that delinquency could be viewed as a normal activity in the culture of a slum ("interstitial") neighborhood and that most offenses—almost 95 per cent—were committed with others in a gang. Tannenbaum made a more detailed analysis of the ways gangs induct members into criminal subcultures and again emphasized the familiar theme that the gang is a by-product of family disorganization :

The family, by its internal weakness, may have been a contributory factor. The father or mother or an older brother may have been delinquent or there may have been a sharp conflict of opinions and attitudes in the family, or constant bickering and incompatibility between the parents, or the father may have died and the mother forced away from the home so that the children were left unsupervised, or an ignorant and poverty-stricken mother may have encouraged the child to bring in food or money whether earned or stolen, or the father may have been a drunkard and given to seriously mistreating the child and breaking down the loyalty and unity which are essential to the slow maturation of systematic habit formation. In these and innumerable other examples that might be cited of family inadequacy we have a source for the acceptance by the child of his playmates—and gang affiliates—*as a substitute for the home*.[26]

Thus it became clear that, in lower class urban life, the gang was replacing the family as the adolescent's and young adult's primary identification group. This general picture was strongly supported by a later study, influenced by, but not carried out at, the Chicago school. This was W. F. Whyte's *Street Corner Society,*[27] a participant-observer study of a young adult gang and its social environment in Boston. But Whyte's study represented a theoretical break with the Chicago tradition in that it made clear what was implied by the facts uncovered in the Chicago research, that is, that lower class urban culture is not so much disorganized as organized differently from middle class society. The research documented again the restricted role of the family and the extended role of the gang in influencing the socialization of adolescents and young adults. "There was," said Whyte, "a kid's gang on Norton Street for every significant difference in age. There was a gang that averaged about three years older than Doc; there was Doc's gang . . . ; there was a group about three years younger . . . ; and there was a still younger group . . . ."[28]

Studies such as those reviewed above stimulated attempts to construct theories to explain and predict the emergence of delinquent gangs and the kinds of delinquent behavior they would habitually exhibit. Theories proposed have approached the problem from both psychological and sociological directions. More work seems to have been done from sociological directions, and most of it is based on the theories of Emile Durkheim and Robert Merton. Merton's viewpoint was developed from Durkheim's classical theory in the area of another form of deviant behavior, suicide. Merton's argument is that U.S. society, in particular, maintains the ideology of an open-class system and the possibility of "success"— economic affluence and social prestige—for everyone, but that the structure of U.S. society makes this unrealistic for most lower class members. The combination of high success aspiration, with little opportunity for achievement, creates *anomie* among those whose aspirations are blocked. Merton holds that when legitimate access to social goals is denied, illegitimate means of achieving the same goals will be used. High rates of criminal behavior are the result.[29]

Cloward and Ohlin have developed Merton's theory farther.[30] They hold that there is differential access to illegitimate means as well as to legitimate means, and that a major variable which determines this is the relative integration of the community—criminal and non-criminal—where disadvantaged youths are growing up. We will examine this theory more closely in chapter 2.

A somewhat different theoretical orientation has been adopted by Cohen, and more recently by Miller.[31] Both of these authors put forward an argument that is, at least on the surface, contradictory to the theories of relative deprivation reviewed above. The argument essentially denies that lower class adolescent culture accepts middle class goals and values but necessarily must use alternative means of pursuing these. It is argued instead that lower class youth culture has its own distinctive values and goals that are different from those of the middle class. Cohen argues that this is more characteristic of youth culture than adult culture and that the delinquent tradition is kept alive by successive age groups. As Cohen sees it, this tradition is a revolt against exposure to the middle class norms of teachers, police and other authoritative representatives of more privileged society. Miller argues for a strong, semi-independent cultural tradition in the lower class as a whole. For Miller, "lower class culture is a distinctive tradition, many centuries old with an integrity all of its own." [32] We shall evaluate these different theories in a wider perspective when we discuss the integration of primary groups into their social context, but it is sufficient here to note that the conflict in explanatory models exists and is not yet fully resolved.

The middle class adolescent peer group: The Chicago studies focused mainly on lower class deviant behavior and did not investigate middle class or upper class society to determine whether cultural equivalents of the group occurred elsewhere in the class structure. But from about the 1930s on, there was increasing attention devoted by social scientists to the emergence of a general urban youth culture. The Conference of the Research Planning Committee of the American Sociological Society in 1934 and in its subsequent reports [33] emphasized the necessity for research in this area, but in fact little research was initiated. The first major contributions to social theories about adolescence appeared in 1944 with the publication of the Forty-third Yearbook of the National Society for the Study of Education and the November 1944 issue of the *Annals* of the American Academy of Political and Social Science.[34] In these volumes, Davis, Tryon and others treated youth culture as a series of transitional institutions and emphasized the important socializing functions of the peer group in adolescence. In 1949 *Elmtown's Youth* [35] by Hollingshead appeared along with Havighurst and Taba's *Adolescent Character and Personality*.[36] For the first time an empirical sociological study had been undertaken to investigate the social life and culture of normal middle class teenagers.

Hollingshead located 259 cliques in Elmstown and classified them into three types on the basis of function : school, recreational, and institutional cliques. He identified the modal sizes of these types of cliques and concluded that school grade—or age—and social class in the community were prime determinants of clique membership. Beyond that, commonly shared likes and dislikes drew the members of a particular clique together. He noted however that "although members of different cliques may be enemies in a social sense, they commonly work together when an issue involving class interests is at stake." [37]

As a result of empirical and reflective studies, the importance of the peer group in the socialization of the urban adolescent was clearly recognized. Ausubel stated this succinctly in 1958 :

Like home and school, the peer group is an important socializing, enculturative, and training institution. It is here that children learn most of their poise in dealing with persons outside the intimate family circle; acquire approved techniques of sociability, self-assertion, competition and cooperation, and develop sensitivity to cues indicative of group expectations, censure, and approval. By interacting with their peers they learn the functional and reciprocal basis of rules and obligations, how to play differentiated roles, and how to subordinate their own interests to group goals. Only the peer group can furnish suitable models and occasions for children to observe and practice the social skills and behaviors they must know in order to enact their appropriate age and sex roles both in their subcultures and in the wider community.[38]

More recent books, such as Smith's *American Youth Culture*,[39] have continued to stress the importance of examining the structural aspects of adolescent life, but research lags behind such exhortations, as Smith himself points out :

However in spite of the awakening alertness to the importance of youth culture phenomena, sociological structures involved in the socialization of the adolescent are still overlooked because the theory finding research is not gauged to uncover and disclose these structures. Over-emphasis on the formal structures of the family, school, and church, as well as adult patterned recreational and character-building organizations, has concealed the informal institutions that characterize youth culture.[40]

Two studies exist which are first attempts to fill the gap described by Smith. I made a study of adolescent leisure-time peer groups in which I mapped the informal structure of adolescent groups and examined some of their dynamics.[41] In this field investigation of adolescent peer groups, I was able to locate hierarchies of groups in suburban areas and to study their component structures and dynamics over an extended period of time. Networks of cliques were discovered within each hierarchy and there were clique leaders and crowd leaders who maintained the structure through their reciprocal role relationships. These leaders were taken as role models by their followers and exerted pressure on their followers to maximize the rate at which members learned a mature heterosexual role. Here was a clear example of the process of group formation which Freud postulated in outlining his group psychology, but I examined the process in primary groups rather than in the secondary groups which Freud used to illustrate his arguments.

More recently, Sherif and Sherif [42] have published a book summarizing their field research into the leisure time peer groups of adolescent boys. This research attempted a more systematic sampling of social class environments than my study. The study indicates that peer group values vary systematically from one sociocultural setting to another and that peer groups exhibit a differentiated status structure which operates to induce social conformity within the groups.

Studies of adolescence were begun on the basis of European social theories which posited the increasing disorganization of family life and the possible disappearance of primary groups in the emergent industrial culture of modern cities. These studies led, however, to the discovery that the progressive removal of the function of adolescent socialization from the family did not result in a huge aggregation of atomized individuals being absorbed into the vast secondary structures of modern society. Instead it resulted in the creation of a new range of primary groups in communal settings—groups sufficiently integrated with each other and sharing enough common values to be referred to as "youth culture." The formation of a youth culture had been interpreted as a consequence of family disorganization or disintegration but, although the family was changing form, it showed no signs of disappearing. Rather it was becoming more specialized. It retained the function of childhood socialization but relinquished much of the responsibility for adolescent socialization to the adolescent peer group and to the school.

The adult peer group: With the rise of the nuclear family and the disappearance of the extended family, the responsibility of the parents for early socialization of the child has actually increased. Grandparents, uncles and aunts, sisters and brothers are far less often available to mind and train the child. Similarly the mobility of the nuclear family in urban society increases the dependence of the spouses on each other, and the nuclear family, therefore, assumes an increased responsibility for the stabilization of the adult personality.[43] This process has been accompanied by the rise of suburbia which provides an environment specializing in these two functions. Suburbia is a result of the splitting off of economic functions from the family. In the proliferating reaches of suburbia and other community settings, social scientists began to discover that primary groups are important for parents as well as their children.[44]

What these studies showed was that social class expectations are also mediated to the adult through primary groups. Thus one of the best indications of social class equality is frequent visiting between families, particularly informal, casual visiting. Davis, Gardner, and Gardner, for example, writing of adult cliques, point out that:

. . . these persons conceived of themselves as being members of a small very intimate group—"our little crowd" (the clique)—to which, for certain types of affairs, they were willing to add a few more couples to form "our large crowd" (the extended clique). Beyond these there was a somewhat wider circle of persons with whom they were willing to participate, who could not be ignored, and whose opinion mattered, but with whom they were not willing to associate intimately.

A very large affair should include the entire extended clique and to omit a member suggested discrimination. Members of the wider participation circle, however, might be deliberately excluded and there would be no ill feeling, while beyond this latter group there were types of people who, under no conceivable conditions, could be invited to a social affair.[45]

In their particular study, the authors identified sixty cliques, extended cliques, and intermediate groups and concluded that clique behavior was definitely "class-typed." Each clique had definite behavior patterns of the particular class level in which it functions.

In upper class and middle class settings, the family seems to be the central component in informal adult peer associations. These informal associations may also be supplemented by membership in formal voluntary associations. Wright and Hyman demonstrate that the latter tendency is most characteristic of urban, middle class parents with children of school age but that, even with this group, the notion of Americans as a nation of "joiners" is considerably exaggerated.[46] Lower class communal interaction, by contrast, seems to take place on a much more sex-differentiated basis. Adult peer groups at this level tend not to be composed of multi-family units. Adult men meet either in a fixed locale, in bars or on street corners, while cliques of women meet in their homes, or chat over fences, from windows, or in doorways.[47]

Communal cliques at all levels of society select members along social class lines. Even within social classes such groups maintain even finer distinctions which tend to stabilize intra-class structure. For instance, Hollingshead and Redlich[48] describe the social cliques of the upper class of New Haven, Connecticut. They use the term "core group" to refer to families whose ancestors have been in Class I for several generations and the term "arrivists" to refer to the families whose male heads have almost achieved membership in Class I in their own generation.

Three distinct types of clubs characterize this stratum: the one-sex club, the family club, and the special interest club. "Gentlemen's" and "ladies'" clubs represent the first type. The family club is designed to meet the social and recreational needs for all family members. The special interest club is for persons with particular tastes and hobbies. Three "gentlemen's" clubs maintain club houses where the members may meet, relax, read, have a drink at the private bar, or eat with their equals. Two of these clubs are "exclusive"; the acknowledged members of the core group, the Gentile professional and business elites, are divided between them. No exclusive "ladies'" club maintains a club house. Their members meet in private homes, parish houses, or other clubs. The most exclusive one meets in the home of some member. It has no name other than the one the members have traditionally accorded themselves, namely, Our Society. This is truly a core group of equals where memberships are passed down from mothers to daughters and daughters-in-law with few exceptions. There are a half-dozen acceptable family clubs in the community, but Gentile members of the core group are concentrated in one, the *arrivists* are clustered in another, professional families in two others, and Jewish *arrivists* and professionals in another. Several yacht, fishing, hunting, and beach clubs are maintained by Gentile families; in like manner groups of Jewish families maintain beach and country clubs. Some 97 percent of the Class I families have at least one membership and 75 percent belong to two or more clubs. The husband belongs to a men's club, the wife to a ladies' club, and the family to a family club. A relatively small number of leisure time interests are represented in the special interest clubs—tennis, golf, polo, sailing, fishing, and hunting among the men and the raising of flowers and purebred livestock or thoroughbred horses among both sexes.[49]

Thus we can view a social class as a kind of "galaxy" of primary groups. Membership in the "galaxy" is determined by a combination of historical, geographical, and economic factors but the galaxy itself is only very loosely organized. Its organization consists in the more or usually less formalized relationships between families, peer associations, and clubs. Memberships in these cliques, and relationships between cliques, are constantly shifting and reforming, groups are solidifying and disintegrating as individuals and families move and mature. Despite this fluidity, there is usually enough stability over a period of time for the development of different life styles which are internally consistent within a particular social class. Communal primary groups ensure that these life styles are transmitted to the incoming members of the social class, that is, to those individuals who are born into the class and are maturing within it and to those individuals who were born outside it but are achieving membership in it. The picture presented shows that adult and youth clique structures support social class stability.

The discovery of primary groups in organizations

Nineteenth century social theorists correctly perceived the massive changes in traditional family and community life of their time, but misperceived the significance of these changes. We suggest that what they interpreted as the lessening importance and possible disappearance of primary groups can now be seen as the first stages in the differentiation and proliferation of primary group structures accompanying urbanization and industrialization. Through these changes, the family became more limited in size, but the nuclear family gained increased responsibility for the initial socialization of the child. At the same time it lost a large part of its responsibility for the latter stages of socialization. Students of modern communities discovered, and have begun to chart, the structure of the extensive youth culture which has emerged to take over many of the functions of adolescent socialization. It is clear that the adolescent subculture is rooted firmly in

Durkheim

primary groups which play an important part in socializing youth for the demands of the new social order. And it is also clear that in many communities, similar groups, existing among adults, tend to solidify the social class structure and to influence the political life of communities. Thus the evidence we have so far indicates that primary groups in communal society have undergone a process of differentiation rather than extinction.

But the problem which Durkheim in particular had posed was the problem of the integration of the individual within the multiplicity of secondary organizations which represent the backbone of urban industrial culture. Social scientists were somewhat slower to study organizations than they were to study communities.

Industrial organizations: Elton Mayo must be given the major credit for directing the attention of social scientists to the study of industrial organizations. In 1926 the Harvard Department of Industrial Research was set up within the Harvard Graduate School of Business Administration. In 1927 Mayo began the first major study initiated by the department. This study was conducted at the Hawthorne factory of the Western Electric Company over a period of five years. The company was interested in the relation of worker fatigue to productivity and had already carried out some inconclusive experiments concerning the effects of lighting on productivity, when they called in the Harvard researchers under Mayo. The main investigator in the field was Fritz Roethlisberger who collaborated with William Dickson (head of the Western Electric Company's Employee Relations Research Department). The result of their research was subsequently published under their joint authorship as *Management and the Worker*.[50] This work has had far reaching and continuing effects on management policies and social theory.[51]

The field experiments described in *Management and the Worker* began as an attempt to assess the effects of such factors as lighting and incentives on productivity, but finally led the investigators to the point where they regarded such factors as less important in this regard than the normative systems of the informal primary groups of workers within the factory. These primary groups were viewed as mechanisms by which the workers were able to exercise some control over the environment and so protect themselves from excessive demands by management. They were also seen as providing important social rewards for the individual workers. Traditional management theory regarded the workers in a factory as a collection of isolated individuals solely oriented to maximizing their earnings. In the 1920s, in particular, European and American managerial theory emphasized rational principles for the efficient structuring and functioning of developing organizations. This early theory, for example, pointed out that the number of men who can be closely supervised by a particular superior is extremely limited. From this observation a "principle" relating to "span of control" was developed which advocated that the ratio of supervised to supervisor should be minimized. Formal organization charts were developed to prescribe relations between positions in the organization. Time and motion studies were carried out to determine the most efficient ways to organize the workers' physical environment to maximise productivity.

The work of Mayo and his associates presented a fundamentally different picture of the organization, emphasizing the fact that the rewards sought by workers were far wider in scope than money alone. Productivity was shown to depend on the worker's integration into an informal work group and on his perception of the social status of the work group in the organization. Thus, as Shils has pointed out in reviewing this work :

His [the worker's] attitude depended on whether he felt himself to be part of a respected group, i.e., one which was apparently respected by the representatives of management with whom the group came into contact. Without the latter relationship, the workers felt themselves to be viewed with either indifference or hostility, and in that event they responded with hostility. As a result, for most workers the absence of a personal relationship with some symbol or agent of the management resulted in a reduction of output below the level made possible by their skill and intelligence.[52]

This new "organic" view of the organization has continued to develop through a series of field studies carried on over the years by various faculty members of the Harvard Business School and others elsewhere who have been influenced by their work.

W. F. Whyte followed his *Street Corner Society* by a penetrating analysis of human relations in the restaurant industry.[53] He analyzed the kitchen as a small work unit and paid particular attention to the way in which human relations were influenced by technology, the physical layout of the restaurant, and different patterns of supervision. Much of Whyte's experience in this and other industries is summarized in an article he published in 1951 under the title "Small Groups and Large Organizations;"[54] the particular focus in the article is on the effects of primary work groups on organizational effectiveness.

Whyte's restaurant study was followed by a series of field analyses of work groups in a variety of settings. Homans[55] studied a group of ten "cash posters" in a clerical group; Lombard[56] studied a group of twenty sales girls in a large department store; Walker, Guest, and Turner[57] studied the interaction of foremen with their work groups; Zaleznik[58] studied a work group of fourteen men and their foreman in a machine shop, and later, with Christensen and Roethlisberger,[59] the formal and informal relationships among fifty workers in a medium-sized manufacturing company. All these studies are notable for the use of systematic first-hand observation of social interaction between workers on the job. With the work of these researchers, a new foundation was laid for an industrial psychology based on something more than armchair theorizing, simplistic moralizing, and anecdotal information.

The "human relations" approach has consistently stressed the importance of informal relationships, particularly affective relationships. The studies document the fact that managerial planning which does not take these factors into account can have important *unintended* consequences influencing the attainment of managerial goals. The studies have been confined mainly to the lower strata of organizations with blue collar and clerical workers receiving most attention. The role of the foreman has received particular attention because the foreman's role was readily seen as the crucial link between the work group and the larger organization. The peculiarly stressful nature of the foreman's role has been well documented.[60] As the "man in the middle" he is caught between the expectations of management and the expectations of the workers. How he reacts to this tension—by accepting it or trying to resolve it—is a key variable in the work group into the larger secondary structure.

Studies of executive groups are rare. There are some exceptions, such as Caudill's study of a psychiatric hospital,[61] and my own study of executive decision making groups (reviewed in Chapter 8). It is too early yet to be certain which particular characteristics mark executive groups off from groups of workers lower in the hierarchy, but in the next chapter we shall advance a theory predicting some of these characteristics.

The Tavistock Institute of Human Relations in London is another important center of research which has contributed to our knowledge of the operation of primary groups in industrial settings. The Institute was founded in 1947 by social scientists who had worked together in World War II. Their experience in the war suggested that applied social science could make a useful contribution to organizational effectiveness in peacetime and so they founded the Institute to undertake research, and to consult and teach in the field of the social sciences. They were aware of the work of Mayo and others at the Harvard Business School and, in fact, the two centers have kept up a lively exchange of ideas and personnel.

Two major studies at Tavistock have made a particularly decisive contribution to the understanding of the functioning of primary work groups in organizations. One was carried out by Trist and a number of associates [62] and focused on the national coal industry in Britain; the other study by Rice [63] considered the organization of weaving mills in India. Diverse as these studies might appear, they nevertheless led to similar conclusions concerning the functions of work groups. We will summarize these studies in some detail.

Trist describes traditional coal mining methods in Britain as follows: Miners formed groups of three by mutual selection and were allocated to a particular work place by drawing lots. Each miner worked a different shift and performed three basic steps—coal getting, tub filling and advancement of the coal face. The three team members were paid jointly on the basis of output. Trist and his co-workers were able to institute a comparative study of the relative effectiveness of different forms of the required organization, some spontaneously evolved variations, and an innovation called "composite longwalling." They showed that the plan designed by management was inferior to the composite longwalling scheme. The new organization by management led to extreme specialization where the workers lost sight of the whole cycle, were too concerned with performing their own specialized duties to correct imbalances, and competed with each other for special privileges and pay increases. Composite longwalling maintained the common payout for the three man group, tied pay to production, allowed one man to perform more than one task, and provided for more work group regulation of the mining cycle. As a result, output was higher, absenteeism and accident rates were lower, and there was less need for managerial intervention. Thus the longwall method designed the job so as to increase the solidarity of the work group and give the work group more control over its environment. It also ensured that work group goals would be tied in with management goals by relating pay to production.

In his study of the organization of Indian weaving mills, Rice showed that a similar process of job specialization resulted when automatic work methods were introduced and that this led to similar problems. Because tasks were interdependent, disorganization resulted from differentiation along mechanical lines. Rice himself reorganized the automatic shed so that work groups of seven could be responsible, as groups, for sixty-four looms and the supporting tasks needed to keep them running effectively. The work groups developed their own leaders who undertook the organization of their groups and as a result efficiency and quality increased. Non-automatic weaving was also reorganized in an experimental shed established for the purpose. Workers in non-automatic weaving had been performing a whole task but they were socially isolated. In this case the task was broken down into specialized sub-tasks which were performed by different men now working in a group where interaction and cooperation were required. The experimental system established higher performance norms which spread to other parts of the mill. At the end of the experimental period, production and quality had increased markedly and individual earnings had also risen sharply.

Haberstroh has written an excellent summary of the main implications of empirical research at Tavistock which relates to the utilization of work groups in the planning of industrial organizations. We quote it here as an apt conclusion to the research we have reviewed in this section :

A work group that has been allowed to develop a sense of group identity, autonomy, and cohesiveness is a sound social structure for the acceptance of responsibility and interdependence. If the group can be given a psychologically complete task in an adequately factorized organizational scheme, these qualities can be utilized to make the work group a fundamental organizational component of known capabilities and characteristics. Among the necessary characteristics are that the group has successfully internalized the task model and role system appropriate to its functions. To regulate successfully, the group needs full information on its own performance relevant to goals and to any factors that may contribute thereto. Under these circumstances the group can be expected to respond not only with a suitable level of work but also by taking responsibility to a substantial extent for self-regulation of efficiency and effectiveness.[64]

Military organizations: The studies reviewed so far have been primarily undertaken in business, industrial and governmental bureaucracies. But there is a further tradition of organizational analysis which has centered about the problem of maintaining the morale and combat effectiveness of military personnel in armies. Morale has always been a central issue in military organizations, and military organizations have often been organized in small units. However, it was not until World War II that the crucial role of primary groups in maintaining military morale and effectiveness was seriously studied.

A number of excellent studies,[65] appearing since World War II, present information on the role of primary groups in military organizations in both the allied and German armies. However, we shall focus on Shils and Janowitz's study [66] of the Wehrmacht because their conclusions are most succinctly stated and are representative of those found in other studies.

Shils and Janowitz set out to explain the reasons why German army units continued fighting even after central command disintegrated, supplies ceased, and it was obvious that German capitulation was inevitable. During this time, there was remarkably little desertion or active surrender by individuals or groups. It had been suggested that the morale and resistance of the German forces could be attributed to the effectiveness of the Nazi propaganda machine. Shils and Janowitz reviewed the extensive studies made by the Intelligence Section of the Psychological Warfare Division of SHAEF and came to conclusions which challenge this assumption. They stated their basic hypotheses, which are confirmed by their analysis, as follows :

1. It appears that a soldier's ability to resist is a function of the capacity of his immediate primary group (his squad or section) to avoid social disintegration. When the individual's immediate group, and its supporting formations, met his basic organic needs, offered him affection and esteem from both officers and comrades, supplied him with a sense of power and adequately regulated his

relations with authority, the element of self-concern in battle, which would lead to disruption of the effective functioning of his primary group, was minimized.

2. The capacity of the primary group to resist disintegration was dependent on the acceptance of political, ideological, and cultural symbols (all secondary symbols) only to the extent that these secondary symbols became directly associated with primary gratifications.

3. Once disruption of primary group life resulted through separation, breaks in communications, loss of leadership, depletion of personnel, or major and prolonged breaks in the supply of food and medical care, such an ascendancy of preoccupation with physical survival developed that there was very little "last ditch" resistance.

4. Finally, as long as the primary group structure of the component units of the Wehrmacht persisted, attempts by the Allies to cause disaffection by the invocation of secondary and political symbols (e.g., about the ethical wrongness of the Nationalist Socialist system) were mainly unsuccessful. By contrast, where Allied propaganda dealt with primary and personal values, particularly physical survival, it was more likely to be effective.[67]

From the point of view of the conscripted soldier, this had the following meaning :

For the ordinary German soldier the decisive fact was that he was a member of a squad or section which maintained its structural integrity and which coincided roughly with the *social* unit which satisfied some of his major primary needs. He was likely to go on fighting, provided he had the necessary weapons, as long as the group possessed leadership with which he could identify himself, and as long as he gave affection to and received affection from the other members of his squad and platoon. In other words, as long as he felt himself to be a member of his primary group and therefore bound by the expectations and demands of its other members, his soldierly achievement was likely to be good.[68]

The authors pointed out that the German general staff instituted a replacement system which maintained the integrity of the primary groups in the army. Units which had undergone a victory were maintained as units as far as possible and when replacements were necessary, the entire personnel of a division would be withdrawn from the front as a unit. Replacements were made while the unit was out of the front line so that a unit was given time to assimilate new members before going into battle again.

Janowitz and Little also suggest[69] that the existence of cohesive primary groups does not necessarily contribute to the goals of the military organization. If this is to happen the primary group must actively espouse the goals of the larger organization of which it is a part. Essentially the same conclusion was reached by Speien. He noted that studies of U.S. soldiers during World War II showed that they had little knowledge of and little verbalized commitment to the war.[70] He then raised the question :

why, if this were true, did they fight so well? He concluded, on reviewing the evidence available, that this was due to the fact that primary group relations sustained morale and supported a generalized commitment to the military and its goals. Janowitz and Little illustrate this with the case of segregated Negro units in World War II, which were very cohesive but developed "defensive norms" which broke with the general commitment because these groups interpreted military authority as depreciating their personal dignity. Shils has also argued along the same lines stating that "primary group solidarity functions in the corporate body to strengthen the motivation for the fulfilment of substantive prescriptions or sense of obligation. . . . it cannot be said that goals are set by membership in the primary group but only that efforts to achieve the legitimate, formally prescribed goals may be strengthened by such membership." [71]

A key position in terms of the integration of primary group goals and organizational goals is that of formal leader of the unit, for example, the platoon leader. The leader occupies the classical position of middle man similar to the role of foreman of a work team in industry. He must be close enough to the men for them to identify with him and yet at the same time he must also represent the demands of higher authority. Shils has stressed the enlisted man's desire for a protective personal relationship with an authority figure in this kind of position, and emphasized the effectiveness of "an exemplary and protective leader" in raising morale in U.S. military units.[72]

Shils and Janowitz give evidence which indicates that the primary group in the army acts as a family surrogate, and that a man's real family loyalties were one of the most substantial threats to the solidarity of the army unit.[73] The captured German soldiers themselves identified with the family-like nature of their units with statements like : "We were a big happy family." In addition, it became clear that soldiers were most likely to desert while on furlough, or after receiving distressing news from their families. Similarly the members of units were most likely to discuss surrendering among themselves after concretely recalling family experiences. Because of these factors, families of soldiers were instructed to avoid mentioning family deprivations in letters to the front and, as Allied bombing of the civilian population became more severe, personal messages to the front were censored to prevent distressing family news reaching the men. Thus the soldier was able to transfer his primary loyalties to his unit while physically with the unit, providing he felt secure about his family. While actually with his family, his loyalties to them tended to be reactivated at the expense of those to his military unit. Interestingly enough, it was those men who had the most normal identification pattern in the family who were able to identify most firmly with the military unit. This same point is also supported by evidence presented by Grinker and Spiegal.[74] It is the person with a faulty family identification pattern who is most likely to be a deviant member of a military unit and a deserter to the other side in a stress situation.

A limiting variable influencing the cohesiveness in military organizations, as in factories, is the technology with which the military unit is working. Different weapons systems require different kinds of team relationships. A submarine, for example, demands continued close contact among the crew over lengthy periods of time and virtually cuts off outside social contact. An airplane is similar but returns more quickly to base and so allows more frequent contact with non-crew members. By contrast, the members of a rifle squad in battle may readily lose contact with one another and so experience a sense of isolation from the expectations and support of other group members.

Evidence to clinch the importance of primary group cohesion as a basis for morale and effectiveness comes from those German units whose integrity was not established or adequately maintained. As the war progressed, it became increasingly difficult to maintain the integrity of primary groups. The survivors of groups suffering severe casualties were regrouped and new units of recruits were thrust directly into battle without the opportunity of solidifying primary group ties. It was in units of these kinds that desertions and active surrender occurred. In these situations the individual seemed to readily remove his emotional ties and identifications from the group and refocus them on himself. The individual regressed to a narcissistic state and became concerned with saving his own skin—a marked contrast to situations where men in intact primary groups would fight to the bitter end.

Shils has argued that the primary group reduces a soldier's fear of death and injury by counterposing against such fear a need for approval by his comrades.[75] As evidence he quoted the fact that replacements to U.S. combat units were more likely to say "prayer helps a lot" whereas veterans looked to concrete support from their comrades.

Thus ideology had only an indirect effect on fighting effectiveness in both the U.S. and the German armies. The crucial variable was the degree of preservation of the cohesive primary unit. The soldier fights to protect the primary group and to live up to the expectations of his fellow group members. The army in battle is the prototype of the organization under stress, and military studies illustrate most vividly the crucial role of the primary group in preserving organizational cohesiveness and goal directedness.

Educational organizations: We have reviewed research on primary groups in industrial and military organizations. But there are other important kinds of formal organizations which we have neglected, for instance, political parties and trade unions, hospitals and prisons. The main reason for neglecting these is that empirical research on organizations of these kinds is very limited and any investigation of primary groups virtually non-existent. However, there is another type of organization which is so crucial to the socialization process that it cannot be ignored. This is the school, where the organization of students into classes produces large numbers of primary groups.

In the 1930s Moreno [76] made the first attempt to quantify some aspects of primary group relationships in educational and therapeutic institutions. He believed that education and therapy were facilitated when those involved were allowed to group themselves for work, play, or living according to their spontaneous choices. Moreno developed the socio-metric test to facilitate the process of primary group formation. The method is a simple one, consisting of rating scales which map the direction and intensity of personal attractions and repulsions in groups. These choices are then summarized by pictorial or mathematical models. Sociometry quickly became very popular in schools, both because it is simple to administer and because it is quantitative in character. The method em-phasized emotional attractions and repulsions and its use led to a new emphasis on the study of primary relationships in classroom groups.[77]

Lewin's work in the 1930s also reinforced the trend to the analysis of the class as a small social group. Lewin developed what came to be known as "field theory" which was a topological approach to human relationships similar in some ways to that of Moreno. Lewin was a Gestalt psychologist who led a group of social scientists at the University of Iowa Child Welfare Station and later at the M.I.T. Research Center for Group Dynamics. His most famous study was an experimental inquiry into the causal factors underlying different "emotional climates" in children's groups.[78] He set up children's clubs and subjected them to authoritarian, laissez-faire, and democratic forms of adult leadership. He was able to show that these authority roles produced markedly different emotional climates in the groups.

This demonstration of the effect of adult authority roles on the developing culture of children's groups had obvious implications for the classroom, and it was not long before these implications were being syste-matically investigated. In the 1940s, Thelen and others at the Chicago Human Dynamics Laboratory tried to develop a theory of instruction using Lewin's field concepts. Withall,[79] for instance, followed up Lewin's research by developing a research tool called the "Climate Index." This was employed to characterize and quantify verbal behavior in the class-room. The development of group dynamics theory and research, particu-larly at the University of Michigan where Lewin's group moved after his death, has continued to reinforce and influence the study of primary group processes in the classroom.

These theoretical and methodological developments gave shape to a growing emphasis on the use of group processes to make teaching more effective. The main philosophical justification for this can be traced to John Dewey's writings, his laboratory school at Chicago, and to the writings and educational practice of some of his outstanding followers such as W. H. Kilpatrick. (Kilpatrick's "project method" stressed that group problem solving was central in effective education.)

It is interesting that traditional educational theorists regarded a class as an aggregate of individual pupils in the same way as traditional industrial theorists regarded the members of organizations as aggregates of individuals. The combination of progressive educational theory and educational research on classroom behavior brought a new understanding of the importance of viewing a class as a primary group and working through group processes rather than ignoring them.

Thelen's *Group Dynamics in Instruction* (1949)[80] was the first full treatment of this break with an individualistic tradition. Thelen developed a plan for the social organization of learning whereby the classroom was divided into small sub-groups in which the students collaborated in joint productive enterprises. Particular stress was given to placing students with complementary skills in the same group. The following year, Trow, Zander, Morse, and Jenkins published an article under the title "Psychology of Group Behavior: The Class as a Group." [81] They asked the question: "What are the implications of viewing the class not merely as a number of individuals in the same room but as a group?" In the course of answering this question, they developed a comprehensive and systematic model of the classroom group, covering such variables as "objectives, atmosphere, climate and morale, group structure, leadership, and dynamic processes." They also reviewed existing research relating to the classroom as a group and listed findings such as the following:

1. the attitudes of an individual have their anchorage in the group to which he belongs;
2. the conduct and beliefs of pupils are regulated in large measure by the small groups that form the classroom;
3. failure to learn may be conceptualized as resistance, especially on the level of group standards;
4. the difficulties of transforming verbal learning into social action can be met by role playing in "reality practice."

They went on to suggest that increased motivation in learning can be produced by group determination of goals, the building of a supportive group atmosphere, and the encouragement of participative membership. They also attempted to describe the major roles played by teachers in the classroom and to estimate their effects and appropriateness under various conditions. These two publications introduced a fundamental break with the individualistic approach to classroom instruction and laid the foundation for a full recognition of the importance of understanding and using group processes in teaching. The articles were complemented in 1951 by a methodological contribution made by Wright, Barker, Nall, and Schoggen.[82] They gave a detailed example of the use of Wright's technique of behavior setting analysis, the description of behavior "episodes" and the categories which could be used to analyze descriptive data from classroom groups.

With research tools derived from various theoretical viewpoints becoming available, educational researchers began to make an increasing number of studies of the aspects of pupil interaction and pupil-teacher relationships. However, such studies have generally considered the relationships of only two or three variables. A few studies undertaken in elementary or secondary schools have made a holistic examination of the classroom as an ongoing social unit which is a functional subsystem of the larger society. But theoretical contributions have been made, too, which stress this viewpoint. Parsons,[83] for example, has analyzed the elementary and secondary school class as a small social system, and the way in which it functions as an agent of socialization and social selection. Other systemic approaches to understanding the internal dynamics of classroom groups have been advanced in Henry [84] where, in particular, the model outlined by Getzels and Thelen represents more of a social psychological approach than that of Parsons.

However, the most thoroughgoing *empirical* analyses of particular classroom groups have been made, not in elementary or secondary schools, but in college courses. One such study was undertaken by Orth [85] who followed two 100-man first year classes through the first year M.B.A. program at the Harvard Business School. Although these class groups are large, they assume many primary characteristics because the members of the class are together throughout the day, classes are run on a participative basis, and many members also meet in small study groups in the evenings. Orth analyzed the emerging social structure of these groups, paying particular attention to the development of group norms. He found that, in order to cope with their environment, section groups developed norms defining such things as the maximum and minimum levels of active participation in the classroom. He was also able to demonstrate a significant relationship between the degree of support a class member received from his peers and the grades he received at the end of the year. Peer support is an important causal factor in determining high and low final grades.

A number of other studies have been made of twenty-man class groups in a course in Social Relations at Harvard College. The course, called Analysis of Interpersonal Behavior, runs for a full academic year and various classes have been intensively followed by Mills, Slater, Mann, and myself.[86] These studies will be described in some detail in chapter two. It is worth noting here, however, that these studies represent a major advance in primary group analysis because they have applied a variety of sophisticated, quantitative research procedures to fully fledged, longterm groups. Considered together, these studies give what is to date the most comprehensive outline of the development of primary group structures and subcultures. They trace the evolution of group norms, the major developmental phases through which the groups move, the generalized sequence of topical concerns, the processes of role differentiation, and the evolution of authority relations. It is certainly time that similar methods were applied to classroom groups of children and middle adolescents.

The self-conscious creation of new primary groups

So far we have traced the process by which social scientists "discovered" that primary groups of new kinds were spontaneously forming within the developing structures of urban communities. We have shown how these studies indicate the integrative role played by primary groups at all stages of the socialization process.

The evolution of the social patterns which can support this socialization route has been, like most evolutionary development, a rather slow and haphazard process. It has taken place initially apart from the cognizance of social theorists and within organizations almost despite the conscious efforts of many administrators. Consequently the full cycle of group participation is not always present in the socialization of a given individual and has often not functioned effectively to change the individual in a way that allows him to adapt to society. In addition, the greater reliance on the nuclear family to effect the initial socialization of the child has had a high cost. This reliance demands a stable marital relationship between spouses during the initial socialization of children. At the same time, the rapid pace of industrialization and urbanization has placed major strains on the marital relationship. A child whose personality was formed by incorporating parental tensions spends a good deal of his later life performing defensive rather than adaptive maneuvers. One of the key problems in a society which has institutionalized a rapid state of technological innovation, is how to produce stable personalities able to take up, even thrive on, the rapid changes in social structure and social values that must necessarily accompany such innovation. In fact, it has become evident that large numbers of people cannot cope with this kind of society and that the existing structures do *not* adequately socialize even a large majority of the members of society.

In response to growing numbers of "disturbed" people who represent such a failure in socialization, there has been a phenomenal rise in primary groups deliberately designed and constructed to "resocialize" adults so that they can live more effectively in a rapidly changing society. This quiet but extensive social revolution has not been adequately documented. This is partly because the efflorescence of these primary groups, which we shall refer to as resocialization groups, has not been centrally planned but represents a fairly spontaneous response by individuals and institutions to an apparent social need.

By "resocialization groups" we mean groups, such as many therapy groups, sensitivity training groups, academic courses in human relations run as self-analytic groups, Alcoholics Anonymous and Synanon groups, and house church groups. Members of these groups devote a considerable amount of time to participating in a discussion and evaluation of their own personality processes—interpersonal processes within the group itself—and of their behavior in concrete life situations external to the group. There has been a phenomenal growth in the number of these groups, particularly in the United States, but also in Britain and Europe, in the last decade. Such groups have risen out of very different social situations and from diverse cultural traditions and have operated until recently with remarkably little formalized administration, mutual awareness, or exchange of information. The most deliberately planned and centrally organized group programs have been conducted by the National Training Laboratories originally associated with the National Educational Association. These have been groups organized primarily for business, academic, and religious professionals.

What do these groups do? Because socialization takes place predominantly in primary groups, resocialization must also take place in primary groups. Resocialization groups function to change the ways in which people view their behavior by providing "open feedback" from fellow participants about the meaning of each individual's behavior for them, by increasing the range of behavioral phenomena consciously perceived by the individual, by making apparent and challenging in a variety of ways the working assumptions about human behavior held by him. In addition, resocialization groups more or less actively teach or indoctrinate members with some values which are functional for an open-ended, rapidly developing society—values of consensual and empirical rather than authoritative validation, respect for the legitimacy of differing viewpoints, dialogue as a way of confronting and exploring different viewpoints versus dialectic debate as a way of defending one viewpoint as superior to others, collaboration and interdependence rather than individualistic competition; recognition of the individual's responsibility for the personal growth of others and an emphasis on self-realization through activism rather than resignation to the status quo; openness to and acceptance of emotional responses of others to oneself as legitimate data for evaluation of one's action rather than irrelevant trivia to be ignored or dismissed.

The proliferation of small groups which function to resocialize individuals in a period of rapid change is not a new phenomenon. One has only to think, for example, of the role played by the small groups, which made up the Methodist revival in England, in producing the kind of personal values required to serve the needs of the new technology and social structure of the early industrial revolution. The groups of the Methodist revival met in each others houses and engaged in prayer and the mutual examination of their spiritual lives. Like the Quaker groups—and contemporary resocialization groups—they were prepared to "share the truth" with a member who didn't see the implications of his words or actions. A similar example is to be found in contemporary Communist China which is now at a similar stage of development. China, in authentic Communist fashion, has organized the process from the top down. At the lowest level, the Chinese population is now organized into small groups of generally seven to thirteen, but not more than twenty, members.[87] These groups function essentially as resocialization groups, examining inner motivations, group effectiveness, and so on. In Chinese terms they engage in "study" which is the intensive application of group and self-criticism to individual group members in the light of Communist precepts. They appear to be functioning to move what was a personality system based on external control by shame to an internal control by guilt. The emphasis, as in early Methodist groups, is on right thinking, self-criticism and *faith*. In the Chinese case, faith is in the party as exemplified by a mystical Mao-image while in the Methodist case it was faith in a mystical Christ.

On the other hand, the U.S., Britain, and much of Europe are moving out of the initial stages of the industrial revolution into what might be appropriately named the "cybernetic" revolution. As this occurs, there is increasingly a chronic lag between the values and meanings acquired by the individual in his initial socialization and the values and meanings needed by a society that continues to change radically within the individual's lifetime. This problem is compounded by the gaps which occur in the socialization process through the failure of emerging structures to provide primary groups either soon enough or sufficiently effective to change the individual as he moves toward new experiences and new demands. It is our impression that the use of resocialization groups represents a social mechanism which will become increasingly institutionalized, elaborated, and effective, and probably a permanent feature of our society. Such groups will produce a basic personality type which will not simply adjust readily to change, but will deliberately seek to utilize change effectively by discriminating between alternatives, seeking feedback from others to achieve in the short run the consensual validation to make coordinated, interdependent action possible and, in the long run, to evaluate policies and programs by their results. In addition, such groups will become a permanent or intermittent feature of particular secondary institutions, acting to socialize people within these institutions, and to make the institutions more responsible for and responsive to the developmental needs of those in them and those whom they serve.

But how do resocialization groups work? We shall discuss later in some detail the processes by which such groups involve members in a common emotional life. It is sufficient to note here that resocialization groups recreate primary ties originally formed in the family. They reactivate family identifications and make use of transference relationships to modify personality by redefining the social meaning of specific action patterns. When deliberately established within an organizational setting, resocialization groups can also transmit common personality needs to the organization and in some cases successfully modify organizational structure and relationships to increase the personal satisfactions of those in the group.

Summary: add to

The significance of the primary group

Empirical studies of primary groups make it clear that they operate as mediating mechanisms or buffers between personality systems and social systems. It is through the primary group that social expectations are mediated to the individual and internalized by him. Primary groups are, therefore, crucial at all stages of the socialization process. The socialization process begins in the family of orientation, is carried further within the classroom and recreation peer group, completed within the organizational work group, the adult recreational peer group and the family of procreation. Whereas nineteenth century theorists saw primary groups— especially the extended family—as disintegrating under the impact of industrialization, it is clear now that this process has led and is still leading not to the disappearance of primary groups but rather to the creation of new and more differentiated types of primary groups. The emergence, for example, of a distinctive and prolonged adolescent subculture based on a primary group structure is one example of this. Similarly, the proliferation of "self-analytic" groups at the adult level, in many different societies and in different social strata, increasingly acts to modify deviant behavior and resocialize normal adults in a rapidly changing society.

Because primary group structures are changing radically and new structures are being deliberately created to direct the course of socialization and of social change, it is important that social scientists understand more clearly the processes which take place in such groups. While primary groups perform certain basic social functions, the results vary greatly according to the environment in which a group operates, its structure, and the extent to which it is consciously created to serve a purpose or emerges in response to social pressures. This understanding is even more important if a society decides, for one reason or another, to maximize the creative potentialities which groups offer.

We must now ask ourselves: Given the theory and research briefly reviewed thus far, what more specific conclusions and hypotheses can be advanced about the primary group? Another way of approaching the question is to ask: What would be an adequate theory of the primary group? If we can answer that question, then we can go further and see what data has been accumulated that would support such a theory in a satisfying way.

An adequate *theory* of the function of primary groups would explain:

1. the dynamic mechanisms which enable the individual to identify with a group, to participate emotionally in it, and to be influenced by it;
2. the major variables within primary groups—and their interrelationships —which can be used to explain and predict group behavior; and
3. the ways in which primary groups are integrated into the larger social structure—organizations, social classes, etc.—so that they respond to social demands and transmit pressure to modify the larger social structure.

A good deal of knowledge relating to (2) and (3) is to be found in the extensive literature on small groups in field and laboratory situations. As far as (1) is concerned, an adequate theory can only be derived from major developments in personality theory, along with studies of group processes in therapy and sensitivity training groups.

The following chapter will attempt to outline an answer to (1) and (3); that is, propose a theory of the way in which the individual relates to the primary group and of the way the primary group relates to its own social environment. In chapter 2, the primary group itself will be regarded largely as a "black box" and only those internal elements which are directly important in external relationships will be dealt with. We shall then outline in chapter 3, a model of the internal structure and processes of the primary group. Chapter 4 will discuss the basic methods for measuring the variables in the model.

Notes

[1] Charles H. Cooley, *Social Organization: A Study of the Larger Mind* (New York: Scribners, 1909), p. 23.

[2] Ibid., p. 29.

[3] Charles H. Cooley, Robert C. Angell, and Lowell J. Carr, *Introductory Sociology* (New York: Scribners, 1933), p. 53.

[4] Edward Shils, "Primary Groups in the American Army" in Robert K. Merton and Paul F. Lazarsfeld, Eds., *Continuities in Social Research* (Glencoe, Ill.: Free Press, 1950), pp. 16–25.

[5] Edward Shils, "The Study of the Primary Group" in Daniel Lerner and Harold Lasswell, *The Policy Sciences* (Stanford, Calif.: Stanford University Press, 1951), pp. 44–69.

[6] Ibid., p. 44.

[7] Charles H. Cooley, *Introductory Sociology*, p. 32.

[8] Ferdinand Toennies, "Gemeinschaft and Gesellschaft" in Talcott Parsons,

Edward Shils, Kasper D. Naegele, and Jessie R. Pitts, *Theories of Society* (New York: Free Press, 1961), pp. 191–201.

[9] Ibid., p. 191.

[10] Georg Simmel, "The Metropolis and Mental Life" in Kurt Wolff, *The Sociology of Georg Simmel* (Glencoe, Ill.: Free Press, 1950), p. 422.

[11] Max Weber, "Types of Social Organization" in Parsons et al., *Theories of Society,* pp. 218–29.

[12] Ibid., p. 219.

[13] Pierre G. LePay, *Les Ouvriers Européens,* 2nd ed., 6 vols. (Tours: Mame, 1877–79), first published, Paris, 1855.

[14] Emile Durkheim, "On Mechanical and Organic Solidarity" in Parsons et al., *Theories of Society,* pp. 212–13.

[15] Emile Durkheim, *Division of Labor in Society,* trans. G. Simpson (New York: MacMillan, 1933).

[16] Emile Durkheim, *Suicide* (Glencoe, Ill.: Free Press, 1951).

[17] Durkheim, *Division of Labor in Society.*

[18] Sigmund Freud, *Group Psychology and the Analysis of the Ego,* trans. J. Strachey (London: The International Psychoanalytic Press, 1922).

[19] Cooley, *Social Organisation,* p. 30.

[20] William I. Thomas and Florian Znaniechi, *The Polish Peasant in Europe and America,* 5 vols. (Chicago: University of Chicago Press, 1918–20).

[21] Robert E. Park, *Human Communities: The City and Human Ecology* (Glencoe, Ill.: Free Press, 1952), p. 51.

[22] Ibid., p. 32.

[23] Ibid., pp. 32–3.

[24] Frederic M. Thrasher, *The Gang,* 2nd ed. (Chicago: University of Chicago Press, 1936).

[25] Clifford R. Shaw and Henry D. McKay, *Juvenile Delinquency and Urban Areas* (Chicago: University of Chicago Press, 1942).

[26] Frank Tannenbaum, *Crime and the Community* (Boston: Ginn, 1938), pp. 12–13.

[27] William F. Whyte, *Street Corner Society,* 2nd ed. (Chicago: University of Chicago Press, 1955).

[28] Ibid., p. 3.

[29] Robert K. Merton, *Social Theory and Social Structure,* rev. ed. (Glencoe, Ill.: Free Press, 1957), esp. chapters 4 and 5, pp. 131–94.

[30] Richard A. Cloward and Lloyd E. Ohlin, *Delinquency and Opportunity: A Theory of Delinquent Gangs* (Glencoe, Ill.: Free Press, 1960).

[31] Albert K. Cohen, *Delinquent Boys: The Culture of the Gang* (Glencoe, Ill.: Free Press, 1955), p. 25; Walter B. Miller, "Lower Class Culture as a Generating Milieu of Gang Delinquency," *Journal of Social Issues,* vol. 14, no. 3 (1958), pp. 5–19.

[32] Miller, *Lower Class Culture,* p. 19.

[33] Edward B. Reuter, "Sociological Research in Adolescence," *American Journal of Sociology,* vol. 42 (July 1936), pp. 81–94; idem, "The Sociology of Adolescence," *American Journal of Sociology,* vol. 43 (November 1937), pp. 414–27; Jessie R. Runner, "Social Distance in Adolescent Relationships," *American Journal of Sociology* vol. 43 (November 1937), pp. 428–39.

[34] Nelson B. Henry, ed., "Adolescence," 43d *Yearbook of the National Society for the Study of Education,* pt. 1 (Chicago: University of Chicago Press, 1944; James H. Bossard and Eleanor S. Boll, eds., "Adolescents in Wartime," *Annals of the American Academy of Political and Social Science,* vol. 236 (November, 1944).

[35] August B. Hollingshead, *Elmtown's Youth* (New York: John Wiley, 1949).

[36] Robert J. Havinghurst and Hilda Taba, *Adolescent Character and Personality* (New York: Wiley, 1949).

[37] Hollingshead, *Elmtown's Youth,* p. 450.

[38] David P. Ausubel, *Theory and Problems of Adolescent Development* (New York: Grune and Stratton, 1954), p. 461.

39 Ernest A. Smith, *American Youth Culture—Group Life in Teenage Society* (New York: Free Press, 1963).

40 Ibid., p. 226.

41 Dexter C. Dunphy, "The Social Structure of Urban Adolescent Peer Groups," *Sociometry,* vol. 26, no. 2 (June, 1963), pp. 162–74.

42 Muzafer and Carolyn Sherif, *Reference Groups* (New York: Harper and Row, 1964).

43 See Talcott Parsons and Robert F. Bales, *Family: Socialization and Interaction Process* (Glencoe, Ill.: Free Press, 1955), for a discussion of this process.

44 Allison Davis, Burleigh Gardner, and Mary Gardner, *Deep South* (Chicago: University of Chicago Press, 1941), p. 138.

45 Ibid., p. 169.

46 Charles R. Wright and Herbert H. Hyman, "Voluntary Association Memberships of American Adults," *American Sociological Review,* vol. 23 (June, 1958), pp. 284–94.

47 Walter B. Miller, "Implications of Urban Lower-Class Culture for Social Work," *Social Service Review,* vol. 33 (September, 1959), pp. 219–36; William Lloyd Warner and Paul S. Lunt, *Social Life of a Modern Community* (New Haven, Conn.: Yale University Press, 1941); Elizabeth Bott, *Family and Social Network* (London: Tavistock Publications Ltd., 1957); Peter Willmot and Michael Young, *Family and Kinship in East London* (London: Routledge, 1957).

48 August B. Hollingshead and Frederick C. Redlich, *Social Class and Mental Illness: A Community Study* (New York: Wiley, 1958).

49 Ibid., p. 82.

50 Fritz Roethlisberger and William Dickson, *Management and the Worker* (Cambridge, Mass.: Harvard University Press, 1939).

51 An excellent summary and discussion of this work may be found in J. Madge, The Origins of Scientific Sociology (Glencoe, Ill.: Free Press, 1962).

52 Edward Shils, "The Study of the Primary Group" in Lerner and Lasswell, op. cit., p. 48.

53 William F. Whyte, *Human Relations in the Restaurant Industry* (New York: McGraw Hill, 1948).

54 William F. Whyte, "Small Groups and Large Organizations" in John H. Rohrer and Muzafer Sherif, eds., *Social Psychology at The Crossroads* (New York: Harper and Brothers, 1951).

55 George C. Homans, "The Cash Posters: A Study of a Group of Working Girls," *American Sociological Review,* vol. 19 (December, 1954), pp. 724–733.

56 George F. Lombard, *Behavior in a Selling Group* (Boston: Harvard University, Division of Research, Graduate School of Business Administration, 1955).

57 Charles R. Walker, Robert H. Guest, and Arthur Turner, *The Foreman on the Assembly Line* (Cambridge, Mass.: Harvard University Press, 1956).

58 Abraham Zaleznik, *Worker Satisfaction and Development* (Boston: Harvard University, Division of Research, Graduate School of Business Administration, 1956).

59 Abraham Zaleznik, C. R. Christensen, and Fritz J. Roethlisberger, *The Motivation, Productivity, and Satisfaction of Workers* (Boston: Harvard University, Division of Research, Graduate School of Business Administration, 1958).

60 Burleigh B. Gardner and William F. Whyte, "Man in the Middle," *Applied Anthropology,* vol. 4, no. 2 (1945), pp. 1–28; Charles R. Walker, Robert H. Guest, and Arthur Turner, *The Foreman on the Assembly Line* (Cambridge: Mass.: Harvard University Press, 1956); Donald E. Wray, "Marginal Men in Industry: The Foremen," *American Journal of Sociology,* vol. 54 (January, 1949), pp. 298–301.

61 William Caudill, *The Psychiatric Hospital as a Small Society* (Cambridge, Mass.: Harvard University Press, 1958).

62 Eric L. Trist and K. W. Bamforth, "Some Social and Psychological Consequences of the Longwall Method of Coal-getting," *Human Relations,* vol. 4 (February 1951), pp. 3–38.

63 A. K. Rice, "Productivity and Social Organization in an Indian Weaving Shed," *Human Relations,* vol. 6, no. 4 (1953), pp. 297–329.

64 Chadwick J. Haberstroh, "Organization Design and Systems Analysis" in James G. March, ed., *Handbook of Organizations* (Chicago: Rand McNally, 1965), p. 1190.

65 Edward S. Shils and Morris Janowitz, "Cohesion and Disintegration in the Wehrmacht in World War II," *Public Opinion Quarterly,* vol. 12 (Summer, 1948); Samuel A. Stouffer, et. al., eds., *The American Soldier,* vols. 1 and 2 (Princeton, N.J.: Princeton University Press, 1949); Morris Janowitz and Roger Little, *Sociology and the Military Establishment,* rev. ed. (New York: Russell Sage Foundation, 1965), particularly chap. 4, "Primary Groups and Military Effectiveness," pp. 77–99; Robert K. Merton and Paul L. Lazarsfeld, eds., *Continuities in Social Research: Studies in the Scope and Method of the American Soldier* (Glencoe, Ill.: Free Press, 1950); Roy R. Grinker and John P. Spiegal, *Men Under Stress* (Philadelphia: Blakiston, 1945).

66 Shils and Janowitz, "Cohesion and Disintegration in the Wehrmacht," pp. 280–315.

67 Ibid., pp. 281–82.

68 Ibid., p. 284.

69 Janowitz and Little, *Sociology and the Military Establishment,* p. 78.

70 Speien in *Continuities in Social Research.*

71 Shils in *Continuities in Social Research,* op. cit., p. 22.

72 Ibid.

73 Shils and Janowitz, "Cohesion and Disintegration in the Wehrmacht."

74 Grinker and Spiegal, *Men Under Stress,* chap. 2.

75 Shils in *Continuities in Social Research.*

76 Jacob L. Moreno, *Who Shall Survive?* (Washington: Nervous and Mental Disease Publishing Co., 1934).

77 *See:* Margaret E. Bonney, "A Sociometric Study of the Relationship of Some Factors to Mutual Friendships on the Elementary, Secondary, and College Levels," *Sociometry,* vol. 9, no. 1 (1946), pp. 21–47; Helen H. Jennings, "Sociometric Differentiation of the Psychegroup and the Sociogroup," *Sociometry,* vol. 10 (February, 1947), pp. 71–9.

78 Kurt Lewin, Ronald Lippitt, and Ralph K. White, "Patterns of Aggressive Behavior in Experimentally Created Social Climates," *Journal of Social Psychology,* vol. 10 (May, 1939), pp. 271–99.

79 John Withall, "The Development of a Technique for the Measurement of Social-Emotional Climate in Classrooms," *Journal of Experimental Education,* vol. 17 (March, 1949), pp. 347–61; John Withall, "The Development of the Climate Index," *Journal of Educational Research,* vol. 45 (October, 1951), pp. 93–100; John Withall, "An Objective Measurement of a Teacher's Classroom Interactions," *Journal of Educational Psychology,* vol. 47 (April, 1956), pp. 203–12.

80 Herbert A. Thelen, "Group Dynamics in Instruction," *School Review,* vol. 57 (March, 1949), pp. 139–48.

81 William C. Trow, Alvin F. Zander, William C. Morse, and David H. Jenkins, "Psychology of Group Behavior: The Class as a Group," *Journal of Educational Psychology* (May, 1950), pp. 322–38.

82 Herbert F. Wright, Roger G. Barker, Jack Nall, and Phil Schoggen, "Toward a Psychological Ecology of the Classroom," *Journal of Educational Research,* vol. 45 (November, 1951), pp. 187–200.

83 Talcott Parsons, "The School Class as a Social System: Some of Its Functions in American Society," *Social Structure and Personality* (New York: Free Press, 1964), pp. 129–54.

84 J. W. Getzels and Herbert A. Thelen, "The Classroom Group as a Unique Social System," in Nelson B. Henry, ed., "The Dynamics of Instructional Groups," *Yearbook of the National Society for the Study of Education* (Chicago: University of Chicago Press, 1960), vol. 59, pt. 2.

85 Charles D. Orth, *Social Structure and Learning Climate* (Boston: Division of Research, Graduate School of Business Administration, Harvard University, 1963).

86 Theodore Mills, *Group Transformation: An Analysis of a Learning Group*

(Englewood Cliffs, N. J.: Prentice Hall, 1964); Philip Slater, *Microcosm* (New York: Wiley, 1966); Richard D. Mann, *Interpersonal Styles and Group Development* (New York: Wiley, 1967); Dexter C. Dunphy, "Social Change in Self-Analytic Groups," in Philip J. Stone, Dexter C. Dunphy, Marshall S. Smith, and Daniel M. Ogilvie, *The General Inquirer* (Cambridge, Mass.: M.I.T. Press, 1966); Dexter Dunphy, "Phases, Roles and Myths in Self-Analytic Groups," *Journal of Applied Behavioral Science,* vol. 4, no. 2 (1968), pp. 195–225.

[87] H. F. Schurmann, "Organization and Response in Communist China," *Annals of the American Academy of Political and Social Science,* vol. 321 (January, 1959), pp. 51–61.

chapter 2

The subsystem and suprasystem of the primary group

Introduction

How are individuals, previously unknown to each other, able to establish binding emotional relationships and form primary groups which exercise a degree of control over their actions? Why are people apparently so ready to relinquish a degree of individual self-determination to a group? In the first part of this chapter we will try to find answers to these questions. We have pointed out that the central feature of primary groups is the affective bond among members, and we shall concentrate on explaining how affective bonds are formed. However, primary group membership sometimes holds other rewards than affective, and we shall deal with some of these in the latter part of the chapter.

The coordination of the individual with the primary group

The development of personality in primary groups

To understand how emotional relationships are formed, we need to go back to early childhood and examine the first relations with others formed by the infant. Studies of childhood increasingly reveal the importance of such early "object relations," as they are frequently called. It is the nature of these early relationships which determines whether or not the growing child will be able to relate to others at all as he matures and it also strongly influences the character of those relationships he does form. For example, if Erikson and others are correct in their analysis of the impact of socialization in the first year of life, an attitude of basic trust or distrust in others is laid down at that period.[1]

Out of relationships in the family and subsequent primary groups there develops what we shall refer to as the "integrative core" of the human personality. What does this integrative core consist of? We shall argue that it is a system of images of people and groups to which consistent reaction patterns have been built up in the life of the individual in primary groups. The integrative core of the individual's personality results from the linking of originally undifferentiated drive states with the structure of successive systems of social objects—at first the nurturant mother, later the family as a whole as it presents itself to the child at different stages of his development, and from there to the other primary groups which become significant to the maturing individual.

Recently there have been attempts to synthesize Piaget's work on the early cognitive development of the child with Freudian and neo-Freudian theories of the early development of object relations. The results of the first attempt to do this empirically as well as theoretically have been published recently by Decarie.[2] Decarie adapted methods for her research which Piaget had used to study the way infants respond to physical objects. The methods were used by Decarie to study the way infants respond to people. According to Decarie, the child must learn to "construct" people from the evidence of his various senses. In the initial world of the child—the "narcissistic" period—there are no permanent objects : the child has to learn to distinguish objects from the surrounding field and then to conceptualize them even when they are physically absent. As far as persons are concerned, the child has to achieve "object constancy," that is, he has to learn to distinguish an object, conceptualize it, and eventually love it to the extent that the love object will not be rejected or exchanged for another even when it does not provide immediate or total satisfaction. Moreover, Decarie finds that for the child with normal development, there is a rough parallel between Piaget's stages of (physical) object construction and psychoanalytic stages of (social) object relations.

The first stage of social object relations, distinguished by Decarie, occurs at about the age of five weeks when the child reacts affectively (with a smile) to a smiling human face. We have all seen the delight of a mother when she is first able to elicit this response. At this stage, the infant cannot conceptualize an inanimate object which is permanent, substantial, and separate from the self, but he can recognize a person. This is presumably because persons are more rewarding. The next stage of social relations occurs when the child can recognize a *familiar* person from the rest of his environment, that is, he no longer smiles automatically at anyone who smiles at him but only at someone whom he recognizes. This again contrasts with the child's perception of physical objects for, at the same stage, the child is *not* able to attribute permanence to a physical object which has shown even the slightest visible displacement. Next, at about six months, the child is able to visualize a displaced physical object and deduce its whereabouts, and also seems capable of formulating a concept of a loved person, even in the absence of that person, and to be able to respond in a differentiated way to that person. He will cry, for example, when his mother leaves him. Finally, the child abandons the idea of his own omnipotence and acts to please the loved person in a way indicating that the wish for approval is stronger than the wish for physical gratification. The child moves at this time from a reactive response to a loved object to an active initiation of overtures of affection. He will even play imitative games when the loved object is not present and, in these games, will respond to the mental symbol of the loved person as if the person were in fact there. It is at this point in the child's development that we can begin to speak realistically of internalized social objects. The child has begun to create an inner social world which can control his behavior in the same way as the outside social world.

In Piaget's terms, at this point in the child's development, he has achieved "the symbolic evocation of absent realities," which is both the basis of conceptual thinking and the basis of forming emotional ties with others.[3] He is now able to form stable, cooperative relations with other people.

On the basis of studying children from foundling homes, Decarie also presents evidence that the lack of a normal family environment can result in irregular development of object relations and an impairment of the ability to relate to others. Decarie's work confirms the idea that the ability to relate to others is fashioned in the most primary of primary groups, the family. It also suggests that this ability does not develop automatically and can be impaired. [Spitz's work on institutionalized children shows that it can also be completely destroyed.[4]] If, as psychoanalysts suggest, the core of the self consists of internalized object relations, it is not an audacious claim to say that the self is born in the family and that the ability to form adequate emotional relationships with others is determined early in life, literally in the first year.

Psychoanalytic theory holds that this initial relationship with a love object—usually the mother—is subsequently differentiated and modified by later human relationships. It is not within the scope of this book to outline the stages by which the self develops as new emotional ties are formed and old ones are modified. However, we will point out that the standard stages of psychosexual development are closely tied to the maturing of the child in the family and that, in addition, the peer groups of childhood and adolescence play an important part in reinforcing these stages. The play groups of childhood, for example, are usually formed early in the oedipal period and reinforce the demands on the child for self-dependence and self-control experienced during the preceding anal period. Similarly, the "gang age" corresponds with the latency period and continues through prepuberty. The gang reinforces the child's learning of his basic sex role, acquired through the identification with the parent of the same sex—an identification which was initiated at the preceding oedipal stage. The adolescent peer group is in large part responsible for the adolescent learning an appropriate heterosexual role. Thus, group membership strongly reinforces the stages of internalization which are initiated in the family.

The core of the interior world of the individual consists then in the images of those persons which have been most relevant to the satisfaction and to the frustration of drives. This has two implications. First, a new external object of the same class as an internalized object can produce the same reaction as the internalized object. In addition, because concrete images are associated with a drive, an increase in the intensity of the drive may be sufficient to produce the image of the satisfying object, so that fantasies are the normal accompaniment of states of arousal. Such fantasies often activate behavior designed to satisfy drives and needs, and so the individual seeks to externalize his fantasy life, although sometimes it may be too threatening to do this directly.

The nature of internalized images

Internalization is the result of active manipulation of objects with the sense organs and the image of an object is, in fact, actively constituted by "fitting together" the impressions of the various sense organs. Consequently, internalized social relations are imbued with rich, emotive, sensuous associations in the form of stored sense reactions. (Sociologists tend to overlook this in their writings, whereas it features strongly in the writings of psychoanalysts.) Thus it cannot be too strongly emphasized that it is not the external object which is internalized, or necessarily an objective and accurate picture of that object, but the individual's experiential image of the object. The infant's image of the breast is not what the adult perceives and it certainly contains important components of both frustrated rage and drive satisfaction. As Heimann puts it :

It is through the medium of his sensations that the child experiences his objects, and sensory experience forms the matrix of both unconscious fantasy and conscious perception. Since the elementary categories of sensory experience are pleasurable or painful, these are also the primary characters of the infant's object relations.[5]

The individual's interior world is, therefore, not a simple reflection of the successive sets of primary groups through which he has passed. There are often considerable differences between external and internal objects, that is, between the outer real object and the inner subjective image of it. The distortion arises from the emotions experienced as the object is encountered in the process of satisfying one's needs. Because significant social objects are more or less frustrating or satisfying, they become invested with affection and love, or fear, hostility and hate, or sometimes with all of these emotions (ambivalence).

Because images are associated with particular sequences of behavior, they tend to produce these behavioral sequences when called to mind. Language forces us to distinguish between objects and relationships with objects, but this useful distinction is in some ways artificial. For, in the process of socialization, objects are defined for the learner in terms of his relationships with them, that is, by what he does to them and what they do to him. Children indicate this clearly when they define objects in terms of appropriate actions : milk, for example, is for drinking and a chair is for sitting on. Since objects are defined in terms of relationships with them, the nature of the relationship can be expected to have a major impact on the image which is formed, and particular behavioral sequences or learned responses are associated with internal images.[6]

When images are recalled in fantasy, these behavioral sequences tend to recur. Adults often inhibit action of this type when it attaches itself to fantasy and try to keep the action internal. Despite this, ongoing fantasies are often revealed by unconscious movements, irrational slips in speech, displaced symbolism, and other deviations from the norms of rational behavior. These processes become clearest in dreams, in expressive behavior such as lovemaking, and in the arts.

The developing personality is differentiated in response to changes in the structure of the child's social environment : new relationships evolve from or are imposed upon older relationships. Old relationships are not, however, erased from the cumulative store of learned responses. A major problem, therefore, is how integration of the personality is maintained when new objects are internalized. As Heimann has pointed out in the article quoted above, there is both continuity and change :

the early introjected objects differ greatly from the later super-ego yet have certain features in common with it. The climax of a process differs from the preceding stages, but the preceding stages belong together and to the climax. There is a genetic continuity between the persecutory fears of the infant, roused initially by his cannibalistic impulses, the anxiety of the latent child in connection with the disapproving internal voice of his parents, and the sense of guilt, mortification, and remorse of the adult who has failed to act in accordance with his ideals.[7]

Because fantasies are associations between internalized images, they are not necessarily dependent on words, although they may involve words and may be capable of expression in words. Operating largely on a non-verbal level, fantasy is a mode of generalization of internal object systems through which new object images are related to those which exist. A concrete incident may clarify the importance of this for understanding group behavior.

On the first day of a class I was teaching one year, a student entered the classroom somewhat late. He perceived the class seated in a circle with the instructor seated at a desk, which was noticeably different from the others and designed for an authority figure. It is obvious that the student, in perceiving this, will probably act toward the authority figure in terms of the normal definition of appropriate behavior for such a situation. This student did—he chose an empty seat, pulled it up to the circle and sat in it, waiting for the instructor to proceed. In this case, however, it was interesting that the student passed up two empty places nearest to him, walked behind the instructor, chose a chair somewhat apart from the table and pulled it into the circle so as to interpose himself between the instructor and the only three female class members, sitting to the instructor's right. In terms of the theory being proposed here we will assume that his behavior is being influenced by his generalized image of authority figures in the context of those fantasies of his which concern authority figures. What could be the general character of these fantasies? A further clue is given in the ensuing discussion when he contributes a remark to a controversy about the nature of leadership: "Leadership is s . . . s . . . seduction of others to your own point of view." This suggests that the fantasy is of a sexual nature, and from the previous incident, one surmises that it concerns the relationship of the instructor to the female members of the group. This suggestion acquires some strength when he writes in his first weekly analysis of group behavior that he feels particularly attracted to one girl—who consistently sits near the instructor—finding her even more appealing when he realizes she is married. When some weeks later the same student remarks that "he always disliked his father intensely and felt very close to his mother, that when she came up for a weekend it was great fun, just like having a date," the nature of the fantasy is fairly apparent. The point of the anecdote is that the series of object relationships the individual has had in the past are by no means irrelevant to present situations and that the images which comprise the personality core and the fantasies which link them exercise an important influence on day-to-day action.[8]

Projection as the basis of emotional relationships with others

Given that the personality core is formed in this general manner, we must ask why internalized images are so important. It is our belief that people attempt to maintain a psychological equilibrium by establishing patterns of relating which are consonant with their fantasy relationships. These patterns may be "adaptive" or "maladaptive" from the point of view of a "healthy" course of development, but they represent persisting modes of adaptation worked out by the individual in the past. The internal world is maintained intact by establishing connections with new people and groups in a way that grants them "equivalence" with internal objects. In his initial maneuvering to obtain a "best fit" between internal and external systems, the individual relates through actively projecting internalized objects. One of the clearest demonstrations of this mechanism is the infant's oral manipulation of any object which is given to him—as the breast is the one significant object internalized, all other objects are manipulated in the same way.

This process of "matching" internal and external phenomena is frequently referred to as "projection." While projection has often been referred to as a defense mechanism, it seems better to distinguish it from defense mechanisms and to view these as primarily attempts to block or disguise projection. Projection is the more normal and fundamental process. Thus Ezriel states :

Our behavior therefore is not only governed by conscious needs and environmental demands but also by unconscious needs. . . . One individual meeting another will try to establish the kind of relationship between them which will ultimately diminish the tension arising out of object relations which he entertains with unconscious phantasy objects.[9]

Recently there has been a tendency to use the concept of projection in this wider sense, that is, to refer to a more general process underlying social learning rather than to a pathological symptom. Weiss, for instance, points out that

. . . the term projection, in current usage, refers to every kind of externalization, particularly to every process in which ideas, impulses or qualities belonging to oneself are imputed to others.[10]

Actually this usage does not represent a new departure, but simply an emphasis of one aspect of Freud's work which he did not develop fully, owing to his concern with abnormality rather than normality. In *Totem and Taboo* Freud wrote :

But projection was not created for the purpose of defense; it also occurs where there is no conflict. The projection outward of internal perceptions is a primitive mechanism, to which, for instance, our sense perceptions are subject and which therefore normally plays a large part in determining the form taken by our external world.[11]

Similarly, Anna Freud, after dealing at length with projection as a defense mechanism, remarks :

At the same time, identification and projection are normal activities of the ego and their results vary greatly according to the material upon which they are employed.[12]

The notion of projection and introjection as basic to normal learning processes in social situations is, of course, also implicit in the work of Charles Cooley and G. H. Mead. In developing the implications of this view of projection as part of the normal process of social learning, theorists such as Murray, McClelland and Fromm have stressed that not only repressed impulses but also idealized images may be projected. Once again this does not seem to be a radical departure from tradition since it is consistent with Freud's notion of the "replacement of the ego ideal with an object" and Melanie Klein's "identification by projection." Concerning this latter phenomenon Klein writes :

In the course of further work, I also came to recognize the major importance for identification of certain projective mechanisms which are complementary to the introjective ones. The process which underlies the feeling of identification with other people, because one has attributed qualities or attitudes of one's own to them, was generally taken for granted even before the corresponding concept was incorporated in psycho-analytic theory. . . . The mechanisms underlying such phenomena, however, had not been investigated in much detail when, in my "Notes on Some Schizoid Mechanisms," I suggested the term "projective identification" for those processes which form part of the paranoid-schizoid position. . . . Here I wish to go somewhat beyond my paper on schizoid mechanisms. I would suggest that a securely established good object, implying a securely established love for it, gives the ego a feeling of riches and abundance which allows for an out-pouring of libido and projection of good parts of the self into the external world without a sense of depletion arising. . . . In other words in such cases there is a balance between giving out and taking in, between projection and introjection.[13]

That is, while projection was orginally conceived as a pathological mechanism, it is now seen as a normal mechanism of relating to others.

We would go farther still and propose that the degree to which the individual can change or modify his set of projected objects is a measure of the adaptability of his personality at this level. Rigidity implies compulsive projection of the same object or sets of objects in all situations, that is, projection of inappropriate objects, or the inability to project at all. The normal individual seeks to resurrect earlier object relationships and to reestablish them in the external "real" world. The stronger his emotional involvement with the internal objects, the more he will attempt to project them into reality. An instance of this is the fond lover waiting for his loved one and seeing her in every other approaching woman. Play, art, and religion are the prototypical forms of active externalization of internal objects.

"Externalizing" and "internalizing" are relative words which need qualifying because they imply a clearly defined ego boundary which is "crossed" in projection. As adults, we forget the long process through which a sense of separate identity is created and how fluid is the normal ego boundary even in adulthood. It is, in fact, relative to situations encountered and subject to redefinition, and it may be more appropriate to refer to projection as "ego-extension." The mother who experiences a sharp, stabbing pain in the arm as her child receives an injection has extended her ego boundary to include the child—the child's pain is experienced as her own pain. The clearest example of the fluidity of ego boundaries is the process of hypnotism, where the ego of another literally replaces the ego of the individual. Unfortunately, we understand relatively little of the conditions which determine the strength and weakness of ego boundaries in specific situations. We know most concerning the functioning of projection from therapy situations, particularly in the form of "transference." Once again, this has typically been regarded as pathological but, in fact, the therapeutic process represents an attempt to modify *rigid* forms of projective identification so that the individual may relate to others more normally. However, he will still rely on projection to accomplish this.

In situations where we do not feel threatened, projection is part of our normal pattern of responding to and being influenced by others. In situations of extreme threat, however, we sometimes repress our unwanted reactions, attributing them wholly to outside sources. It is this latter response, for example, which is particularly marked in the phenomenon of the "scapegoat," a common social phenomenon and an important one in small groups.

The processes of projection and internalization are central to the development of cohesion in primary groups. It is the activation of similar internalized objects through the construction of a "shared group fantasy" which is the affective basis of social order. Group integration occurs through the "matching" of similar internalized objects with external objects so that a delimited range of modes of relating is established, i.e., the group arrives at a consensus about the class of internal objects to which links will be made and the range of appropriate responses which will be brought into play. Through the sharing of fantasies, the group constructs a common mythology which, when attained, gives the members a satisfying sense of meaningfulness in group life. Agreement may be reached about matching internalized persons or internalized groups. The significance of projection or transference of the internalized image of a *person* has been widely recognised and discussed, for it is the form of projection occurring in individual therapy. The therapist is frequently, for instance, reacted to as a father figure. The significance of the projection or transference of the internalized image of *groups* has been treated in less detail; it is, however, a characteristic feature of therapy and self-analytic groups, where the whole constellation of family roles may be projected so that one person is seen as a father figure, another as a mother figure, and other members as siblings. In this manner, a complex projective fantasy concerning oedipal rivalry and sibling rivalry may be created. Other important groups, such as the adolescent peer group, or the romantic dyad, may also be projected at different times. In a recent publication, Wolf has made a clear statement concerning this process :

[Therapy groups] reflect a microcosmic society and, of course, tend to reproduce that much-abused institution—the family, which, since it probably ushered in the patient's neuroses, is the logical agency for checking it. . . . The presence of both sexes enables each participant to project more readily maternal, paternal, and various sibling relationships out of the past on to various people in the group. . . .[14]

A crucial question to be asked here is : What determines the particular object or object system which will be projected in any situation? And, since we are concerned particularly with group situations, how is it possible for groups to arrive at a consensus about projecting a common set of internalized objects? Presumably, the system of object relations selected represents a response to both internal and external forces—in the development of the individual, relative fixation may occur at one or more developmental levels, and some systems of object relations will assume greater emotional significance than others. We will posit, therefore, an internal hierarchy of object systems : If external conditions were invariate, the individual would choose to project one object system rather than others. As we know from psychiatric studies, for some individuals one set of internalized object relations is so important that it will be projected regardless of major changes in the external situation and despite maladaptive consequences. Presumably, however, the normal individual has differing and alternative sets of object relations which can be brought into play according to the particular external situation. In this case, external cues will be responded to which will serve to "pull" appropriate internalized relationships into play. In social situations, considerable use is made of such cues to define situations for the "actors" involved. The elevated seat of the judge in court, for instance, indicates a position of authority and, therefore, normally calls forth appropriate deferential reactions. The suppression of emotive symbols in the doctor's surgery emphasizes the fact that it is not a place for amatory play. Normal response to such symbols is so smooth that individuals are not conscious of the rapid switches in projective systems. It is chiefly in situations where individuals perceive competing cues that they become conscious of their responses. In such situations, or where cues are indistinct, the person actively seeks for cues which will allow him to respond to others in a meaningful way. This was brought home to me most clearly by a member of a class who said :

When I first came into the group everyone was completely a stranger to me. So for each person in the group I tried to think of someone I had known who reminded me of them in some way, and I thought of them as those persons until I was forced to revise my opinion by something they did or said.

Such a deliberate and consciously conceived form of projection is probably uncommon, but it does illustrate a process which occurs less consciously in situations of uncertainty. The easy transition in dreams of one person into another or their fusion into a single person are clear examples of the generalization of images which takes place in fantasy.

The formation of affective bonds in group development
We are dealing here with the problem of integration of the action of the different individuals who comprise a group. Individual action can only be coordinated by the creation of a common culture which is able to attract or compel the loyalties of group members and guide their actions in areas relevant to group functioning. At this point we would like to introduce the idea of the "focal conflict" as the matrix out of which culture develops.

There are some basic issues which are central to the nature of groups, over which conflict is likely to develop, and which must be resolved more or less adequately if the group is to hold together and function minimally, adequately, or effectively. Because these issues are basic to group life, and every individual begins life in a family group, each person comes to a new group situation with some preferred solutions to these problems. These preferred solutions are often not held consciously, but are predispositions to actions along particular lines. They usually bring with them strong emotional investment in the preferred solution.

Let us examine a well-documented regularity in the early stages of leaderless experimental problem solving groups as an example of one of these focal conflicts. It has been noted that when groups of students, previously unknown to each other, are assembled as experimental groups for six or eight sessions of problem solving, the second session is particularly fraught with interpersonal conflict. During this session there is a marked drop in task-oriented behavior, there is relatively little friendly behavior, but there is the highest level of hostile behavior. Careful analysis of this phenomenon has shown that what is occurring in these groups is a struggle for leadership status. As these groups have no formal leader or leaders, establishing a consensus on the relative status of group members is a necessary preliminary to effective problem solving. The conflict in the second session consists largely in some members fighting verbally for a dominant position in the group. Not all groups are able to achieve status consensus in a single meeting, and conflict is then extended into subsequent meetings; in these cases the group product has been shown to be significantly poorer as a result. The allocation of status and power among the group members is, therefore, a focal conflict that one can confidently predict for groups in formation and one which will recur over a period of time as groups mature and change. It should not be assumed from this, however, that everyone in a group necessarily prefers to be in the most dominant position. In fact, these studies present evidence that not all members engage in the struggle; some are apparently content to occupy, or actively prefer, subordinate rather than dominant roles in a group. There is also evidence that some of those who find themselves in a dominant position, initially, will subsequently abandon it as they perceive other consequences of occupying the position.

Can we then specify the most significant focal conflicts or issues for primary groups—what might be called the central integrative problems? Four such issues seem almost universally important:

1. the distribution of "attention," usually indicated by the amount of time the group spends "focused" on a particular individual;
2. the distribution of power and prestige, usually indicated by the attributed or actual influence the individual exercises in the group, particularly on group decisions;
3. the distribution of "goods" or the fruits of the group's instrumental activity—these may be tangible or intangible—;
4. the distribution of love and affection, usually indicated by the amount of liking group members express for an individual.

Each individual, over his lifetime, has built up certain underlying preferences as to a *desired* position in these dimensions. He has also built up a more realistic *expectation* as to what may actually result. There may be a discrepancy between these two—a particular person, for example, may *desire* to be the most popular person in the group but he may *expect*, on the basis of his past experience, to be somewhat disliked by most members. Both his desires and his expectations will probably influence his behavior—he may strive to be popular but the anxiety with which he does this may betray his expectation that his hopes will not be fulfilled.

The listing of these focal issues is meant to indicate the order in which they generally assume predominant importance. We do not have space to review research evidence for this, but newly formed groups seem to work on these issues in the sequence indicated. Members struggle initially to establish their desired share of the group's attention by monopolizing their optimum proportion of the total rate of interaction in the group. The satisfaction of whatever interpersonal needs predominate in the individual depends largely on establishing a sufficient exchange rate with others that may subsequently be qualitatively refined to deliver the kind of interpersonal "goods" the individual wishes to exchange. Next, mobilization of the group and its stabilization depend on establishing consensus in the group on the relative status of those in it. The stabilization of the status hierarchy is in turn the major determinant of the distribution of resources among group members. Those higher in status receive a greater proportion. Finally, emotional ties develop and strengthen over time, with each individual receiving more or less of the affective rewards and punishments.

The process of group integration can be viewed then as a successive series of focal conflicts centering about these issues. A particular focal conflict represents an attempt on the part of all or a significant proportion of group members to establish a solution to the conflict which will maximize their particular desired solution, or, failing that, minimally establish their expected solution. The nearer the individual approaches to his desired solution, the more satisfied he will be. To approximate this expected solution is to achieve an adequate level of satisfaction, but to fail to establish an expected solution will lead to dissatisfaction. Of course, a group may reach a solution that is close to the optimum for everyone. On the other hand, it may reach a solution that is not particularly satisfying to anyone, but which simply reduces the frustration which derives from seeing some few members actively enjoying commonly desired group resources.

Projective specialist and the processes of group formation
While we have identified a set of central ideas of integrative conflict, and outlined a sequence with which they frequently occur, we have not yet described the mechanisms by which these conflicts are worked through and resolved in the form of a particular group subculture. It is obvious that agreement on the solution of these conflicts is seldom arrived at by deliberate, conscious group decision making. Conflict is minimized in some cases by adjustment to particular cues in the social situation. For example, group members may accord superior status to one member who exhibits the dress and mannerisms of a higher socio-economic background. This may occur at a predominantly unconscious level because the members react as they have in past situations to similar cues. But, as the size of a social system increases, the possibility of differing cues being identified by different participants obviously increases. Since a good deal of projection operates unconsciously, how is it then possible for groups to reach concensus about the common internalized objects which will be projected, especially in cases where cues are contradictory or indistinct? The answer to this question is that specialized roles emerge which function to make cues more salient to members of the system. This has been clearly expressed by Jaques :

Individuals may put their internal conflicts into persons in the external world, unconsciously follow the course of the conflict by means of projective identification, and re-internalize the course and outcome of the externally perceived conflict by means of introjective identification. Societies provide institutionalized roles whose occupants are sanctioned, or required, to take into themselves the projected objects and impulses of other members. The occupants of such roles may absorb the objects and impulses—take them into themselves and become either good or bad objects with corresponding impulses—put them into an externally perceived ally, or enemy who is then loved or attacked.[16]

In this passage Jaques indicates the importance of the non-rational or projective specialist in the integration of social systems; in fact, one might regard his statement as the cornerstone of a dynamic theory to explain "charisma" or "charismatic leadership." The sociologist generally feels that charisma is an attribute of the leader's personality, some kind of "animal magnetism" which, therefore, as a sociologist he does not have to explain. Jacques' viewpoint leads one instead to see charisma as essentially the resultant of a mutual emotional awareness of cues transmitted between the leader and his followers. Implicit in Jaques' characterization of the process of projective identification is the division of the group into two parts—the individual or individuals who "act out" the problem and the more passive majority whose role is largely limited to the transmission of emotive signals, often at an unconscious level, of underlying emotional concerns. Thus the role of the projective or non-rational role specialist is crucial to the cohesiveness of the group; it is through the differentiation of such roles that emotions are channeled or "processed" in the group situation, that conflicts are worked out, that values and norms emerge, and are internalized by the group members.

To arrive at an adequate understanding of the way in which projective specialists emerge and are used by group members, it is necessary to make use of both Freud's concept of "identification with the idealized leader" and Jacques' idea of "the use of common object as a defense against psychotic anxieties." The two processes may be viewed as alternatives or supplements. Thus images are projected in such a way that concrete persons become living symbols of solidarity or conflict. Inner tensions are externalized and certain group members assume significance as models of parts of the self. The perceived compatibility of other persons with internal objects defines their suitability as targets for the projection of these good or bad objects.

The projective specialist plays an important role in channeling the emotional drives of others by focusing them on himself or by deflecting them on another object. He does this through the manipulation of acts and symbols which have acquired emotional meaning in the socialization experiences of group members. The problems of social integration do not find a solution primarily through an intellectual debate about appropriate values and norms to guide group action. Affective involvement and loyalty are achieved in a group as agreement is reached on who will be taken as appropriate self or non-self models and how these will be related to the individual's existing images of himself. Each group member participates vicariously as conflicting emotional propositions are worked through to a point of resolution; the group solution is then internalized, and becomes the common denominator underlying subsequent action in the group. It is this common denominator which is the primary basis for group cohesion.

Fantasy and mythology in group integration
The previous socialization experiences of members are vitally important in

group integration. Common structural features in families create common object types and common fantasies available for recall in conflict situations within groups. Focal conflicts developing in the group will be resonant with nuclear socialization conflicts; they will produce heightened emotional states involving the arousing of such emotions as hostility, sexual desire, and anxiety accompanied by fantasies such as aggression, sexual fulfillment, and escape. It is the communication of these states through expressive words and gestures which "sparks off" the action of projective specialists, whose dominant forms of expression are actional and who, therefore, play out group members' fantasies in a visible drama. The results of this drama are then internalized by the group members and become part of the developing mythology of the group. Such a mythology acts as a unifying and controlling force in the further development of the group, for it subordinates the images and plans of individual members to a superordinate image and plan which is a group rather than an individual product. As Malinowski has pointed out: "Myth is . . . a vital ingredient of human civilization; it is not an idle talk, but a hard worked active force; it is not an intellectual explanation or an artistic imagery, but a pragmatic charter of primitive faith and moral wisdom. . . ."[17]

Individual fantasies resemble mythologies in many ways, for example in symbolism and "logic," and group mythologies orginate in individual fantasies. However, while individual fantasies are the source of mythologies, mythologies represent those aspects of individual fantasies which are shared and persist because they have their basis in common life experiences. A group mythology develops from selection among individual fantasies; the particular fantasies which are chosen are then modified over time in accord with the general needs of the group members. Those members who are most influential in the creation and development of a group mythology are those who produce fantasies resonant with the individual fantasies of most members.

But it may well be asked: What functions do fantasy and mythology perform for a group? Mythology centers about persisting current focal concerns or areas of strain in the group, in the way that individual fantasy, for instance a dream, centers about current focal concerns of the individual. Both individual fantasy and mythology arise in situations of conflict and tension, represent conflict and tension in symbolic terms, and serve to resolve or alleviate the tension. Mythology, like individual fantasy, may be regressive, stabilizing, or creative, i.e., it may embody destructive infantile wishes and represent the triumph of social values over infantile wishes, or be an active form of imagining through which new patterns of action are forged. Collective *fantasy* is thus a method of communication which will be resorted to when members find a focal concern too threatening to handle directly or are unable cognitively to identify the nature of the focal concern. *Mythology* is the outcome of this process—the *institu-*

tionalized product of the communication of fantasy. Mythology is a symbolic representation of concerns which members of the group possess in common. As such, it exercises a powerful effect on group behavior because the elements of the myth are also elements of the inner emotional life of those in the group. Thus when mythology is made salient, it makes salient to the individual the inner images which it represents and, therefore, is a compelling force in drawing forth appropriate behavior.

For societies, mythologies are closely associated with important roles in the society, and are usually given over to the magical and religious specialists whose task it is to preserve and embellish the mythology and represent it to the social group. These magical and religious specialists not only serve the mythology, the mythology also serves them. Because of their association with the central symbols of the group—symbols invested with strong emotional resonance—the specialists themselves acquire some of the mythological power of the "gods" or "spirits," that is, the externalization of the inner images. This power, referred to by sociologists since Weber as "charisma," is a type of compulsive control exercised over the individual by an external object, a control similar in character to that exercised by internal objects with strong emotional investment. We can surmise, therefore, that the external object has gained this power through projection—the role specialist now "stands for" the internal object, his actions correspond to the internal fantasies of his followers who can then follow their dramatization in the world outside. The rapidity with which charisma can be lost is also explicable in terms of this theory, for when a role specialist acts "out of character" with the inner image he is no longer able to symbolize it effectively and so his ability to use the accompanying fantasy is broken. Similarly, if there is a radical change in the prevailing group emotion and the role specialist fails to change his behavior correspondingly, his source of power disappears.

The same process can be seen on a smaller scale in primary groups. Focal conflicts emerge as a significant majority of group members seek to establish a group solution which will optimally maximize their need satisfaction or minimally recreate an approximation to a group environment which is familiar enough to be predictable. More often than not these conflicts about relative status and power, achievement and self-expression, and emotional satisfaction and deprivation are resolved by group processes guided by role specialists who represent alternative solutions to these conflicts. The working through of these issues becomes embodied in a group mythology which preserves the solution and solidifies it as the mythology is internalized by group members. The clearest evidence for this view comes from studies of therapy groups and self-analytic groups in academic settings.

A number of students of processes in resocialization groups have documented the fact that there is a tendency for these groups to pass through qualitatively different phases of interaction and culture building in the course of group development. These phases are similar to those discussed above except that the phases are more prolonged and the conflicts more obvious. There now seems general agreement[18] that there is a tendency in such groups for the following sequence to occur :

1. A concern with leadership participation versus objective observation, the issue being whether to participate or withdraw, whether to involve oneself in the group or not.

2. Attempts, by those who decide to participate, to confront and control others and establish a status hierarchy in the group. These attempts are usually responded to with resentment and anger even by those who have not opted for an active role. This, in turn, leads to high rates of aggression and withdrawal, and attempts to defend oneself from the group by concealing one's emotions and fantasies. A status hierarchy is usually established by the end of this phase, although the hierarchy may not be willingly accepted.

3. Concern with task achievement accompanied by feelings of impotence and an inability to achieve, the expression of frustration and depression is high. One problem behind this is that when effective task leadership emerges, it emphasizes the stratification of the group, and arouses resentment which then leads to lowered morale and group loyalty.

4. Concern with affection between members and a rise in group identification; the internalization of the group and its norms by many members; the development of group cultural life in the form of extended expressive symbolism.

5. Concern with the ending of the group, with evaluating its successes and failures, with dissolving emotional ties. Depression is again high and leads to further internalization of the group culture.

Some evidence has also accumulated which indicates that this process is accompanied by a form of role differentiation which is crucial to group integration through the working out of a set of cultural solutions to the basic conflicts which these phases represent.

Bennis and Shepard,[19] for example, analyze recruitment to leadership roles within each phase of the development of therapy groups. They suggest that there are various personality types which are more or less congruent with the roles demanded by the unconscious needs of the group at each stage. They postulate that individuals vary considerably on dimensions about which conflict will occur. In particular, they regard two problems—authority and intimacy—as of crucial importance. They indicate that when authority emerges as an issue in the early stages of a therapy group's development, there will be some members who will attempt to find comfort and security in rules of procedure, in an agenda, or in an expert. These are referred to as dependent members. Others are discomforted by authoritarian procedures and they react to the same conflict by counterdependent behavior. Similarly, when intimacy becomes a group issue some will seek to create a stable situation where there is a high degree of intimacy (the overpersonal members), while others are threatened by this (the underpersonal members). Bennis and Shepard suggest that some members are "unconflicted" on a particular issue, that is, they will emerge as leaders who actively work to create one of the alternative solutions to the conflict. There will usually be other members, however, who are ambivalent or "conflicted" about what they want and whose participation will not be so clearly oriented to one solution or the other. Bennis and Shepard suggest that major swings in the cultural solution to these issues occur as one or other of the unconflicted members takes the lead and draws the group in the direction he feels impelled to go.

I have gathered some empirical evidence from academic self-analytic groups which supports the kind of analysis made by Bennis and Shepard. In a study of two self-analytic groups,[20] I used a content analysis of member reports of group meetings and showed that, in the groups studied, role specialists emerged who became symbols of the major alternatives faced by each group in the evolution of its culture. Thus the problems of attention and status are worked out through the interaction of two role specialists named the "scapegoat" and "aggressor." The scapegoat represents an excessive dependency along with a demand for an inordinate amount of attention. With the emotional support of the group members, the aggressor symbolically "puts down" the scapegoat or "cuts him down to size," thus rejecting simple dependency as a solution to the authority problem and also underlining the idea that centrality in the group will be shared out among members in a somewhat equitable fashion rather than seized unilaterally by the person who talks most volubly. The resolution of this conflict symbolizes the fact that the group has the power to exert control over members, particularly by punishing them, and that its emergent norms can be enforced. The group creates a myth about this event which centers about the group and its leadership. Because the formal leader —instructor—in these groups refuses to adopt the usual role of authority, the group feels out of control and feels the leader is weak and impotent. This is portrayed vividly in various imaginative stories or fantasies told in the group at this stage which usually center about groups, experienced in the past, which were immobilized and had ineffective leaders. The scapegoating of a disliked member is a way of resolving the authority issue in such a way as to emphasize the authoritative power of group norms. Thus group cohesion at this point is achieved by projective identification by most members with the aggressor in his attempts to silence and control the scapegoat who represents weakness, anxiety, and deviance from emergent group norms.

The next major conflict faced by the group centers about the amount of individual gratification which will be allowed members within the structure of group control. Is the system of control emerging in the group going to center about the punitive inhibition of impulse gratification or are members going to be able to express their impulses relatively freely within the group context? The aggressor continues to symbolize punitive control over impulses, while a new role, that of "seducer," comes to the fore to symbolize impulse gratification. For a time, action in the group swings from one pole to another as a symbolic dialectic discussion of these alternatives takes place. Some members polarize around one or other of these figures, while the majority of the group members are progressively immobilized by their inability to resolve the pull between the two extremes. Over time, however, group support swings to the side of the aggressor and once again the power of the group to control the behavior of individuals is demonstrated. This resolution produces a new myth expressed in fantasies in which the group and its formal leader are portrayed as cold and rejecting with the result that emotional satisfaction is stultified. Control has been established but at the cost of spontaneity and emotional communication. Finally, a new period ensues where identification with the formal authority figure takes place. The recreation of the image of the authority figure is instrumental here. Now members project their ego-ideal onto the authority figure and create a new myth expressed in Utopian fantasies of groups marked by personal affection and productivity. This period in the life of the group is marked by the emergence of religious imagery and a harnessing of motivation to task achievement. It is as if the group has finally succeeded in creating an "ego" for itself.

This particular study shows that there are major shifts in the development of primary groups and that phasal shifts are accompanied by changes in the current myth which the group develops to rationalize and integrate its behavioral assumptions. A myth in this sense is a view of the nature of authority and group relationships which is meaningful to members in terms of their previous experiences of primary groups, going back ultimately to experiences in the family. In the shift from one phase to another, nonrational role specialists play a crucial part. The individual is able to project his inner conflict onto group members who play roles representing distinctive alternatives and to watch them work out a solution in the inner conflict through their actions. He is not, however, only a passive observer in this process for he can, and usually does, both consciously and unconsciously communicate support or opposition for one or other proponent at various stages of conflict resolution: People feel meaning even when they cannot freeze it into words, and the symbolic expressions of the role specialist communicate meaning at an emotional level, building a bond of identity between members and creating a consciousness in the individual that the images of his heart and mind are those of others as well. It is by this means that the collection of individuals brought together to perform a task, or thrown together by force of circumstances, come to share a common identity and common goals, and will sacrifice self-interest for the interests of the group. It is by sharing in what Piaget called "the symbolic evocation of absent realities" that a novel cultural reality is created, and this reality can be internalized to form a new center of control over personal behavior.

But the process of relating to the primary group does not proceed in a social vacuum. Each group is not an isolated unit. It is also a sub-system of a larger social order which influences its basic character. In particular, the relationship of the primary group to its social environment exercises a marked influence on the needs which the individual can satisfy through his relationship with the group. While all primary groups center around the affective involvement of members, the environment of the group can be a powerful influence on limiting or enhancing the emotional satisfaction of membership. If workers are strung out along an assembly line, for instance, or working on different floors of a plant, they may form primary groups but the extent of the interaction and hence their need satisfaction can be severely limited by technology. Similarly, the structure of authority may limit the control of the group over its environment so that it is powerless to ameliorate poor conditions.

So far, we have developed a theory of the way in which the individual relates to the primary group, as if all primary groups existed in the same milieu. In fact milieux differ widely and we shall now consider some of these differences systematically, inquiring in particular how these differences affect the processes we have been discussing. We shall also deal with the ways in which individuals use primary group membership to pursue interests which extend beyond emotional satisfactions and are more "rational" in character.

The coordination of the primary group with the larger social system [21]

Previous approaches

Despite a sizeable body of literature on small group processes, little work has been done to formulate a theory of the relationship between small groups and the larger social systems which encompass them. The titles of some articles sound very promising,[22] and contain useful ideas; but none of them present what might be called a comprehensive theory of the relationship of primary groups to larger social structures. More promising is a recent paper by Wilson.[23] He proposes that to understand more complex social systems, it is necessary to understand the relations between small groups, on the one hand, and social structure and institutionalization on the other. He proposes in particular that "the structure of role relationships in a social system corresponds to a network of overlapping small groups" and that "the total network of small groups is a complex system in which the state of any one group depends in general on the state of all the others." [24] This is strongly supported by the literature reviewed in chapter 1, and it is a far more realistic view of the nature of secondary structures than the idea that they are collections of atomized individuals controlled by organizational charts, formal principles of supervision, and economic incentives. However, it tells us little that would help predict, for example, whether or not the members of small groups will act to support or subvert the goals of the larger system of which they are part.

And, after all, that is a crucial question, for we have advanced the idea that the small group is a vital element in social integration or, as is sometimes the case, in social disintegration and reintegration. We might state at this point, therefore, that an adequate theory dealing with the relationship of the primary group to secondary structures would help us to predict whether the group culture will tend to integrate members into the culture of the secondary structure or will mobilize them to ignore, modify, or transform it.

In preparing this section, the authors reviewed some of the few studies which have dealt directly with this issue and, were struck by a remarkable parallel between two studies from diverse sources. One of these works was Cloward and Ohlin's *Delinquency and Opportunity*.[25] Cloward and Ohlin review previous theories of the origins and causes of gang delinquency and develop a theory which is intended to account for—and to a limited extent predict—the different forms of deviant behavior in lower class gangs. These authors distinguish three distinct types of delinquent gang :

1. The criminal gang, which engages primarily in organized crime, particularly theft. The delinquent behavior of these gangs reveals rational planning and well-disciplined behavior on the part of gang members.

2. The conflict gang, which engages in sporadic violence rather than systematic theft. Behavior in these gangs is marked by long periods of relative passive, law-abiding behavior broken by sudden outbreaks of "pointless" violence.

3. The retreatist gang, which centers primarily around drug taking.

Cloward and Ohlin advance a theory which relates gang behavior to two main factors (1) the nature of the adult community, particularly whether it is in a stable, socially integrated area, and (2) the availability of legitimate means to attain culturally-valued goals. Criminal gangs, in Cloward and Ohlin's theory, arise in communities which are sufficiently stable for patterned roles and skilled crime-oriented behavior to be learned, but in which it is difficult or impossible to attain culturally-valued goals. Cloward and Ohlin emphasize that American society stresses material success and teaches that it is available for all. The experience of the lower class adolescent is, however, that the legitimate means of obtaining material success are not available to him. Lacking legitimate means, some adolescents choose to obtain the ends by illegitimate means and obtain training and role models from the criminal infra-structure.

In socially unintegrated areas, the same kind of relative deprivation applies, but the adolescent is doubly disadvantaged. Neither the legitimate nor the illegitimate means are available to him because of the disorganized nature of his "community." Gangs of adolescents form, but they are unable to develop systematic instrumental means for obtaining desired ends. All they can do is to relieve their frustration periodically in outbursts of emotionally-directed violence. Such violence is useless from an instrumental viewpoint, but operates as a catharsis to relieve the buildup of tension.

Retreatist gangs are seen as being formed by the "dropouts" from both criminal and conflict subsystems. In both systems, some individuals are not able to achieve or sustain gang membership and fall back into retreatist subgroups which center around narcissistic gratification through group fantasy and drug taking.

The other study which attempts to predict deviant primary group behavior, but in a very different context, is by Sayles.[26] Sayles is concerned with behavior of industrial work groups which can be considered deviant from the point of view of management's goals. Sayles considers four kinds of work groups which can be described as follows:

1. The conservative work group, which usually consists of highly skilled workers holding strategic positions in the work flow. Work groups of this kind usually conform to management expectations, but occasionally exercise restrained but effective pressure on management for highly specific objectives of benefit to the employees rather than management.
2. The strategic work group, which usually consists of semi-skilled workers who cannot be promoted but have a realistic opportunity for improving their conditions if the job is upgraded. Such groups are "strategic" in the sense that they usually develop rationally designed strategies for exerting continuous, well-controlled pressure on management.
3. The erratic work group, which usually consists of workers who have unskilled jobs which are technologically interdependent but very similar in nature. Such groups are erratic in the sense that they exhibit long periods of docile behavior punctuated by unpredictable emotional outburst often accompanied by wildcat walkouts.
4. The apathetic work group, which is usually made up of workers who hold low paid jobs, or who work in the same area on unrelated jobs. Groups of this kind seem unable or uninterested in forming pressure groups, but they create a problem for management by their high turnover rate.

The correspondence between Cloward and Ohlin's and Sayles' theories is more apparent if they are summarized as in table 2.1.

Both theories are similar in that they suggest that the kind of deviance in lower status groups can be predicted from knowing their status

Table 2.1: A comparison of two theories of deviant behavior

SAYLES	CLOWARD AND OHLIN
1. Conservative work group—restrained pressure for specific objectives.	1. No equivalent to Sayles.
2. Strategic work group—continuous, rationally-oriented, well-controlled pressure for continual upgrading.	2. Criminal gang—rationally-oriented, well-controlled and organized crime, particularly theft.
3. Erratic work group—sporadic, unpredictable wildcat walkouts, or other emotional outbursts.	3. Conflict gang—sporadic, irrational, violent outbursts.
4. Apathetic work group—high desertion, withdrawal rate.	4. Retreatist gang—narcissistic, withdrawal into drug taking.

and certain key aspects about the organization of their environment. They are also similar in that they suggest that rationally-oriented deviant behavior is most likely to emerge in that part of the social hierarchy where : (1) members share common interests derived from a feeling of relative deprivation—that is, members share the aspirations of upper groups but are denied legitimate means to realize these aspirations; and (2) members, through group organization, can formulate means which stand a realistic chance of being at least partially successful. The theories are also similar in suggesting that there are some environmental conditions where instrumental interdependence is difficult to achieve or group organization cannot realistically bring substantial realization of aspirations. Under these conditions, the theories suggest that irrational, expressive behavior will occur that is instrumentally useless but emotionally satisfying in relieving an accumulation of frustration and anger. Finally, the theories provide a place for those rather poorly integrated groups made up of individuals who have not "made it" in the higher levels of the system and who no longer attempt to realize their culturally-induced aspirations.

The effect of the larger environment on the primary group. At this point we inquired whether these basic ideas could be used to construct a more general theory that would encompass many types of primary group behavior and allow us to predict : 1. where in the social system primary groups will support or deviate from the norms of the larger system, 2. what form deviance will take if it occurs, and 3. how some key factors in the internal structure of the group, such as group cohesiveness, leadership style, and the complexity of informal organization will vary. We will not trace the various steps by which such a theory was developed, but in the remainder of this chapter such a theory will be advanced, supported and illustrated with some of the more pertinent evidence gathered from empirical studies.

Our theory follows Cloward and Ohlin and Sayles in focusing on the relationship of the primary group to its environment. Underlying both of these works is a theme which depicts individuals using the primary group as a means for pursuing, within the larger system, personal goals which the system was not designed to fulfill. Like these authors we see the structure or organization of the secondary system as placing limits on the patterns of primary group relationships which can develop within it. We also agree that primary groups are used as instruments for coping with the secondary system in the interests of members, but that the effectiveness of primary groups in this regard varies with different levels of the hierarchies which control the secondary systems. A very important factor in this regard is the degree to which the environment renders communication and interaction difficult, prescribes the kinds of communication and interaction which can occur, and facilitates the development of varied patterns of communication and interaction. In community settings this is strongly influenced by social mobility, and in organization settings by technology. The ability of the individual to predict, cope with, and exercise control over his immediate environment, either singly or in cooperation with others, is an extremely important factor in his conformity to and deviance from the formal goals of the secondary system.

The most important motivating factor in the formation of primary groups is the desire for a personal, affective response from a few other individuals. The need for an emotional response from others is basic, as we have shown in the earlier part of this chapter, but the attainment of satisfying interpersonal relations in secondary systems is often limited by an emphasis on rational, instrumental behavior. Primary groups help fulfill the need for affective relations and would, therefore, exist in secondary structures even if this were the only need they fulfilled. But primary groups also form because secondary roles do not always enable the individual to attain other goals that are important to him but which he may be able to obtain by collaborating with others. Similarly, primary groups also help the individual to cope with the system by informing him of the way the system works and, in some cases, by influencing the system to work to his advantage.

There are, therefore, two basic reasons for the existence of primary groups : (1) the need for emotional relations with others and, (2) the need to cope with and control the secondary environment as effectively as possible. We have discussed the need for affective response in some detail in the first part of this chapter but we wish to point out two very important motivating factors in group participation. The most important form of control is that which allows the individual singly, or through group membership, to exercise control over the official *goals* of the secondary system. This kind of control is most effective because it allows an individual to influence the orientation of the secondary system so that its goals coincide with, supplement, or at least do not contravene his own. Another form of control can be exercised : this is control over the means by which secondary goals are implemented. (Even if I cannot influence the goals of the secondary system in which I find myself, if I have control over some of the strategic resources needed to pursue these goals, I can bargain for more attention being paid to my interests.)

Most individuals are influenced to pursue two goals from primary group membership—to gain an affective response from others and to enhance control over the secondary system in their own interests either by modifying its goals directly, or by bargaining for more attention to their needs by threatening the attainment of the system's goals. An individual's formal role in the secondary system may ensure the satisfaction of one or both of these needs, but secondary roles are seldom totally efficient in these respects. Consequently, there is always a push for primary group behavior where people of similar status interact within a larger secondary system. But, more importantly, the *way* primary groups serve their members can be determined in general terms by noting the way in which the secondary roles of the group members are least efficient as a means for attaining the goals we have discussed. For instance, given a secondary role which gives its encumbent little opportunity to develop satisfying emotional relationships with others, little or no control over the goals of the secondary system, and a great deal of control over secondary system processes, we would predict that a primary group developed by this person, along with others in similar roles, would use its control over system processes to enhance satisfaction in these other areas.

We have worked from and extended the theoretical systems of Sayles, and Cloward and Ohlin to give a broader coverage of the upper echelons of the social systems with which we are concerned. The resulting six category system is designed to predict primary group characteristics given environmental constraints, or to predict environmental constraints given primary group characteristics. Three of the categories are similar to those three which Cloward and Ohlin and Sayles hold in common. The other three include Sayles' fourth category and involve other groups which are found in the upper reaches of organizational hierarchies not considered by these authors. It appears, however, that deviance from formal organizational goals is not the sole prerogative of low status workers.

Table 2.2 summarizes the following discussion.

Each category will be taken in turn, and four different aspects of it will be discussed : (1) the relationship of the typical member to his environment will be considered in terms of the extent to which his secondary role provides social-emotional satisfaction and an opportunity to influence the goals of the secondary system or the means by which these goals are realized; (2) how the secondary roles of the members place limits on the amount and kinds of satisfaction the member can gain from a primary

Table 2.2: The relationship of primary groups to their social context

NAME OF GROUP	EXAMPLES	DOMINANT ROLES	CHARACTERISTICS
apathetic groups	retreatist drug addict groups apathetic work groups in industry deserter groups in armies geographically mobile lower-lower class families	the seducer	A subjugated position with no control over the environment. A sense of failure coupled with mobility reduces social inter-action and leads to retreatism.
erratic groups	conflict gangs small crews and short assembly lines in industry unintegrated Negro units in U.S. Army some lower class families in stable areas	the aggressor	A subjugated position with no control over the environment. The environment encourages interaction which leads to solidarity; frustration is shared and irrational, explosive behavior results—for example wildcat strikes, scapegoating.
strategic groups	criminal gangs engaged in organized theft middle class social clubs semi-skilled workers in industrial work groups regular military units	Instrumental and expressive leaders, or "The Great Man" leader	The environment encourages solidarity; group-controlled deviance emerges. It is instrumental and effective in inducing environmental change if limited when collective action is undertaken. Groups have some control over the means by which social goals are realized.
cabal groups	rising community power cliques upper middle class families lower officer groups in army cliques of men occupying strategic staff and line positions in industrial organizations	the wheeler-dealer	The environment encourages limited solidarity because differential skills and secondary roles allow a trading-off process between members. The creation of a new power center allows the enhancement of individual positions. Control over means is high and, if collective action is undertaken, goal setting can sometimes be influenced.

Table 2.2 (continued)

NAME OF GROUP	EXAMPLES	DOMINANT ROLES	CHARACTERISTICS
organizer groups	groups of top executives in business and industrial plants established community power elites chiefs of staff	The chief	The environment allows solidarity and solidarity facilitates the effective implementation of policy. There is some control over goals and a high degree of control over means can be maintained if the groups are solidary.
conservative groups	upper elite families the independently wealthy large stockholders	The idol	The ownership of resources is the main source of power mainly for affective reasons. and solidarity is sought Control over goals is very high, but control over means is exercised through organizers.

group will be described; (3) how the primary group develops and operates under these conditions will be discussed, and, in particular, how the emerging structure encourages behavior which supports or deviates from the formal goals of the secondary system; and (4) some examples will be given from empirical research relating to the type of groups we have in mind for the given category.

Apathetic groups: Members of apathetic groups occupy roles of complete subjugation in the larger social system. They are given little opportunity to attain goals personally important to them or to influence the goals of the total system. Their roles in the attainment of goals set by others are relatively insignificant in that, with little cost to the system, they can be readily replaced, if indeed they are wanted at all. In an organizational setting their formal role in the secondary system generally permits little social interaction among peers. This is, therefore, a situation where group life is stifled and group life exists only when secondary role requirements are not in effect or are flouted. Yet flouting role requirements invites heavy sanctions, such as being fired from the job. Members are powerless to resist such action and collective attempts to modify the larger system are difficult or impossible. This is in contrast to other groups which do possess the ability to fight back when the system threatens sanctions. The apathetic group is not in a position to do this.

Group cohesion depends on affective communication. But affective communication is only possible where members can assemble to communicate. However, assembly is sometimes denied by the secondary system—laws against "consorting" and "loitering" in community areas are examples and are mainly enforced in relation to lower class groups.

In organizational settings, the nature of the technology may reduce opportunities for social contact. Often, for example, machines have to be tended in isolation and, if neglected, stoppages and breakdowns are likely to occur. In such situations, any group activity encourages members to deviate from the norms of the secondary system. Consequently, sanctions may be employed to reduce social interaction and so group activity is often sporadic and group cohesiveness correspondingly low. Thus apathetic groups are particularly apparent where the larger system interferes with spontaneous assembly, and makes those groups that are formed essentially illicit.

In such cases, environmental constraints prevent group life from serving as anything but a source of social-emotional satisfaction and even this is achieved at the risk of separation from the larger system. Because the primary group, in this case, possesses no power over the secondary system, group members resort to fantasy as a substitute way of gratifying needs which cannot be fulfilled in the real world. Thus, the main activity of apathetic groups is fantasy building, sometimes supported in communal settings by the use of drugs.

Cloward and Ohlin have described apathetic groups, in communal settings, which take the form of "retreatist" gangs of drug addicts. Sayles' "apathetic" work groups also meet the criteria outlined. One can also point to the deserter and surrender groups in military systems which are made up of soldiers cut off from supplies, separated from their original units, and under enemy fire.[27] The social debris of W. L. Warner's community studies,[28] that is, those he designates as members of the lower-lower class, and citizens of poverty cultures such as those studied by Robert O. Lewis in Mexico City,[29] and which other writers have studied in the slums of London, Paris, New York and Moscow, also form groups of this type. Such groups generally exist at the very bottom of secondary systems, since there are few other areas in the hierarchy where role constraints are so severe. These group structures are usually ephemeral, their membership unstable, their normative systems relatively undeveloped and capable of exercising little sustained control over individual member behavior.

The most prominent leadership role in the apathetic group is that of "seducer," for the seducer is the member who symbolizes the group's wish to escape from unrewarding constraints imposed by the outside world. He leads other members in a "flight" reaction away from reality into a less threatening world of fantasy. Gang studies[30] show that the fantasies of retreatist gangs are filled with imagery of "instant success"—the term "flight" is very descriptive in that it has the meanings both of escape and of soaring. The wish to rise immediately and effortlessly to fame and fortune is clearly expressed and even drug taking is referred to as "getting high." By using appropriate imagery, the seducer is able to reinforce the inner wishes of the apathetics to escape and rise above reality. Since reality cannot be constantly avoided, the seducer's leadership role in any group is usually a transitory one, for his charismatic qualities inevitably fail to produce the longed-for Utopia. The transitory character of leadership in these groups fits in well, however, with the general pattern of drifting, bumming, and casual labor.

Erratic groups: The secondary roles shared by typical members of erratic groups are somewhat similar to those of the apathetics. The main difference is that erratic groups are more able to operate as groups while members are performing their secondary roles. The consequence of this reduction in one major environmental constraint has both positive and negative aspects. On the one hand, it promotes group stability by encouraging group activity and leading members to act on a more reality-oriented level, for example, to try to use the group to adapt more effectively to the larger system. On the other hand, the primary group can still exercise little control over its environment. It, therefore, offers low satisfaction of needs other than those which are affective, but it facilitates the communication of frustration. As a result, it reinforces resentment through a process of emotional contagion. Meeting others while performing one's role serves to heighten one's sensitivity to the group's lack of control over the institutional setting. As the subservience and insignificance of the group and its members are emphasized, there is a gradual build-up of frustration and hostility which may be released in explosive, irrational, and sometimes violent ways.

Thus group behavior typically consists of long periods of verbal—sometimes adaptive, sometimes fantasy-oriented—activity followed by violent emotional outbursts. Such outbursts perform two functions. First, they have a cathartic value, for in releasing pent-up tensions, they make it possible for group life to continue at a more peaceful level and enable members to continue trying to adapt to reality. Second, they constitute a weapon which the group uses to remind the controllers of the secondary system that all is not well at their end of the field. The weapon is not very effective because its timing is unplanned and usually not organized on a scale large enough to change the system. But it does ensure the group's existence is known and, as a result, members' problems are sometimes taken into consideration by system leaders. More often, however, negative sanctions are levied upon group members, especially if the destruction of property is involved.

The most important dimension of group life for the erratics is thus the affective one, with a heavy emphasis on the discharge of mounting tension. Consequently, the group leader is usually the individual who responds most directly to the build-up of tension by providing outlets for mounting hostility. Such a leader can maintain his power by manipulating symbols of hostility and aggression, but he cannot effectively control the timing of tension release. He must act when tension is high and so cannot readily mobilize group emotion for instrumental purposes. We refer to this type of leader as "the aggressor."

Elsewhere I have provided a description of the role of the adolescent gang leader in triggering aggressive activity. In a taped interview, the informal leader of a delinquent gang described, in his own words, the way in which his group damaged a club room which had been set up by community organizations for youth in the area. The incident led to the closing of the club room.

It was quite a good turn out down there that night. The night we went down there, there was judo on early and it finished down there at eight o'clock. A man came in with the records. He turned on the record player and we put a couple of rock 'n roll records on and he turned it off, and wouldn't let us play any more. So we all walked outside and he told us to come back inside and locked the door again and put up some table tennis. No one would play table tennis. They wanted to play records. "All right," he said, "you can go if you don't want to join in the games." So at any rate we all walked outside and Bob and I went up to the hotel and when we came back I got a bottle of coke poured down my back. "All right," he said, "if you want to run the place like that you'd better go home." We were just about ready to go when he gave me a broom and dustpan and told me to clean up the floor. I got a nice big tin full and Bob tipped it on the floor again, and he threw it over again, and the old bloke came over and said, "Come on, what are you doing?" So I threw the dustpan at him and the broom smashed the window. Then Bob came charging down with the broom and put it straight through a window. Then we got the legs off the chairs, both of us, and broke every leg on the chairs, the mops, the sink, tore the curtains down and smashed the coke machine. He [the adult club leader] was standing out the front at the door watching. We tore the curtains down off the stage. "All right," he said, "you'd better go." So he put us out and locked the place up.[31]

The role of the gang leader in sensing the group's rising hostility and summing it up in direct action is shown clearly in this incident as is the dependence of his leadership on the existence of such emotions.

Cohesion in these groups varies over time but is markedly increased for short periods while aggression is directed to a scapegoat within the group or a symbolic object outside the group. Unity comes through finding a common object to hate and attack. The group combines to fight rather than to engage in flight like the apathetic groups.

The type of "conflict gang" described by Cloward and Ohlin is certainly the most publicized type of erratic group found in the modern city. Gangs exhibiting this kind of behavior have been studied at first hand and clearly described by a number of social scientists and others in the field.[32] Typically such gangs spend lengthy periods "hanging around" on street corners, but these lengthy periods of passivity are inclined to erupt into the sporadic violence of gang fights or beatings.

Such gangs are found in areas of the city which are disorganized by transience or, if organized, do not provide gang members with opportunities to pursue wealth and community power in a systematic way.

Sayles' "erratic" work groups are also of this type. In industry, members of erratic groups often hold jobs involving low-status, small-crew work controlled by machinery, for instance, short assembly lines involving a high level of worker interdependence. In this case, workers must act in each others' presence with the recognition that a machine controls them all. The ability of the group to assemble but not to control its own action creates considerable frustration.

Many of Warner's upper-lower class families also display erratic characteristics. This is presumably because they espouse social aspirations which they are unable to fulfill while living in communities where communication with other families is facilitated. Similarly, segregated Negro units in World War II developed strong cohesiveness but displayed erratic characteristics. In U.S. cities rioting and looting emerges most frequently in upper-lower class areas. In general, therefore, erratic groups are formed among individuals who are low in a social hierarchy, can communicate with each other, but cannot influence the system in such a way as to promote their own real interests. Such groups can undertake occasional concerted group action in response to the build-up of frustration, but the group action generally takes destructive forms.

Strategic groups:　The members of strategic groups are likely to hold roles in the secondary system which differ from those of erratic group members in two ways. First, the roles are more crucial for the operation of the system in that they require the incumbents to exercise more discretion or control over the means for achieving secondary goals. Second, the roles involve few technological constraints such as interdependence in a work flow or control by a machine. As a consequence of these two factors, the strategic group is usually a far more complexly organized system than are either the erratic or apathetic groups.

As in the case of the apathetic and erratic groups, the secondary roles of the members of strategic groups are still relatively subjugated to the roles of status superiors. Use of the group to affect the secondary system in the interests of maximizing personally-desired goals is not legitimated by the formal leaders in the system. But unlike the other groups discussed, environmental constraints are sufficiently weak to make the group activity a realistic way of achieving results in this direction. As the secondary roles of group members do not dictate the nature of the interdependence between members, there is the possibility for greater flexibility in group organization and better use of the personal resources within the group. The possibility of exercising some control over the system, rather than being completely subjugated to it, reduces frustration so that group behavior does not center around tension release. Because members' roles are relatively important in maintaining the wider system, those who control the system are more likely to alter aspects of the system so that the central processes will not be seriously disrupted. Those who control the system eventually realize that negative sanctions used in response to deviance by members of these groups often provoke further deviance. Expelling them from the system and replacing them—at least in large numbers—is costly because their roles require more selective recruitment and more training than is the case with workers lower in the hierarchy. Their absence during the replacement process can also seriously affect the operation of the system. Because of these factors, the members of strategic groups are likely to employ tactics of systematically controlled collective deviance to bargain with superiors who have more legitimate control over the system. Such behavior makes the system pay a price for their conformity, a price which constitutes progressive achievement of the goals of the strategic group.

However, there is a limit to the extent and frequency with which collective deviant acts can be undertaken by the strategic group. Too great a deviance in any one instance, or too frequent deviance over an extended period, will incur costs to the system greater than those of complete replacement. Replacement then becomes the lesser of two evils and is more likely to be used. In line with this we can posit a need in the strategic group for a well-developed system of internal control to keep deviance at its most profitable level, and this is what is generally found.

Strategic groups are instrumental groups *par excellence*. They develop more complex normative systems than apathetic or erratic groups and more clearly defined leaders. Like most instrumentally-oriented groups, they are likely to develop differentiated instrumental and expressive leaders who play mutually supporting roles. The instrumental leader forces the pace of task achievement while the expressive leader builds up and maintains the solidarity of the group. Sometimes these roles are combined by the exceptional or "great man" leader who can perform both functions effectively, but this demands considerable flexibility of leadership style. The leaders of the strategic group must be able to guide group members through complex strategies which reap benefits for the group as a whole. They must also be able to control group emotions despite the discipline and delayed gratification which are involved.

Before considering some examples, it should be made clear that the strategic group does not seek control over system processes as an end in itself. While groups sometimes act informally to block the means of goal-attainment in the secondary system, this is done for the purpose of pursuing the group's own goals rather than for the sake of controlling the means themselves.

One example of a strategic group is Cloward and Ohlin's criminal gang. Here rational, disciplined, deviant behavior is used to gain material resources unattainable through members' secondary roles in the community. The limit on the extent and frequency of deviance is especially evident here. Thefts must be well timed and carefully executed. Members must also understand secondary norms and, in fact, conform to some of them to ensure that tracing the theft becomes too costly to be worth carrying through to the apprehension of the criminals. What often occurs as a result is an unwritten agreement, between the police and suspected criminals, for the criminals to keep to their own territory and the police to let them alone within it as long as they commit "acceptable" crimes and keep the crime rate at a "reasonable" level.

One of the criminal gang's counterparts in polite society is the middle-class social club. The members of these groups aspire to belong to higher social elites. However, they can only do this relative to other middle class persons. They can be elitist by becoming trend setters, but they cannot stray far from the middle class morality nor can they downgrade the latter to any great extent without fear of being expelled from the social network which buoys them up. Their goals are gained by breaking protocol in minor and acceptable ways, but the protocol as a whole must be recognized and peers have to believe that basically the groups support it and contribute to its maintenance. The same is true for the cliques and crowds of middle class youth where strategic group behavior is so studiously learned.

Sayles' "strategic groups" in industry are, of course, prototypical, and the strategic group is also the typical small work group studied by industrial sociologists from Mayo to Zaleznik at the Harvard Business School. The systematic restriction of output is especially germane to these groups, as is the well-disciplined strike. Members of these groups are known to accept the authority of the factory system and their jobs are deeply imbedded in the production process. As a result their deviance is most tolerated and most profitable. Less skilled workers are more easily replaced. More highly skilled workers are given more individual power to attain personal goals and, consequently, these men are apt to form groups of another type which we shall discuss later.

The typical combat team in the armed services is also a strategic group. The extended and thorough training in obedience to authority which is given the members of such squads certainly attests to the potential source of systematic deviance which they represent.

Cabal groups: A cabal is a factional group, with emphasis on secrecy and confidentiality, which engages in power maneuvers in order to advance the interests of members. The roles held by members of this group differ from those of strategic group members in that they give their incumbents a good deal of power over the processes by which the system achieves its goals and even some control over goal-setting if they act in concert. They are also relatively free from environmental constraints on moving about and interacting freely with others.

The power of a cabal member's secondary role enables him to pursue many of his own interests quite effectively without group support. Because of this the cabal member is less dependent on his group. But he must maintain as much power as possible over system processes if he is to extend this capability. Consequently, while the strategic group threatens to dislocate system processes in order to attain specific goals, the cabal generally attempts to support system processes but to bring them more under the control of the cabal. Given this control, however, cabal members like to use it to achieve personal goals that are not formally recognized, particularly to enhance their own personal power in the system. But often those who have the resources which will most benefit the cabal member are other members of his own group. Within the cabal is a mixture of conflicting and complementary interests and what results is a continuous process of exchange. This process of exchange is enhanced by the fact that different members of cabals tend to hold secondary roles at somewhat different levels and in different areas of speciality—thus I may provide you with some important "inside information" about plant politics if you use your influence to upgrade my position.

Deviance in the cabal takes the form of a steady push to take a good deal of organizational decision making out of the formal, relatively "public" structures set up for this purpose. Members express considerable resentment with "red tape," "bureaucratic procedures," and "committee processes." They advocate the virtues of individual decision making and individual responsibility. By bypassing formal processes, these groups operate to reduce the oversight and control exercised over their activities by higher administrators and hence to enhance their freedom to negotiate informally and build up informal power centers lower in the organizational hierarchy.

If members are sufficiently motivated, as they usually are in times of rapid organizational expansion or major environmental change, this type of group can develop the most complex pattern of behavior of any type in the secondary system. Each member may hold several roles within the group, for example, an instrumental one in one area, a coordinating one in another, and an expressive one in a third. For the purposes of prediction, however, this group type is also the most problematic. Because members can achieve a good deal on their own, they may be sufficiently satisfied with their lot to forego group activity. A good deal depends on the nature of their personalities—a high need for power, in particular—and the stability of the secondary system. Change in the recruitment pattern and/or change in the structure of the system are likely to activate or reactivate cabals.

The key leadership role which is likely to develop in the cabal is the "wheeler-dealer." This is usually a person with a high activity rate who is constantly on the move developing personal contacts in strategic positions. He is an object of regard within his group because of his personal contacts with people in key positions and because of his ability to facilitate trade-offs of information and power. He sees interaction as a process of bargaining and exchange, and while ready to do favors, does them because they represent credit which can be drawn on in the future.

Examples of cabals are community power cliques which often arise from the upper-middle class. Similarly, the informal groups in industrial management referred to by Melville Dalton as "vertical symbiotic cliques" [33] exhibit the characteristics of cabals. Burns[34] has also given a detailed description of their operations and functions within organizational settings.

Organizer groups: Members of this type of group directly control the secondary system; they are the captains of industry, the community power elites, the chiefs of staff. Unlike members of cabals, these people are not motivated to form a primary group to attain control over secondary goals, for goal setting is one of their major functions. Besides seeking the emotional satisfactions of group relationships, they use the primary group to solve their problem of controlling the means by which organizational goals are realized. Their roles not only give them great power, but also place them in positions separate from the day-to-day details of system processes. Apart from emotional support, informal association in a group offers them a chance to coordinate their actions and to consolidate their power in order to prevent the subsystem from resisting their plans for implementing secondary goals.

As the term "organizer" implies, members of organizer groups try to solve this dilemma through the process of organization or, perhaps more correctly, of reorganization. While this tactic has little effect on the behavior of members of the apathetic and erratic groups, it has a very important effect on strategic and cabal groups. Through reorganization, either by changes in role requirements or by interchanging role incumbents in different parts of the secondary structure, organizers can limit or remove the control over system means possessed by cabals and strategic groups. The process of informal reorganization has then to take place among cabals and strategic groups before their control can be reestablished.

The attitude of the organizers is well summarized by a comment from a bank president concerning reactions to his attempts to introduce organization changes :

Being an officer around here is somewhat of a brutal process. We give a person just enough rope to hang himself. That is not to say we fire them, just as we don't fire the people who always run to 'papa,' mainly because of the age-old principles of banking. What we do, however, is castrate them, you know, the age-old game of 'now you see it, now you don't.' We move them around the organization so fast or find a cubbyhole for them so they don't have a chance to get in our way.[35]

Reorganization takes time and energy, and can slow down and dislocate system processes. System heads are obliged to weigh these factors against the gains likely to be derived from initiating such a procedure. Consequently, organizer group behavior can be seen to vary in intensity over a period of time. The base level of activity in organizer groups is provided by the need for affective relations. The varying parameter is consultation and planning in response to the gradual build-up of informal blocks to the attainment of system goals, or to important changes in formal goals, or in the environment of the system. The personal goals pursued by organizer groups revolve around the consolidation of power and the maintenance of the personal authority of group members. Deviance from formal secondary goals, at this level, takes the form of neglecting the larger interests of the secondary system for the narrower interests of maintaining the personal and collective power of the organizers.

The central leadership role in organizer groups can be referred to as "the chief"—a colloquial term in the sense in which it is used in most organizations. The person most likely to emerge as leader of the managerial group is the person who is invested with the most authority in the formal system. As such, he is a fitting object for the projection of images of authority, and his role is one of balancing the various demands and values represented by structural elements in the secondary system while at the same time acting on the system in order to maximize its effectiveness as an instrument for pursuing secondary goals. His leadership style within the group is likely to range from autocratic to benevolently paternal in character. He is treated with deference by those in the organizer group.

Conservative groups: On the upper periphery of the secondary system one more type of group can be found. Members of this group do not control processes at all, but usually control the ultimate goals of the system. They are served by the system and are also related to it by the fact that they own some of its resources and expect a return on their investment.

Behavior in these groups is based largely on affect. This is similar to the apathetic groups, but in this case members have the material resources to act out or live many of their fantasies. Expressive *activity* is restricted in favor of fantasy in the apathetic groups, but conservative groups facilitate expressive activity. Leadership in these groups is based on the expressive dimension. The leader of conservative primary groups might best be referred to as "the idol," for he cultivates a style of leisure consumption which others in the system tend to copy on a lesser scale. Unfortunately, there are few thorough studies of groups of this kind, probably because middle-class social scientists are more likely to cast their analytic eyes downward while their aspirations fly upward.

The combined resources of conservative group members constitute the base upon which a given secondary system rests, and members can, therefore, exercise considerable control over the operation of the system. Such activity is rare, however, and usually occurs only in periods of crisis where the returns on members' resources are threatened. The tactic used by members in such cases is usually the simple threat to withdraw resources, which greatly affects the behavior of organizer and cabal groups, as they see the possibility of their ability to affect goal setting and to control means being reduced by such intervention.

Except in times of crisis when the value of their resources is threatened, conservative groups often exhibit a low level of cohesiveness. The secondary system is not organized in such a way as to require cohesiveness for the effective pursuit of individual interests. The "ties that bind" are primarily affective and are strongest when they support or, at least, do not interfere with the playing out of individual fantasies.

Summary:
The group as an open system

In this chapter, a theory of the way in which individuals develop affective relationships within and to primary groups has been outlined. Affective relations are the central characteristic of primary groups wherever they are found, and projective identification is the central process by which an individual is able to relate to others in such groups and be controlled by developing group norms. The roles of projective specialists are central in the process of group formation and integration because they are the focus of projected images of strong emotional significance to group members. In the second part of the chapter, it was suggested that individuals also use primary groups to pursue interests beyond the gaining of affective satisfaction. These interests can only be pursued by bringing the secondary environment under some degree of control. The position in the control hierarchy is an important determinant of the degree to which needs other than affective ones can be satisfied. A theory was developed to predict how these interests would be pursued at different levels and the implications of this for primary group structure and consistent forms of deviation by primary groups from the goals of secondary systems. Generally speaking, this theory assumes that most individuals form primary groups to satisfy affective needs and use such groups to help them control their secondary environment by influencing goal-setting for the total system and by controlling the means of implementing these goals. Most secondary systems are constructed in such a way, however, that those at the bottom are subject to environmental constraints which make it difficult to form cohesive primary groups and so attain even a minimal level of social-emotional satisfactions. Groups at the lower levels find their control over the secondary environment is negligible. Consequently, the primary groups at this level have a tendency either to withdraw into fantasy—apathetics—or if they can become solidary to react against the system—erratics. Higher in the secondary system, environmental constraints on group formation are usually less severe and affective satisfaction is fairly readily achieved. However, secondary roles give the individual little effective control over system goals or over the means used to pursue these goals. However, group control over means is a possible source of bargaining power and the strategic group is the result. Beyond this level, secondary roles provide greater individual control over means, but cabals emerge to consolidate this control, and to attempt to influence goal-setting in the interests of group members. Above the cabal level, organizers find that their secondary roles give a high degree of control over goals, but that their positions remove them from direct control over the means by which these goals are pursued. They, therefore, use primary groups to consolidate their power against attempts to control the organization from below. Finally, conservative groups, existing on the upper periphery of secondary structures, use the secondary structures to support their pursuit of enjoyment and self-expression. In stable periods their groups are formed primarily for these purposes and take forms which are not dictated by the constraints of the secondary system. In unstable periods, they may form more highly structured groups in an attempt to consolidate their power over the system. The theory suggests that projective specialists of all kinds, distinguished in part 1 of this chapter, may appear in primary groups, but that the environment of the primary group is a powerful determinant of which roles are likely to be most central for primary groups at particular levels. Similarly, the cohesiveness and complexity of informal organizations vary systematically with the level of the groups in the secondary hierarchy; the most complex and cohesive groups occur in the middle range.

Having examined the *sub* and *supra*systems of the primary group, we turn now to an analysis of its internal structures and dynamics.

Notes

1 *See:* Erik H. Erikson, "Growth and Crises of the Healthy Personality" in Symposium on the Healthy Personality, suppl. 2, *Transactions of the Fourth Conference on the Problems of Infancy and Childhood* (New York: Josiah Macy Foundation, 1950).

2 Therese G. Decarie, *Intelligence and Affectivity in Early Childhood* (New York: International Universities Press, 1965).

3 Jean Piaget, *Play, Dreams and Imitation in Childhood* (New York: Norton, 1962), p. 67.

4 Rene A. Spitz, "Hospitalism: An Inquiry into the Genesis of Psychiatric Conditions in Early Childhood" in *The Psychoanalytic Study of the Child,* vol. I, (New York: International Universities Press, 1945): 53–74; Rene A. Spitz, "Anaclitic Depression: An Inquiry into the Genesis of Psychiatric Conditions in Early Childhood" in *The Psychoanalytic Study of the Child,* vol. 2 (New York: International Universities Press, 1946): 313–42.

5 Paula Heimann, "Certain Functions of Introjection and Projection in Early Infancy," in *Developments in Psychoanalysis,* Melanie Klein, et al. (London: Hogarth Press, 1952), p. 133.

6 This process has been studied in some detail for the child's relationship to physical objects (e.g., Piaget, Bruner) but unfortunately less information is available on the child's perception of significant *social* objects.

7 Ibid., p. 135.

8 Dexter C. Dunphy, "Social Change in Self-Analytic Groups," Ph.D. diss. Department of Social Relations, Harvard University, 1964.

9 Henry Ezriel, "A Psychoanalytic Approach to Group Treatment," *British Journal of Medical Psychology,* vol. 23 (1950): p. 61.

10 Edoardo Weiss, "Projection, Extrojection and Objection," *Psychoanalytic Quarterly,* vol. 16 (1947): p. 353.

11 Sigmund Freud, "Totem and Taboo" in *The Complete Psychological Works of Sigmund Freud,* J. Strachey, ed. (London: Hogarth Press, 1955), p. 64.

12 Anna Freud, *The Ego and Its Mechanisms of Defense* (New York: International Universities Press, 1946), p. 129.

13 Melanie Klein, *Our Adult World* (New York: Basic Books, 1957), p. 59.

14 Alexander Wolf, "The Psychoanalysis of Groups" in *Group Psychotherapy and Group Function* in Max Rosenbaum and Milton Berger (New York: Basic Books, 1963), p. 275.

15 Christopher Heinicke and Robert F. Bales, "Developmental Trends in the Structure of Small Groups," *Sociometry,* vol. 16, no. 1 (1953): 7–38; Hugh Philp and Dexter C. Dunphy, "Developmental Trends in Small Groups," *Sociometry,* vol. 22 (1959): 162–74.

16 Elliott Jaques, "On the Dynamics of Social Structure—A Contribution to the Psychoanalytic Study of Social Phenomena," *Human Relations,* vol. 6 (1953): 3–24.

17 Bronislaw Malinowski, *Magic, Science and Religion and Other Essays* (Boston: Beacon Press, 1948), p. 1.

18 *See:* Theodore Mills, *Group Transformation* (Englewood Cliffs, N.J.: Prentice-Hall, 1964); Philip Slater, *Microcosm* (New York: Wiley, 1966); Dexter C. Dunphy, "Phases, Roles and Myths in Self-Analytic Groups," *Journal of Applied Behavioral Science,* vol. 4, no. 2 (1968): 195–225; Richard Mann, *Interpersonal Styles and Group Development* (New York: Wiley, 1967).

19 Warren G. Bennis and Herbert A. Shepard, "A theory of Group Development," *Human Relations,* vol. 9 (1956): 415–37.

20 Dexter C. Dunphy.

21 Mr. Eric Neilsen contributed a great deal to the development of this part of the chapter.

22 *See:* William F. Whyte, "Small Groups and Large Organizations" in *Social Psychology at the Crossroads,* R. H. Rohrer and Muzafer Sherif (New York: Harper and Bros., 1951), pp. 291–312; Nicholas J. Demerath and John W. Thibaut, "Small Groups and Administrative Organizations," *Administrative Science Quarterly,* vol. 1 (1956): 139–54; Robert T. Golembiewski, "Small Groups and Large Organizations" in James G. March, ed., *Handbook of Organizations* (Chicago: Rand McNally, 1965), pp. 87–141.

23 Thomas P. Wilson, "Small Groups and Social Organization," August 1966, Annual Meeting of the American Sociological Association, Miami Beach, Fla.

24 Ibid., pp. 7–8.

25 Richard A. Cloward and Lloyd E. Ohlin, *Delinquency and Opportunity: A Theory of Delinquent Gangs* (Glencoe, Ill.: Free Press, 1960).

26 Leonard Sayles, *Behavior of Industrial Work Groups: A Prediction Study* (New York: Wiley, 1958).

27 Samuel A. Stouffer, et al., eds., *The American Soldier* (Princeton, N.J.: Princeton University Press, 1949); Morris Janowitz and Roger Little, *Sociology and the Military Establishment,* rev. ed. (New York: Russell Sage Foundation, 1965).

28 W. Lloyd Warner and Paul S. Lunt, *The Social Life of a Modern Community* (New Haven, Conn.: Yale University Press, 1941); W. Lloyd Warner, *The Status System of a Modern Community* (New Haven, Conn.: Yale University Press, 1942).

29 Oscar Lewis, *Children of Sanchez* (New York: Random House, 1961).

30 *See:* Malcolm W. Klein, ed., *Juvenile Gangs in Context* (Englewood Cliffs, N.J.: Prentice-Hall, 1967); James F. Short and Fred L. Strodtbeck, *Group Process and Gang Delinquency* (Chicago: University of Chicago Press, 1965); Irving Spergel, *Racketville, Slumtown, Haulburg* (Chicago: University of Chicago Press, 1964).

31 Dexter C. Dunphy, *Cliques, Crowds and Gangs* (Melbourne: Cheshire Publishing Pty., 1969), p. 117.

32 *See:* Herbert A. Bloch and Arthur Neiderhoffer, *The Gang* (New York: Philosophical Library, 1958); Lewis Yablonsky, *The Violent Gang* (New York: Macmillan Co., 1962); James F. Short and Fred L. Strodtbeck, *Group Process and Gang Delinquency* (Chicago: University of Chicago Press, 1965).

33 Melville Dalton, *Men Who Manage* (New York: Wiley, 1959).

34 Tom Burns, "The Reference of Conduct in Small Groups: Cliques and Cabals in Occupational Milieux," *Human Relations,* vol. 8 (1955): 467–86.

35 Gerald Leader, "The Determinants and Consequences of Interpersonal Competence in a Bank Setting," June 1965, Graduate School of Business Administration, Harvard University, Cambridge, Mass., chap. 3, p. 29.

chapter 3
A model for researching the primary group *

And now to the black box itself. In the last chapter we concentrated on personality processes and on the behavior of primary groups as a whole. But this book is mainly concerned with what goes on within the groups for the light that can be shed on understanding their internal structures and processes. We turn now to give a preview of what lies ahead in the remainder of the book: discussion and explanation of a model specifying the major variables in the internal system of the group.

The model is designed for the researcher interested in studying ongoing primary groups in their natural environments. We are presuming that interest lies not in the interrelationships of two or three variables alone —a major preoccupation of laboratory experimenters—but in a comprehensive view of the primary group as a system. We assume that the observer is not going to study his group from a mountain top with the aid of a telescope, but rather that he intends to mingle with group members and face the difficult problems of observing and reacting at the same time. What is needed, therefore, is a model which guides the researcher's attention to significant features of group life and which offers practical ways in which he can record and summarize his observations.

The model presented will fall short of an ideal model in this area. There are significant aspects of group life which have been difficult or impossible to conceptualize, let alone model accurately or measure. The

* Ricardo Zuniga contributed a great deal to the discussion of models and to the development of the particular model outlined here.

model we propose is limited in these ways; it is even more limited considering that we would like to go beyond a model and outline a *theory* of the internal structure and dynamics of primary groups. We must face the limitations of the current state of knowledge in the field realistically and content ourselves with the more limited aim of constructing a model which may eventually acquire the status of a theory as propositions concerning its major variables are developed and tested. This chapter will, therefore, outline what we understand by a model, review the origins of our model in both small group theory and general systems theory, and indicate some of its limitations.

The concept of model

Models as analogies and as theories

What is a model?   Answers to this question have created considerable controversy and have often been quite obscure. This is partly because different scientific disciplines make different uses of models, and, therefore, view them in different lights, and partly because the term is used very loosely. Definitions have been placed all along a continuum ranging from models as useless metaphors, to models as full-fledged theories. The most pejorative conception of models considers them simply as partial resemblances :

Models are analogies. Scientific or engineering models are representations, or likenesses, of certain aspects of complex events, structures, or systems, made by using symbols or objects which in some way resemble the thing being modeled.[1]

The definition of a model as simply an analogy can lead very quickly to a deterioration of the term. Chapanis, for instance, has written that :

A model is an analogy and no one expects an analogy to be completely accurate. When we use an electronic computer as a model for the brain, we obviously do not mean that our heads are full of transistors, wires, soldered connections, and magnetic cores. Nor do we believe for a moment that nerve impulses in the brain travel with the speed of electrical impulses in the computer. Neither do we grant that nerve spikes look like or have the manufactured precision of electrical potential emanating from a power supply. With a model it is not even important that any of these conditions be true, for a model can tolerate a considerable amount of slop. It is only an analogy, a statement that in some ways the thing modeled behaves "like this." Modeling is playing a kind of child's game—a grown-up, sophisticated version of a child's game to be sure, but a game nonetheless. The game is called "Make Believe."[2]

If models are nothing more than casual comparisons, examples, or metaphors, we shouldn't expect too much from them, although even analogies of this kind cannot be simply dismissed as unscientific. Miller states, for example, that "the recognition of analogy or formal identity underlies all generalization and all science." [3] If we agree with Miller, then analogies are neither despicable because unscientific, nor present in science only when labeled as such. But is a model only an analogy?

Simon and Newell [4] have gone to the other extreme from Chapanis and elevated models to scientific dignity. Elevated them, in fact, to a point where the concept is again largely useless because it becomes only a synonym for "theory." For these authors, the terms model, analogy, and theory become almost synonymous. Making all three terms equivalent is a solution, but not a very enlightening one. The term "model" must be very restricted if it is to be useful and we shall attempt to do this.

First, a model is not simply an analogy referring to any kind of similarity. It refers only to "the formal identity between a conceptual system and a real system." [5] Second, a scientific model is a particular kind of analogy that has properties which allow it to be used inferentially in scientific research. As Kaplan has pointed out:

No two things in the world are wholly alike, so that every analogy, however close, can be pushed too far; on the other hand, no two things are wholly dissimilar, so that there is always an analogy to be drawn, if we choose to do so. The question to be considered in every case is whether or not there is something to be learned from the analogy if we choose to draw it.[6]

Thus Chapanis is partly right. A poor model *is* a game of make-believe played by adults, but we cannot condemn all models because of that.

If models are more than simple analogies, they are less than theories. Unlike a theory, a model does not necessarily pretend to predict exact relationships which will hold between variables, and it is not meant to be a total explanation of reality. It abstracts some properties from reality and treats others as irrelevant. A model is, therefore, best defined as a formal identity between a conceptual organization and a real phenomenon, made in order to organize the data on the phenomenon in a meaningful way and to suggest important areas for further study. A model will be closer to being a theory in the degree that it attempts to go beyond the description of elements to the quantification of relationships between elements and, even further, to prediction. In the study of primary groups, there is still uncertainty about the variables or elements that are important, and even greater uncertainty about the measurement of such variables. A fully-fledged theory defines variables, shows how they are to be measured, specifies the relationships that hold between variables under given conditions, and predicts relationships when the theory is applied to specific instances. The latter two characteristics make the crucial difference between a theory and a model. For our purposes then, a model is a first necessary, but elementary, step, in a continued process of theory building. It is less than a theory but it can help to organize information into a coherent whole and orient the search for the relationships between important variables. A model is, on the other hand, much more than a simple hunch or a suggestive analogy.

Criticisms of models

We have explained what is meant by a model and why it is useful. But model building has critics who point to pitfalls. Because a clear definition is no guarantee of usefulness, we will discuss some common criticisms of model building and try to learn from them.

First, models often place greater emphasis on similarities than on differences. This can create distortions that will become evident at the stage of interpretation of results: It will lure the trusting scientist into a trap of map reading or pictorial realism,[7] that is, generalizing beyond the area in which the model is analogous to the reality studied. There is clearly a need to create a model which will show differences as readily as similarities and, of course, there is nothing in model building *per se* which prevents this. The answer seems to lie in developing sensitive measuring instruments which can identify differences with precision.

Second, models can lead the scientist away from observation by tempting him with the theoretical delights of model building. As Chapanis caustically puts it, "Scientists are people, too. Doing experiments, building theories, and constructing models are basically fun, in my opinion. Moreover, I am convinced that scientists often entertain models because their models entertain them." [8] Clearly we need to develop a model which will be a useful stepping stone in the development of theory rather than a play thing for the investigator. One way to ensure this is to use a model to develop hypotheses which can be, and are, continually tested. The final test of a model must be its usefulness, although we can continue to hope that it will also be fun.

Third, there is a danger of artificiality when the model is thought of as an adequate analogy to total reality. It can deny the right of existence of data that has no place in it, and [that will] stretch reality artificially so as to fill all the conceptual "boxes" built to receive it. Obviously we need a model that is flexible enough to be modified to successively closer approximations of reality. Those who develop and use the model also need to view it as a tool for understanding reality rather than as reality itself.

While models can be misused, they are necessary and useful in the process of theory building. The final test of a model, we suggest, is whether it is useful and appropriate. When a model is useless, it should be thrown away. When it is a poor model of the reality it is meant to illuminate, it should be criticized and modified or replaced by a more appropriate model. When it becomes primarily an intellectual play thing for the social scientist, it should be rated as such by his colleagues. But we must have a model if we are to begin developing adequate theories to explain and predict primary group behavior.

The next question is : Where shall we turn for the components of the model and how can these components be assembled in the most useful way?

A review of former small group models

This is not the first attempt to construct a comprehensive model of the small group. Outstanding contributions of this kind have been made by others and the most significant have each led to advances in subsequent research. Three outstanding contributions were made by Lewin, Bales, and Homans in a five-year period following World War II. Most subsequent work has elaborated on their approaches and certainly there has been no theorist since whose work has had the same impact. We will touch briefly on each approach and indicate in a general way where we have drawn on the views of a particular theorist for our own model.

Field theory of the small group

Kurt Lewin [9] borrowed from physics the term "field theory" for his approach to studying individual and group behavior. Drawing on Gestalt psychology, Lewin stressed the need of a holistic approach to studying social relationships. This led him to develop a comprehensive set of terms for characterizing a group and its relationship to the environment. Field theory was an attempt to construct a kind of social physics in which the group and its environment were seen as comprising a field of forces, with the behavior of any individual, and of the group as a whole, viewed as a function of the total forces at work in the field.

The field theory of groups depends on a model of the group which emphasizes a group's purposive character. The group is seen as being oriented towards goals and, consequently, as relating to other physical and social objects as resources for reaching these goals or as barriers blocking goal achievement. The stress on the goal-seeking aspect of group life led to the development of various measures of forces tending to unify or disintegrate purposive action. For example, "cohesiveness" was defined as "the sum of the resultant forces on members to remain in the group," [10] and the relationship of this elementary measure of group solidarity to other variables was extensively investigated. Leadership roles were also seen as extremely important because leadership has a direct bearing on goal attainment. The famous studies by Lewin, Lippitt, and White of authoritarian, laissez-faire, and democratic leadership [11] styles were attempts to measure the effects of varying approaches to leadership on goal attainment.

Lewin and his followers at the Massachusetts Institute of Technology —and later at the University of Michigan—specified a model which inspired many researchers to carry out experimental studies. However, some aspects of the approach proved rather unproductive. Lewin's attempt to develop a way of mapping group forces using topological geometry has now been abandoned along with a large number of the terms he introduced—as, for instance, vector, power field. Many of the terms Lewin used were borrowed by analogy from other scientific fields and it proved difficult to specify their meanings in terms of social behavior. But field theory contributed much of lasting value. Its contributions to a viable holistic model are, in our view : (1) a stress on some variables of tested value, particularly variables of a summary or holistic kind, such as cohesiveness; (2) a stress on the importance of examining the relationship of the group to its environment; and (3) an emphasis on two central facets of all group life, namely goal orientation and group integration.

Interaction process analysis

"Interaction process analysis" was the term coined by Robert Bales [12] for his method of observing behavior in groups, and the term is usually extended to cover the theoretical viewpoint from which the method derives. Bales is probably best known for his observational category scheme which has been republished many times in basic social science texts. However, the categories themselves are derived from a system model of the small group as a functioning entity. Bales came to study small groups as a sociologist, unlike Lewin whose training was primarily psychological. With Parsons, Bales developed a concept of a social system and its functional prerequisites which still underlies most sociological thought today. He chose the small group as a convenient and interesting example for testing and developing social system theory.

Bales' model was influenced more by biology than physics and it is consequently more organic than mechanical in character. A group is seen as being in a state of dynamic equilibrium rather like that of the human body. Despite continual movement of energy, there is a tendency to revert to a steady state of balance between the elements of the system. Bales sees equilibrium and social structure as arising out of the desire of group members to reduce the uncertainty of social situations.

A basic assumption here is that what we call the "social structure" of groups can be understood as primarily a system of solutions to the functional problems of interaction which become institutionalized in order to reduce the tensions growing out of uncertainty and unpredictability in the actions of others.[13]

The functional problems to which Bales refers are in his view: (1) adaptation to the environment; (2) the organization and control of the task; (3) the management of individual and interpersonal emotions; and (4) the development and maintenance of integration.

Those who are familiar with the writings of Talcott Parsons will realize that he also advanced and elaborated the same basic paradigm of the functional problems of social systems. From this point, Bales developed a theory covering the bases of role differentiation and the sequence of phases in the development of problem solving groups. Using the categories derived from the theory, he and his students and colleagues provided substantial support for and elaboration of a number of theoretical propositions in both areas.

Bales' model represented a significant advance over Lewin's in that the component concepts could be expressed immediately and directly in operational terms. However, one limitation on the generality of the model is that it was developed primarily with problem solving groups in mind. In fact, Bales spells out quite clearly the conditions for what he describes as "fully fledged problems" and the model is intended to apply in full only to groups engaged in solving such problems. This is a real limitation from our point of view because primary groups are not, in any simple sense, problem solving groups. Primary groups do pursue goals but these are not so clearly defined nor so directly pursued as those of problem solving groups. But despite this, many aspects of the model are relevant. In particular, its dynamic character stressing interaction is vital to any model which attempts to go beyond static categories. Bales' methods of categorizing action and distinguishing phases of group development have also directly influenced our thinking.

Recently Bales proposed an extension of the interaction theory which stresses three dimensions of interpersonal behavior as having central significance in social situations.[14] These three dimensions are examined in some detail in the next chapter for they form the basis of our interaction scoring scheme (however, they are derived from a series of empirical factor analytic studies of small groups).

Homans' model of the group

The third model advanced in the immediate post-war period emanated from another outstanding member of the Harvard Social Relations Department, George Homans.[15] Homans draws heavily on the same basic social system ideas as Bales. He also uses the terms "system," "equilibrium," and "interaction" frequently. But Homans' starting point is with primary groups rather than with the problem solving groups of classrooms and laboratories.

Homans' model portrays the group as having two "faces." The external system of the group represents the group's solution to what Bales calls the "adaptive" problem; it consists of the patterned set of relationships between the group and its environment. The internal system is the remainder of group life and is essentially an expression of the emotional relationships which develop between members. The other major variables in Homans' model are : (1) activities, or what group members do by virtue of group membership; (2) interaction, or the interpersonal communication between one member and another and between members and outsiders; (3) sentiments, or the emotions of group members about what the group is or does; and (4) norms, or the code of behavior adopted by members defining what is good and proper conduct on their part. In addition, while Homans does not stress these terms in his explicit outlines or summaries of the model, he makes considerable use of other concepts such as differentiation, authority, and social ranking.

Through specifying interrelationships between these variables, Homans erects a theory of how equilibrium operates in groups of quite diverse kinds. Our interest, at this point, is not in his theories but in his approach to specifying variables in his model. Here we feel impelled to point out that all the concepts outlined above are basic sociological concepts (partly due to the success of Homans' work) and are important components of any adequate model. However, each concept is too encompassing; Homans makes great virtue out of his sparse use of basic variables but, when he is examining specific cases, even he finds it necessary to make subclassifications of such generalized variables as "sentiment." Being a first-rate field researcher, he is not content to specify that the bank wiring group or the cash posters have norms; he proceeds to describe their content in a fairly systematic manner. But for some reason he balks at making lower-level categories and concepts explicit in his model. The simplicity of the model is, therefore, more apparent than real. While accepting the basic dimensions of his model, we demand a more clearly articulated lower-level specification of the basic dimensions; it is not very helpful to the researcher to proceed as though these kinds of concepts are "obvious."

More recently Homans has stressed the importance of the concept of exchange in groups and has elaborated on the types of exchange which take place.[16] The concept of group resources, their exchange in the group, and between it and the environment, has been largely ignored, and we have tried to build this new emphasis into our model.

More recent contributions by other writers
The 1950s and 1960s have been marked by an increasing emphasis on research on particular kinds of groups, designed in many cases to test aspects of the theories of the writers reviewed so far. Original theoretical contributions have been made in relation to particular aspects of group life, emotional processes for instance, but none of the writers have advanced a comprehensive model of small group structure and processes.

What has occurred is a period of testing, elaborating, and consolidating the seminal work of these writers. The results can be seen in attempts to summarize these developments in introductory texts and review publications.

Golembiewski's *The Small Group: An Analysis of Research Concepts and Operations* [17] is an attempt to state and systematize both the major methods and findings of small group studies. Of particular interest are his distinctions between different types of variables which he refers to as "structural," "style," and "population" panels of variables. These are somewhat like the distinctions we make between "structure," "process," and "content." Similarly, Olmsted's *The Small Group* [18] distinguishes between group "structure" and "culture," including under the latter term much of what we distinguish as "process" and "content." In addition, the book contains an interesting chapter (chap. 4) on the functions of primary groups in society. Shepherd's *Small Groups—Some Sociological Perspectives* [19] covers systematic theories of the small group in more detail than does this book and also attempts to summarize research findings in relationship to some key variables. Hare's *Handbook of Small Group Research* [20] is undoubtedly the best organized, most comprehensive, and clearly-written of all basic texts in the area. It provides the best single introduction to the small group field. The Handbook does, however, lay primary stress on experimental studies rather than field research. The chapter headings can be readily related to various aspects of our model, and, in general, Hare's work can be used as a compendium of research findings and methodological approaches supplementary to those provided here.

Toward a model of the primary group

We have reviewed previous attempts to create and elaborate models of the small group. The reason and justification for advancing yet another model can be summarized as follows : First, all these models are some years old and do not reflect real advances made at both theoretical and empirical levels in the late 1950s and the 1960s. A great deal of thought and research has been devoted, for instance, to emotional processes in group life and this makes it possible to analyze what Homans' treated as "sentiments" and Bales' as "socio-emotional action" in a much more differentiated way. Second, the results and methods of the range of primary group studies reviewed in chap. 1 have not been drawn on. Our review of these studies makes it easier to locate strategic variables and to develop coordinated and flexible measuring procedures. Third, there is no single source to which the field researcher can turn for a systematic introduction to concepts and methods in this field. The models reviewed do not provide such an introduction. Finally, none of the models take into account more recent developments in general systems theory which can explain the basic concept common to all of them, that is, the interrelatedness of group phenomena. We turn now to a review of aspects of systems theory and to an indication of how this, with elements of both small group models and the results of primary group studies, provides the structure of our model for the primary group.

The primary group as a system

The model proposed for the primary group is based on the presuppositions of general systems theory. Some of the most important contributions to the development of this theory have come from von Bertalanffy, especially considering the impact his articles [21] have had on the development of the field interdisciplinary studies in the social sciences.[22] We have drawn heavily on von Bertalanffy's work, but have been influenced by others also. Because of the great overlap in theoretical viewpoints, detailed acknowledgements will not be made for the various concepts outlined.

The initial concept is that the primary group is a system. The concept of "system" is fundamental, but notoriously difficult to define. In general terms, systems can be said to be "complexes of elements standing in interaction." [23] Miller expands on this in a useful way by pointing out what cannot legitimately be regarded as a system :

Our definition of "system" is very general, and at first sight might appear to apply to almost everything in the world. And, of course, the function of general theory is to be inclusive. However, it may be helpful to indicate what is not a system. The opposing lines of two football teams in scrimmage, independent of their backs, would not ordinarily be considered together as a system. If the Headless Horseman of Washington Irving had not been fictional, he could not have held his head in his arm and yet behave like an intact system. All the blondes in the United States are themselves not a system unless they are organized by some sort of communication, like the Red-headed League of A. Conan Doyle. In simple, naïve, commonsense terms, then, a real system is all of a thing. Even though it is possible to construct a conceptual system which includes grandpa's moustache, Chinese haikku poetry, and the Brooklyn Bridge, this would not correspond to a real system of general systems theory, because these things are not surrounded by a single boundary, are not continuous in space-time, and do not have recognizable functional interrelationships.[24]

Miller goes on to define systems as "bounded regions in space-time, involving energy interchange among their parts, which are associated in functional relationships, and with their environments." [25] Thus the problem of boundary definition and of defining the basic dimensions of the system are primary issues in developing a model of the primary group.

The primary group as an open system

Systems theory is appropriate in understanding primary groups partly because of its stress on the *open* character of systems. One of the problems in many theoretical schemes and models that have been proposed for understanding small group behavior is that they treat the small group as a *closed* system. Historically this seems to have taken place because most small group theory has derived from the study of experimental groups where the experimenter has adopted the polite "scientific fiction" that he has controlled all the relevant environmental variables; or if the effect of environmental variables has been studied, one or two are systematically varied and the effects of this variation observed on one or two variables internal to the group. In studying primary groups in field settings, it is seldom possible to achieve such controls, and complex interrelationships between the small group and its environment must be looked at realistically. In the previous chapter, a theory was advanced to suggest which aspects of the environment are most likely to have a major impact on the internal system of the group.

Systems theory stresses that a system such as a primary group not only interacts with its environment but also transacts. As Allport has noted :

If we comb definitions of open systems we can piece together four criteria: there is intake and output of both matter and energy; there is achievement and maintenance of steady (homeostatic) states, so that the intrusion of outer energy will not seriously disrupt internal form and order; there is generally an increase of order over time, owing to an increase in complexity and differentiation of parts; finally, at least at the human level, there is more than mere intake and output of matter and energy; there is extensive transactional commerce with the environment.[26]

Chein argues that Allport could have been more bold in the expression of his fourth criterion : "The real fourth criterion, I suggest, is that an open system has no definite, clear-cut boundary with respect to its surroundings." [27] Yet, despite the existence of interchange, systems often have a considerable degree of independence from their surroundings. The difficulty of formulating the basis of this independence is real, but there have been a number of viable approaches which are directly relevant to the problem at the primary group level. Miller, for example, suggests that the concept of role can be used to define the group boundary :

Boundaries of systems are not always clear-cut and round like the rind of a watermelon. Sometimes they have intricate geometrical design, more like the surface of a branching coral, but even more complex than that. A naval task force maneuvering blind at sea can be a system, even though its boundary is complicated and in continual flux. It is a system organized by communications which require at least a small filament of contiguous space-time of ether, to transmit radio, radar, or other signals. When a typhoon hits the *Caine* and her sister destroyers, wiping out radio and radar contact, then the flotilla is no longer a system, because usual functional interrelationships are impossible. Communications make feasible complex organizations of systems, like the American Psychological Association or the United Nations. A given individual or behaving system can, of course, be part of several systems at the same time, equilibrating at least partially with all of them. To deal with this fact the concept of "role" has been developed in social psychology.[28]

Berrien suggests that communication patterns can define the boundary :

How is a boundary recognized? Several criteria are relevant and necessary. First, the boundary of a human group is defined by the nature of communications; interactions within the boundary are different in quality and/or frequency than those across the boundary. Clearly, the communications within a family, for example, are different from the communications between families in a neighbourhood. The same may be said of a naval task force as contrasted with a task force plus its enemy, or of a work group and the company, or of a church membership committee, or of a U.S. Senate committee and the Senate.[29]

Communications within the group are more frequent, more intimate, and more confidential than communications across the boundary. And this, in turn, leads to the development of, and adherence to, distinctive roles, values, and norms that mark the group members off from others in the group's environment. One result of this is that channels of communication become regularized, communication within the group becomes an easy matter, and others outside become relative strangers. Consequently, as Miller suggests, energy levels can also be used to define group boundaries : "Greater energy is required for a transmission across a boundary than for a transmission in the suprasystem immediately outside a boundary or in the system immediately inside it." [30]

So the distinction between the small group and its social environment is largely one of degree, but this is a problem faced by many open systems. While boundaries may be complex and somewhat ill-defined, it may still be very clear that a system exists. A forest, for example, may be a very distinguishable and real entity, although its boundaries are marked by a gradual diminution in size of verdure and an increase in its spacing. The problem is one of developing appropriate criteria for deciding where to draw a boundary rather than identifying whether or not the system exists.

To clarify this, an open system is one with a boundary sufficient to maintain a certain degree of inner integrity and distinctiveness, yet sufficiently flexible and permeable to be able to use the environment in maintaining and perpetuating its own existence. Consequently, interaction within the group and between the group and its environment will differ both quantitatively and qualitatively. As a consequence of the permeability yet reality of its boundaries, the open system can develop great flexibility in dealing with surrounding systems or objects. Many living systems develop purposive, goal-seeking behavior which maintains and further extends and develops the inner life of the system.

Thus, in speaking of the individual person as a system, Collier writes:

Development of the individual can be characterized by progressive increases in degrees of independence or freedom from the energy pattern of immediate surroundings. . . . The core concept of the living organism is composed of the very characteristics that give rise to individuality which stems directly from the following capacities of the living protoplasm: (a) to maintain itself as a unified organism, (b) to be self-regulating, (c) to achieve a degree of independence from immediate surroundings, and (d) to maintain a degree of identity. These characteristics are shared in some degree by all living organisms.[31]

The same arguments apply to the social systems which evolve out of the relationships between individuals.

As should be evident by now, the concept of the open system has its origin in the realms of biology. It is used to describe characteristics of protoplasm; it is extended to higher levels of live organization not as an analogy but as a principle recurrent at different levels of complexity. It shows a basic isomorphism between the living organism, personality, and the social system, but a distinct difference from non-living matter.

Non-living energy systems tend to break down with mutual impact from interacting energies and drift towards a maximum entropy or smoothing out of differences. Under these conditions identity is not maintained. But the essential point is that the non-living system does not resist in the way that living systems do the invasions of external energy that often finally destroys its individuality. Living energy systems tend to maintain their identity by the following maneuvers: (a) selection of only certain types of energy resources that are compatible with the maintenance of the internal system, (b) discharge of materials when further retention is incompatible with the system, (c) the transformation of admitted energy resources so that compatibility with the internal system is increased, and (d) the storing of reserves and their utilization when external resources are not immediately available.[32]

The idea of transaction with the environment can be broken down into two aspects: What is taken in from the environment by the system and what is given back to the environment. It is important to realize that inputs and outputs are not necessarily equivalent. This has been stated very clearly by Miller:

There is always a constant systematic distortion—or better, alteration—between input of energy or information into a system and output from that system. . . .

The distortion of a system is the sum of the effects of processes which subtract from the input to reduce strains in subsystems or add to the output to reduce such strains. . . . Such alteration can be explained by the fact that every system takes out of its input essentials for the maintenance of its own equilibrium, rejecting all substances that do not contribute to that steady state.[33]

Other elements in the model

In studying groups we need to consider this relationship with the environment and particularly the transactional processes which maintain the group. But how do open systems maintain their identity, especially when their boundaries are highly permeable? They develop a stable structure marked by distinctive channels of communication, differentiation of the component parts of the system, and integrative mechanisms which operate to hold the system together as a coherent, cohesive entity.

Channels of communication: Channels of communication are fundamental to the structuring of the system. Any system which persists over time develops specialized chanels for input and output and for the flow of communication from one part of the system to another. Feedback mechanisms involve sensing and coding processes which result in adjustive responses and allow the system to make necessary changes in adaptive behavior. Special codes prevail which facilitate information processing within the system. This is especially true of primary groups which can develop elaborate codes of general behavior and language behavior, in particular. In fact, it can be argued that the longer a system exists, the more elaborate and unique its codes are likely to become as they adapt themselves to the developing goals of the system.

Differentiation of parts: The increasing independence of a system from its environment allows for increasingly effective control over aspects of the environment through the functional differentiation of parts of the system. The human body is an excellent example of the differential distribution of functions across many millions of cells, some of which specialize in boundary maintenance (skin), others in input and output (alimentary canal), others in communication within the system (nerve cells). Such differentiation allows for much more efficient use of the environment for enhancing the maintenance and growth of the system. It does, however, create problems of coordination and balance for the system. One of the key problems in primary group analysis is to specify the structural elements of the group and to describe their functional interrelationships.

Integration or homeostasis: In Cannon's original sense, homeostasis refers to "the coordinated physiological processes which maintain most of the steady states in the organism." [34] Homeostasis is defined by von Bertalanffy as "the maintenance of balance," and by Rapoport as "the self-regulating properties of a living process." [35] Stagner develops the basically biological idea of homeostasis, applying it to different levels of integration in personality : ". . . The individual, dynamically striving to preserve his inner tissue constancies, moves successively to build a constant physical environment (second level), and a constant social environment (third level). These may be thought of as envelopes protecting the biological constancies."[36] Following this line of thought, it is easy to see that the need to maintain constancy is not only biological, but can be found at different psychological and social levels, including the human group.

When the problems of homeostatic principles and mechanisms are discussed at the level of social relations, it is necessary to be extremely careful not to distort the concept. Berrien has made an excellent analysis of group processes, giving criteria for group homeostasis in terms of near constancy or gradual rise of formal achievement and need satisfaction. He is very much aware [37] of the dangers involved in such an extension whereby the scientist goes from a concept to the postulation of a specific mechanism, a causative force, that provides a verbal answer to the search for actual mechanisms. Toch and Hastorf have posed this problem :

Thus, the main general criticism of homeostatic theory is the assumption implicit in much of this theory of a general principle or force accounting for the result observed, which causes one to overlook the multiplicity of determinants actually involved in every concrete psychological event. The principal corollary of this criticism is that the 'equilibrating force' assumption precludes further investigation, since it leaves no remaining queston.[38]

Such explanations need to be avoided along with the tendency in systems theory, and in functionalism generally, to assume that equilibrating forces exist rather than demonstrating the fact. Similarly, a model must allow for the possibility of change, of disequilibrating forces that may actually disturb the status quo and destroy or fundamentally modify the system. No system is externally constant and eventually all systems are subject to radical change, decay, and destruction.

Four important distinctions from general systems theory must be involved in our model of the primary group. First, we need to develop means of boundary definition along with some global measures of its basic dimensions as a system. These should include its overall relationship to the social environment of which it is a subsystem and to the individual personalities who are involved in the group. Second, we need to describe the basic patterns of communication or interaction between it and its social environment and within the group itself. Third, we need to identify the component parts of the system, their interrelationships, and the different functions they perform. Last, we need to show how these parts and functions are integrated to preserve the stability and/or enhance the growth of the system, or where conflicts occur which lead to disequilibrium, decay, or disintegration of the system.

Further distinctions—structure, process, and content: But how can one distinguish the parts or elements of a system? Everything in a system is interrelated, involved in dynamic processes, and usually in a state of more or less rapid growth or decay. How then can one distinguish parts? This is not a new problem in systems theory, and it is certainly an old problem in social science. The problem is usually solved in social science by making at least a distinction between structure and process. Structure is regarded as the totality of patterned regularities in a system that remain largely unchanged over the period of interest to the social scientist. Thus role structure, for example, consists largely of those prescribed and performed actions which remain constant for those who hold positions in the system being studied. Once one has described structure in this manner it becomes possible to talk of processes which are regulated interchanges between different parts of the social structure. Thus the communication of influence in a system may pass sequentially from higher status levels to lower. A further distinction we would like to make goes beyond the structure/process division to "content." By "content" we refer to the subject matter of communication processes, in other words, the symbolic verbal codes consisting of particular kinds of information, norms, values, and goals. By "content" then we mean the verbal culture of the group.

We would also note that the study of the primary group as an open system requires the study of the interaction of the systems with the subsystems (personalities) and the suprasystems (social environment), but it does not require the study of these two in themselves. Personality and environment are, therefore, to be considered as sources of inputs and receptors of outputs from the primary group, but need not be studied as total systems in themselves. While it is perhaps tempting for the sake of completeness to extend system analysis in toto to these external systems, what we need, if the study of the primary group is to be central, are key summary measures of those aspects of external systems which make the greatest impact on the life of the group.

Classes of variables in the primary group model

In outlining the model proposed for the analysis of the primary group, we begin by indicating the general *classes* of variables in it. From the concept of open systems, we derive the idea that there must be certain parts of the system which specialize in adaptation to the environment. We refer to these variables as *adaptive* variables; they are particularly involved in the maintenance of group boundaries and in interchange with the environment with input and output from the system. Then there are certain parts of the system which remain relatively fixed and constant over time. The totality of these patterned regularities or constants in the system is the *structure* of the system. A third class of variables refers to the *content* of group processes. In the case of the small group this is the class of variables which comprise the group culture, the systems of meanings evolved in the group setting and recognized by the group members by virtue of their membership. Finally, process variables which relate to the dynamic functioning of the group can be distinguished.

Within each of these major classes of variables, there is a further series of subdivisions that represent an increasingly finely grained analysis of the group. The sub-divisions are: the global pattern, which refers to certain gross characteristics of the group considered as an undifferentiated entity; interaction, which is an examination of the interchange within the group and between the group and its environment; differentiation, which is a consideration of specialization of functions within the group; resource allocation, which is a consideration of the way in which resources are distributed throughout the group, and integration which deals with those mechanisms which tend to maintain the equilibrium of the group.

Table 3.1: Classes of variables in the small group model

	ADAPTIVE	STRUCTURE	CONTENT	PROCESS
Global pattern	adaptive stability	group characteristics	group composition	member turnover and attendance
Inter-action	connection network	communication network	communication content	communication processes
Differ-entiation	mediation roles	internal roles	norms	role differentiation role specialization
Resource allocation	adaptive systems	status systems	values, symbols, and goals	resource distribution
Integration	enclosure	cohesiveness and consensus	rituals and myths	member satisfaction and socialization

The combination of four main classes of variables with five subdivisions of each class results in a 4 x 5 table, defining and delimiting twenty areas of research which are shown on the accompanying table. Each of these areas of research represents a *class* of variables in the model : any one box in the scheme would include a number of variables, all of which would match the description of the class. The twenty areas are summarized in table 3.1.

The classes of variables are described below in somewhat more detail than in Table 3.1. Enough detail is included to make the meaning of the categories evident, but the descriptions are brief enough to provide an overview of the scope of the whole model. This is meant to be a simple overview of the scope of the model. After an introduction to the key methods of measurement proposed, subsequent chapters will outline variables in each class in more detail, and show how they can best be measured using specific techniques.

GLOBAL PATTERN

1. *Global pattern—adaptive: "adaptive stability"*
    The major settings in which the group operates and those persons, groups, or collectivities which exercise a significant influence on the group or are influenced by it. The stability of the relationships which are involved.

2. *Global pattern—structure: "group characteristics"*
    The physical, temporal, and membership (personnel) boundaries of the group and the basic activities in which the group members are involved as a group.

3. *Global pattern—content: "group composition"*
    Member characteristics which are properties of individual members but which influence the character of the group, e.g., age, sex, social class, roles held in the secondary system. Differential participation in different settings.

4. *Global pattern—process: "member turnover and attendance"*
    Rates of recruitment, graduation, desertion, and expulsion from the group. Fluctuation in attendance in group settings.

INTERACTION

5. *Interaction—adaptive: "the connection network"*
    The transactional channels between the group and significant social objects in the environment.

6. *Interaction—structure: "the communication network"*
    The interactional channels within the group, i.e., who communicates with whom and how often.

7. *Interaction—content: "the communication content"*
    The major kinds of information circulating within the group.

8. *Interaction—process: "the communication processes"*
    The sequences of information transmission in the group.

DIFFERENTIATION

9. *Differentiation—adaptive: "mediation roles"*
Roles specialized in mediating with the group's environment.

10. *Differentiation—structure: "internal roles"*
The differentiation of functions within the system and their allocation to specific positions in the group.

11. *Differentiation—content: "norms"*
The formulation of requirements for adequate role fulfilment by individuals.

12. *Differentiation—process: "role differentiation and role specialization"*
The processes by which roles become more or less differentiated and/or specialized.

RESOURCE ALLOCATION

13. *Resource allocation—adaptive: "adaptive systems"*
The input and output of resources to and from the system.

14. *Resource allocation—structure: "status systems"*
The distribution of rank or status of various kinds among group members.

15. *Resource allocation—content: "values, symbols, and goals"*
The key systems of meaning and orientation in the system which represent the important cultural resources of the group.

16. *Resource allocation—process: "resource distribution"*
The processing, modifying, and distributing of group resources.

INTEGRATION

17. *Integration—adaptive: "enclosure"*
The degree of definition of group boundaries and the sharing of external reference groups and persons.

18. *Integration—structure: "cohesiveness and consensus"*
The attractiveness of the group to its members and the consensus which exists on this.

19. *Integration—content: "rituals and myths"*
The extent to which developed and accepted rituals, such as rites of passage, exist and the extent to which common myths exist about the nature and purposes of the group.

20. *Integration—process: "member satisfaction and socialization"*
Outputs to the personality from the system which affect the level of individual satisfaction and personal growth.

A critique of the model

The model outlined is a practical compromise between what we would like to include in an ideal model and what may be accurately observed and quantified given the present state of research techniques. In other words, it includes only the *measurable* variables. A model that is open and dynamic in character is strongly favored; the outline above is a compromise between this ideal and previous models which have been, on the whole, relatively closed and static in character. Although this statement may sound extreme, it is supported by the fact that, in researching the literature on small groups plenty of methods were found for measuring the structural aspects of the small group but few for measuring its dynamics. We have strained at the borders of our resources and imagination to invent new methods for measuring dynamic processes where existing methods did not exist or seemed inadequate.

If we have found problems in finding ways of dealing with the dynamic features of group life, we found even greater problems in finding methods and concepts for analyzing the content of these processes. The analysis of the subculture of the small group has been almost entirely neglected by researchers and by most theorists. Nevertheless in this area, too, we have combed the literature for the few exceptional studies and suggested some new approaches which we ourselves have not yet fully implemented.

There are other important areas in group life which receive insufficient emphasis in the model. For example; Theodore Mills has suggested [39] that our grid (fig. 3.1) could well be supplemented by two new columns and an additional row. The two columns he has suggested are one covering "group mechanisms"—major methods of changing the system—and another covering subsystem group relations—the relations of the personalities of individual members to the group. He has also suggested another row covering emotional processes. In setting up the model, we considered the latter two of these three possibilities, but dismissed them only because we felt that the lack of conceptual definition and methodological sophistication in these areas made it hard to provide separate treatment. We decided instead to subsume them in the row labelled "group integration" on the basis that the individual and his emotions represent a major problem of order for the primary group. Similarly, group mechanisms are covered by the column headed "group processes." Such a solution is a practical one which should not be allowed to disguise the necessity for developing the model further in these directions, or for stimulating further conceptualization and research in the areas of mechanisms, emotional processes, and subcultural content. Work of this kind will be necessary to accomplish what Mills refers to as "putting motion in the model."

In the absence of these developments, we have constructed a model which builds on previous theoretical and empirical work and which strains to push the process of systematic conceptualization and quantification in the direction of openness, dynamism, and content. The model is also explicitly operational—it specifies concepts in terms of the operations performed by the researcher. For this reason, a further detailed explication of the variables in the model is put aside until chapter 5, in order to describe the methods which provide operational definitions of particular variables.

Notes

1 Alphonse Chapanis, "Men, Machines and Models," in *Theories in Contemporary Psychology*, ed. Melvin H. Marx (New York: Macmillan Co., 1963), p. 109.

2 Ibid., p. 112.

3 James G. Miller, "Toward a General Theory for the Behavioral Sciences," *The American Psychologist*, vol. 10 (1955): p. 519.

4 Herbert A. Simon and Allen Newell, "The Uses and Limitations of Models" in *Theories in Contemporary Psychology*.

5 Miller, "Toward a General Theory for the Behavioral Sciences," p. 520.

6 Abraham Kaplan, *The Conduct of Inquiry* (San Francisco: Chandler, 1964), p. 266.

7 Ibid., pp. 284–88.

8 Chapanis, "Men, Machines and Models," p. 121.

9 Kurt Lewin, *Resolving Social Conflicts* (New York: Harper Bros., 1948); idem, *The Conceptual Representation and Measurement of Psychological Forces*, Duke University Monograph Series, vol. I (Durham, N.C.: Duke University Press, 1938); *see also* Dorwin Cartwright, ed., *Field Theory in Social Science: Selected Papers* [of Kurt Lewin], (New York: Harper and Row, 1951).

10 Dorwin Cartwright and Alvin Zander, *Group Dynamics—Research and Theory* (Evanston, Ill.: Row, Peterson and Co., 1960), p. 88.

11 Kurt Lewin, Ronald Lippitt, and Robert White, "Patterns of Aggressive Behavior in Experimentally Created 'Social Climates,'" *Journal of Social Psychology*, vol. 10 (1939): 271–99.

12 Robert F. Bales, *Interaction Process Analysis* (Cambridge, Mass.: Addison-Wesley Press, 1950).

13 Ibid., p. 16.

14 Robert F. Bales, "Interaction Process Analysis" in *International Encyclopedia of the Social Sciences*, ed. Alvin Johnson (New York: Macmillan and Free Press, 1968).

15 George Homans, *The Human Group* (New York: Harcourt, Brace & Company, 1950).

16 George Homans, *Social Behavior: Its Elementary Forms* (New York: Harcourt, Brace & World, Inc., 1961).

17 Robert Golembiewski, *The Small Group: An Analysis of Research Concepts and Operations* (Chicago: University of Chicago Press, 1962).

18 Michael Olmsted, *The Small Group* (New York: Random House, 1959).

19 Clovis Shepherd, *Small Groups: Some Sociological Perspectives* (San Francisco: Chandler Publishing Co., 1964).

20 A. Paul Hare, *Handbook of Small Group Research* (Glencoe, Ill.: Free Press, 1962).

21 Ludwig von Bertalanffy, "An Outline of General System Theory," *British Journal for the Philosophy of Science*, vol. 1 (1950), 134–65; idem, "Theoretical Models in Biology and Psychology," *Journal of Personality*, vol. 20 (1951): 24–38; idem, "General System Theory: A New Approach to Unity of Science," *Human Biology*, vol. 23 (1951b): 346–61; idem, "General System Theory," *Main Currents in Modern Thought*, vol. 2 (1955): 75–83.

[22] Roy R. Grinker, *Toward a Unified Theory of Human Behavior* (New York: Basic Books, 1956); O. R. Young, "A Survey of General Systems Theory," *General Systems,* vol. 9 (1964): 61–80.

[23] von Bertalanffy, "General System Theory" (1955), p. 76.

[24] Miller, "Toward a General Theory for the Behavioral Sciences," p. 515.

[25] Ibid., p. 514.

[26] Gordon W. Allport, "The Open System in Personality Theory," *Journal of Abnormal and Social Psychology,* vol. 61, no. 3 (1960): 303.

[27] Isador Chein, "The Image of Man," *Journal of Social Issues,* vol. 18, no. 4 (October 1962): p. 22.

[28] Miller, "Toward a General Theory for the Behavioral Sciences," p. 515.

[29] F. K. Berrien, "Homeostasis in Groups," *General Systems,* vol. 9 (1964): p. 207.

[30] Miller, "Toward a General Theory for the Behavioral Sciences," p. 526.

[31] R. M. Collier, "Independence: An Overlooked Implication of the Open System," *Journal of Individual Psychology,* vol. 18 (1962): 110–11.

[32] Ibid., p. 104.

[33] Miller, "Toward a General Theory for the Behavioral Sciences," pp. 526–27.

[34] Hans H. Toch and Albert H. Hastorf, "Homeostasis in Psychology," *Psychiatry,* vol. 18 (1955): 81.

[35] Young, "A Survey of General Systems Theory," p. 74.

[36] Ross Stagner, "Homeostasis as a Unifying Concept in Personality Theory," *Psychological Review,* vol. 58 (January, 1951), 6.

[37] Ibid., pp. 212–16.

[38] Ibid., p. 90.

[39] Theodore Mills, personal communication.

chapter 4

Methods for the study
of primary groups

Introduction

A veritable multitude of methods have been developed for studying small groups. Yet they are all variants of four basic approaches. First, they can all be divided into measures of some aspect of structure process or of content. Structure and process measures are linked together because, as we noted in the last chapter, structure represents the more persistent and pervasive regularities in process and arises out of the same measures. All measures are, therefore, divided into process measures or content measures. But methods also vary according to who is doing the measuring. In some cases the investigator does the measuring directly; he applies the categories he has derived directly to the ongoing process or its content. In other cases, he uses the group members themselves to apply his categories and utilizes their judgment rather than his own; the group members summarize their impressions for him in some way. Measures differ, therefore, according

Figure 4.1: Types of methods for small group analysis

	PROCESS MEASURES	CONTENT MEASURES
Investigator as source	scoring schemes for interaction analysis	scoring schemes for content analysis
Member as source	questionnaires, rating measures, etc.	interview schedules

to the source of the observation—investigator or member. Figure 4.1 summarizes these distinctions and shows the different kinds of measures which usually result.

It will be seen from the diagram that the methods developed for direct observation can still be used to analyze and summarize member reports, for these usually present the same kind of data which, in ideal conditions, the observer could have measured directly, but which are presented to him in a more condensed and "subjective" form by the group members.

This chapter will concentrate on presenting two generalized schemes for direct scoring by the investigator. One is an interaction scoring scheme, the other a content scoring scheme. Less will be said at this point about the schemes which use the member as a source for data; not because these are unimportant, on the contrary, they are essential, but they involve using categories derived from the other scoring schemes, which may thus serve as an introduction to them. In addition, they are more particularized and it makes for clearer exposition to include them along with the particular variables they are designed to measure.

Categories for the analysis of interaction

In outlining our conceptual model of the primary group, we have already clarified the fundamental distinction between "process" and "content." In this chapter "process" will be dealt with by defining the basic molecular unit of process analysis and outlining a system for categorizing these process units. We will then show how the scores which result from using this category scheme can be assembled into more complex units of behavior to give the most useful description of the structure and sequence of interaction.

The need for a generalized category system
In developing the categories to be outlined, the desirability of a system which can be applied in studying a wide range of primary groups must be kept in mind. Most category systems have been developed for application to one particular type of primary group, for example specifically for family or classroom interaction, interaction in task-oriented discussion groups, or exchanges between members of therapy groups. Because we wish to develop a scheme which will facilitate the comparison of different kinds of primary groups, a generalized rather than a specialized set of categories will be employed.

There are strong arguments to be made for the usefulness of both generalized and specialized category systems. Generalized systems have the advantage of facilitating far-reaching comparisons, but they have the disadvantage of ignoring or misinterpreting unique features of a particular social situation. Specialized category systems are usually "tailor-made" for a particular social situation and, therefore, often yield more detailed data, but it is difficult to generalize beyond the specific situation. This issue has been faced for years by those involved in constructing psychological tests and has received a thorough treatment elsewhere.[1] A more generalized system will be used here because a number of specialized systems exist and there is an unfilled need for a scheme to unify the field of primary group analysis. A generalized scheme does not, of course, preclude the use of specialized schemes to supplement and complement it. In fact, such schemes may be very useful for testing specific hypotheses.

Common problems in category construction
Category systems differ in a number of ways, but there are eight different problems which all interaction category systems must resolve in some way. An outline follows of what seem the most appropriate ways of resolving these problems and also a review of a number of existing category schemes, emphasizing the various resolutions represented there. Finally, a new set of categories will be outlined which attempt to meet the criteria set up for a general system. The eight problems are :

1. Behavioral scope :—What proportion of behavior is to be scored? All behavior? Verbal behavior only? Only some limited types of behavior?
2. Unit :—How is the basic unit of interaction to be determined?
3. Inference level :—What level of inference is required in categorizing basic units? Are the categories largely descriptive or do they require a high level of inference?
4. Multiple scoring :—Are categories mutually exclusive, i.e., if an act is classified as belonging in one category, can the same act also be assigned to another category as well?
5. Theory :—How many categories are there and what is their theoretical justification?
6. Equipment :—What special instruments or facilities are required for scoring?
7. Observer activity :—What observer activity is required?
8. Situational scope :—In what kinds of social situations has the system been used and in what other situations could it be appropriately used?

Behavioral scope: Some investigators are interested in a particular motive, need, or type of action and so, for example, may score only acts of physical aggression in gangs.[2] Because we are interested in studying primary groups as systems, a scoring scheme must contain categories for the most significant theoretical dimensions of the inter-personal behavior in a primary group. Therefore, we limit ourselves to those scoring schemes which attempt to categorize a wide range of interpersonal behavior. There is, of course, a problem here. Such a scheme must be practicable, and, if one attempted to categorize all verbal and non-verbal acts with meaning for others in the group, a single observer could not cope with the work involved in classifying and recording group interaction. Therefore, by "a wide range of interpersonal behavior" we mean all *verbal* behavior and as much *non-verbal* behavior as appears to play an obvious and important part in communication. While this is our population of acts (in a statistical sense), the practical exigencies of research may make sampling inevitable, or often unavoidable, and sampling may sometimes occur in an unsystematic way which is undesirable from a statistical point of view. Ways of minimizing this problem will be discussed later.

Unit: Interaction category schemes differ a good deal in the way they define the unit chosen for categorization. The most widely quoted and used definition is probably that for the basic unit scored in Bales' interaction process analysis : "the smallest discriminable segment of verbal or non-verbal behavior to which the observer, using the present set of categories after appropriate training, can assign a classification under conditions of continuous serial scoring." [3] Steinzor, by contrast, chooses a larger unit, defining it as : "the entire statement a person made that occurred between the statements of individuals immediately preceding and following the person's expression. If the person stopped talking for five or more seconds and then continued, his statement was counted as two units." [4] More recently, Strupp's scheme for scoring interaction in psychotherapy employs a similar unit. Strupp regards each intervention by the therapist as an act unless a markedly different theme from the first is introduced.[5]

Such units can be termed "natural" units, in the sense that they are based for verbal interaction, at least, on linguistic structure. Another possibility which has been employed is a mechanical unit based on a particular period of time. Flanders, for example, divides interaction into three second intervals. The interaction occurring in the three second interval is summarized in a single judgment indicating the preponderant character of the action.[6]

A natural rather than a mechanical unit seems preferable, and one which is rather larger than "the smallest discriminable segment of behavior" which Bales uses. Our unit can be defined as "each distinct uninterrupted flow of communication by an individual and the major category shifts within the flow." This is essentially the same definition of a measurable unit as that used by Mann in his member-to-leader scoring system for self-analytic groups :

We define an act as a single speech or burst of sentences within which the expressed feelings are uniform. One of two events signals the end of an act: (1) the speaker is interrupted by another member or by the leader; or (2) the speaker shifts from expressing one set of feelings to expressing feelings which call for a different array of scored categories.[7]

However, a mechanical unit will be used here to some extent to supplement the natural unit. When a flow of communication continues uninterrupted and without category shift for more than thirty seconds, we arbitrarily regard this as the beginning of another unit.

The preference for a natural rather than a mechanical unit as a prime criterion stems from the feeling that this comes closer to preserving the meaning of an act for the persons involved in the social situation. Later, we will suggest continuing the use of natural rather than mechanical units through to the more complex units which describe social process in macroscopic terms. At the level of the basic unit, a larger unit than Bales used has been chosen because, first, it allows the observer more time to observe holistically than does the rapid scoring of IPA, and second, with an 18 rather than a 12 category scheme the observer needs more time to make a scoring decision.

Inference level: Categories vary widely in the degree to which they require an extended inference on the part of the observer while he is categorizing an act. On the one hand, a category may be virtually descriptive, such as "asks question." Here the observer has only to listen for the standard rise in voice tone accompanied by the standard linguistic structures which signal a question—"Who. . . ?," "What . . . ?," "Did you . . .?." Low inference categories of this kind have the advantage of posing few problems of reliability in scoring. Of course, the problem of inference is not resolved by this solution; it is only postponed to the point where the scores on the category have to be interpreted. Eventually the investigator has to ask himself, "What are the theoretical implications of asking questions?" One of the problems of simple descriptive categories of this kind is that the theoretical implications are often by no means obvious, or, if apparent, not of strategic theoretical interest to the investigator.

At the other extreme, the category scheme may demand that extended inferences be made by the observer while scoring ongoing behavior. An example of a scoring scheme of this kind is Steinzor's system for scoring social interaction. Steinzor scored all verbal behavior into a set of categories which demanded that the observer infer the *intent* of the speaker. Steinzor found it impossible to develop interscorer reliability and concluded that only he could use the system reliably.[8] Mann's scheme, previously mentioned, is also highly inferential but he reported that he and his coworkers were able to achieve quite impressive levels of interscorer reliability.[9]

A system which has categories as descriptive as can be devised while still being obviously derived from and related to important theoretical dimensions is preferred. What these dimensions are will be indicated with the detailed outline of the proposed scheme, but we are not prepared to sacrifice theoretical meaning on the altar of reliability. At the same time, any system which cannot be used with an acceptable level of reliability by a variety of researchers is scientifically useless.

Multiple scoring: Category systems vary according to whether each act can be scored into one or a number of different categories. Statisticians often argue that, from a statistical point of view, it is desirable to avoid multiple scoring so that one can be sure that correlations between types of acts are "real" and not simply an artifact of the scoring system. For example, if a question is scored AB most times a question is asked, it should not be surprising to find that A and B are highly intercorrelated in the results. On the other hand, an act or a statement may perform more than one function at the same time so that reality and statistical simplicity seem to be at odds with each other. A way around this issue opts for multiple scoring on three dimensions which have been shown statistically to be orthogonal to one another. In this way some of the complexity of real life can be preserved while minimizing, as far as possible, the artifactual feature of correlations in such a scheme.

Theory: The crucial question about any category system is what theory or model of human behavior does it represent? A category system always reflects at least a model of human behavior whether or not that model is made explicit. Social behavior is a continuous flow of action; the moment it is divided into discrete units and categorized, there are some principles for classification and these derive from what we believe human behavior is about. The underlying model or theory of human behavior should be made as explicit as possible. We, therefore, view with some suspicion a scheme such as Medley and Meizel's technique for measuring classroom behavior in which the observer records "as many aspects of what goes on in the classroom as possible regardless of their relationship to any dimension." [10] By contrast, there are a number of interaction schemes which do specify clearly the theoretical model from which they derive. Two excellent examples are Leary's system for scoring the interpersonal dimensions of personality [11] and Bales' Interaction Process Analysis.[12]

While the theoretical model does not determine the absolute number of categories in a scheme, it certainly affects the number. Leary's scheme, for example, is basically a two-dimensional scheme and the number of categories are a multiple of four as each dimension has two end points. In fact, the scheme has 16 categories. Similarly, Bales' scheme is essentially two dimensional (instrumental versus expressive) and has 12 categories. The actual number of categories in a scheme is a function of (1) the number of dimensions and (2) the capability of coders to discriminate reliably between intervals on the dimensions and/or combinations of the dimensions. We have chosen a three-dimensional scheme with a total of eighteen separate categories which may also be used in combinations.

Equipment and observer activity: These two issues are closely inter-related. They are very practical issues for any system which is designed to be useful in field settings. Some scoring systems require elaborate mechanical equipment to be used in the field situation, but the introduction of such equipment represents a major change in the situation. It may also be impossible to introduce elaborate equipment into many situations. If a peripatetic gang is being studied, cumbersome machinery for scoring may make it impossible to move about. For example, Washburn's method of recording the social behavior of children requires a time-marker mounted on the left ear like a telephone receiver, a clipboard used on the lap with a sliding ruler that moves freely across the surface of the board, and a stop watch held in the hand.[13] Not only is the observer necessarily pinned to the one spot by equipment of this kind, but he also presents a rather conspicuous and remarkable object in most social situations! Any method chosen must not require equipment which limits the movement of the observer in the field situation or draws an unusual amount of attention to him.

Also of importance is the amount of activity required by a scoring scheme. The method we favor in most situations is the use of a small, portable tape recorder to record verbal interaction along with studied recall of non-verbal behavior associated with the verbal sequence. The tape can then be coded at leisure. If scoring is to be done in a social situation, then it must not require a pace so rapid that the researcher cannot gain a global impression of the total behavioral sequence. Such is the case in the Scoring of Interaction Process Analysis. A method which blinds the observer to phenomena that do not fit neatly into his scoring scheme, and hence precludes serendipitous discovery, may be more of a block than an aid to understanding. The method proposed keeps the observer busy if he chooses to use it directly in the field situation, but not so busy that he cannot gain a general overview of what is occurring.

Situational scope: A scoring scheme is required which is useful for studying as wide a range of primary groups as possible. It is safe to say that the majority of schemes do not meet this criterion. Strupp's psycho-therapeutic interaction scoring scheme, for example, is carefully designed, but in its present form could only be used for scoring behavior of therapists in a therapy situation.[14] Similarly a number of teacher-pupil interaction schemes are specifically designed to measure pupil-teacher interaction and could not be transferred, without modification, to other social situations involving interaction between an authority figure and subordinates.[15] These schemes are extremely useful for comparing the behavior of one therapist with that of another or the behavior of one teacher with that of another. They do not, however, measure how therapists differ from teachers in their behavior toward those in their charge.

There are some schemes which come close to meeting the criterion. Bales' Interaction Process Analysis has been used in a wide range of social situations with resulting insights into phasal processes and role differentiation in a variety of groups. However, IPA was designed for scoring problem-solving discussion groups with specified tasks and is less useful for groups which are largely social in character. Similarly, it emphasizes verbal behavior and is somewhat limited in scoring groups which center around physical activity, sports groups, for instance. Leary's scheme could also be widely applied but does not seem to have gained the popularity it deserves. Lewis, Newell, and Withall's modification of Interaction Process Analysis extends the usefulness of Bales' categories and is certainly close to meeting our criterion of general applicability.[16]

Categories for interpersonal action analysis

A number of small group studies provide evidence which suggests that three dimensions of interpersonal behavior are of key importance in small groups. An important beginning was made in 1952, when Couch and Carter read a paper describing a factor analytic study of observer ratings made on small groups involved in varied tasks. They identified three factors which they named :

1. Individual prominence (such items as confidence and striving for recognition).
2. Group goal facilitation (such items as efficiency, adaptability, and cooperation).
3. Group sociability (such items as sociability and behavior rated as pointed toward group acceptance).[17]

Subsequently, in reviewing studies using interaction process analysis, Bales pointed to the emergence of three main factors which he labeled :

1. Activity (simply interaction rate or rate of participation in the group).
2. Taskability (or ability on the group task).
3. Group sociability (or the degree of liking expressed).[18]

The similarity in the two formulations is obvious. Subsequently Schutz, who was also working with Bales, developed and published FIRO, a three-dimensional theory of interpersonal behavior which defined three similar variables which he labeled inclusion, control, and affection. In due course, I factor-analyzed written reports from the members of self-analytic groups and also distinguished three factors :

1. "Strength," which corresponded with a concern for personal strength in the group and seems related to activity rate.
2. Normative structure, which was a concern for the formal properties of the group, particularly its task.
3. Negativity, or the expression of hostility in the group, which may be regarded as the negative end of the sociability factor.[19]

Bales, in reviewing these and other studies showing similar results, developed a theory of interpersonal behavior based on these three dimensions.[20] This theory provides a substantial basis for adopting a three-dimensional approach to interpersonal behavior.

Therefore, a set of interaction categories was developed, congruent with the specifications outlined above, and based on the three dimensions reviewed. The categories here have been derived as closely as possible from items directly related to the three factors. That this seemed profitable was demonstrated by an exercise in the scope of the three dimensions. All the interaction categories reviewed for this chapter were accounted for in terms of the three dimensions or combinations of the three dimensions. With the exception of some very generalized categories, this could be done in virtually all cases. From the results of this exercise the following interaction categories were developed which provide the advantages of the better category systems reviewed, with faithfulness to the results of the factor analytic studies.

The category system is derived from the three dimensions of interpersonal behavior reviewed which seem to be of central significance to human action. These three dimensions—*dominance, goal direction,* and *affectivity*—are outlined in some detail in table 4.1. Each dimension has a positive and negative pole. For the dominance dimension, for example, the poles are domination and submission. Each of these poles has three levels of intensity which are designated by action names to indicate the type of activity which would rate being scored at that level of intensity. In the domination end of the dominance dimension, for example, the three levels are indicated as follows:

D3. (highly dominating behavior) command, dominate, downgrade other, upgrade self, etc.
D2. (moderately dominating behavior) advise, initiate, counsel, discount, etc.
D1. (slightly dominant behavior) permit, consent, allow, deny, defend self, etc.

Submission represents behavior which ranges from "going along with" to downgrading oneself (*see* table 4.1).

The affectivity dimension has two poles: affiliation and hostility. Table 4.1 gives the kinds of activity which are regarded as instances of affective behavior. Note that affectivity is essentially interpersonal.

Table 4.1: Categories for interpersonal action analysis

Dominance

Domination

D3   Command, dominate, downgrade other, upgrade self, refuse to comply.

D2   Advise, initiate, counsel, discount.

D1   Permit, consent, allow, deny, defend self, attempt to maintain own status.

Submission

S1   Submissive agreement, go along with, admit confusion, excuse self, seek permission or consent.

S2   Comply, seek advice, or counsel.

S3   Yield, submit, downgrade self, upgrade other.

Goal direction

Work

W3   Exhort to task, reinforce group goals, exult in task achievement.

W2   Ask or give opinion or information related to group goals, busy oneself actively with the job.

W1   Signal attentiveness, continue to work, ignore fantasy of other.

Expression

E1   Engage in out-of-field activity, drift, giggle, talk to oneself or engage other in side conversation.

E2   Cry, scream, laugh, joke, express tension, unhappiness, happiness, excitement.

E3   Engage in active play, tell story or extended fantasy, act out at length.

Affectivity

Affiliation

A3   Express affection or love.

A2   Support other.

A1   Accept other, greet.

Hostility

H1   Avoid or ignore other.

H2   Scold, reject, or criticize other.

H3   Attack other.

The dominance and affectivity dimensions are fairly easy to conceptualize and somewhat self-explanatory. The final dimension of goal direction requires more explanation. This dimension has two poles—*work* and *expression*. The work pole of the goal direction dimension is concerned with the active acceptance of task-oriented or goal-oriented behavior. It refers to behavior disciplined by the group goals and group norms. The most extreme kind of behavior here is reasserting the importance of task goals or redirecting attention to them, and endeavoring to enlist motivation in the service of group goals. Behavior on the expressive pole is expressive in the sense of being self-expressive, that is, directed to the expression of one's own inner feelings and fantasies. There is no value judgment involved here. Even successful task performance requires periods of relaxation and tension release. Table 4.1 gives the "calibration" of behavior scored on this dimension. Note that expression is *not* primarily interpersonal in intent—it is aimed at relieving inner tensions although, of course, it has interpersonal effects.

Directions for scoring

We have supplied examples of the types of behavior which can be appropriately coded into these categories. The coding procedures recommended can be effectively illustrated.

The first coding problem centers about identifying the appropriate units to be scored in the flow of communication. The unit of measure is "each distinct, uninterrupted flow of communication by an individual, and major category shifts within it." Such a definition makes impossible the separation of the designation of units from the process of categorization. The first stage of unitization is very simple. A new unit begins each time one person begins to speak after another, or initiates a remark in a new encounter. For example :

Mike: "Hey, Joe, what did you do with the answers to this problem? Are they in this book here?"
Dan: "It's over here."

As Mike's flow of speech was initiated, the observer would score the appropriate category after the first sentence, in this case category W2 : asks for information. Since the second sentence does not represent a category shift, the first score suffices for the whole exchange. Dan's answer then marks the beginning of another unit which is also scored in category W2. We can then imagine the conversation continuing :

Mike: "You stupid ass, didn't I tell you to put them over here? Oh what the hell, I'm leaving!" (leaves)

In this case, the first sentence would be scored H3 : attack. The latter sentence and accompanying behavior E1 : engages in out-of-field activity.

Because this is a three-dimensional scheme, multiple scoring is allowed. Presumably a single act may sometimes express both domination and affection : teacher to pupil : "Good boys like you always put their toys away, don't they?," or in some cases may be weighted on all three dimensions : "Let's all work together on this one, guys" might be scored D2 : initiate, W3 : exhort to task, and A2 : support.

Some limitations, however, are placed on multiple scoring. First, if an act is to be multiply scored, it must reach the second level of intensity on each of the dimensions scored. Thus, "Yes, you're right" cannot be scored S1 : agree *and* A1 : accept, but only S1 *or* A1.

In order to facilitate multiple scoring, the observer should keep a combination of dimensions in mind. Figure 4.2 gives an estimate of the

Figure 4.2: Fusions for combinations of dimensions

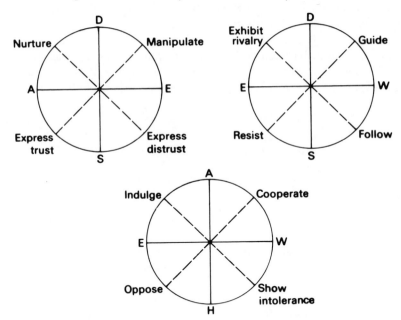

combinations of sets of two dimensions. If the observer keeps the scheme in mind, when he hears, for example, "Let's work on this problem now," he will see this as a clear case of *guidance*. As *guidance* is a fusion of *dominance* and *task advancement,* he will then double score the act in these two dimensions. To be double scored, the intensity of the act must be at least 2.2. We leave it to the observer to judge whether the intensity on either or both dimensions should be raised to 3.

Actually, the scheme is best kept in mind by thinking of it as a three-dimensional space within a globe. Each new act may be placed in a particular position in the space and will be weighted on the three orthogonal axes of the space. As a convention, it is useful to regard the domination dimension as the vertical axis, with dominance upward; to regard goal direction as the forward and backward axis with work forward; and to regard affectivity as the left-right axis with affiliation to the right. One can then memorize fusions of the various dimensions very easily and sense just where in the space a particular act should be scored.

Another way of conceptualizing the scoring procedure is to view it as a set of consecutive decisions. The sequence is as follows: (1) identify the unit to be scored, (2) does it express dominance? If yes, domination or submission? (3) if one of these, how intense is the expression? (level 1, 2, or 3). This is repeated for each dimension until the act is scored for its implication on each dimension.

The rate of scoring can be built up over time and an attempt should be made to score as large a percentage of acts as possible. If scoring is being done concurrently with the ongoing interaction, it is usually not possible to score all acts. If scoring is done from a recording, all verbal acts can be scored, but non-verbal acts will not be scored unless remembered or noted down at the time the action occurred. If scoring is done concurrently, the researcher must note who is initiating the interaction (the speaker) and to whom the act is addressed (the recipient). It is often easiest to assign each group member a number, or initials; it is conventional to designate the group as zero. For instance, if person #2 asks the advice of the group as a whole, the act would be scored 2-0 : S2.

Example application of the IAA categories
The following is a transcript of a few minutes of interaction in a self-analytic group. The group's task is to analyze interaction between members, which makes it somewhat difficult to score the task dimension. However, the heated nature of the exchange between two members, D (a woman) and J (a man), makes it an interesting case of a developing interpersonal interchange. The transcript begins just after J has asked D to summarize the cutting—in his view—remarks she had made about him in the previous session. He has asked her to do this for the benefit of another member who was absent. There is a short interchange among some other members before the conversation is given over to J and D again but the rest of the transcript is largely given over to them.

SELF-ANALYTIC GROUP INTERACTION—The group task is to analyze interaction between members.
(N.B. Members, other than J and D are designated with an asterisk.)
D.   Is it that you want me to repeat what I said about you ? (W2)

J. In a way . . . well, I'm asking you to give us a summary as a start. (D1)

* Did you continue with B after the last time? (W2)

* In the beginning J asked how I felt about what had happened. I responded very briefly. . . . I can't quite remember how I moved from me to D. That was pretty much the topic of the whole period. We went back to you at the end of the whole period. (W1)

* Very, very nice. (A1)

* J tried to say that he was disappointed if I really didn't resent the group, that he didn't want me to feel this way. I was trying to explain . . . he was trying to say (W1) . . . negative criticism could be given for positive purposes in this group . . . maybe a necessary thing to say (W2) . . . I hadn't expressed resentment but J and others . . . (W1)

J. D did say something to me that was a bit of a shock (E2) . . . I tried to consider it impartially, unsure how well I succeeded in convincing myself that her statements were attempts to be analytic and mature. Then I came back with a somewhat futile defense (S3) saying that regardless of what my presentation may have been, I thought that some of the statements were valuable and she said: "Well, that was my opinion" and stuff, so I don't know. But it was quite a sharp thing toward me I thought. At least I felt it was a blow. (E2)

* At least two times individuals remarked "you're a fake" to somebody. Once to D, I think. D and someone else once yelled out "you're a fake" to somebody else. (W2)

* D said, "You're a fake" to J. (W1)

* Yes, that's right. (S1)

* This was something I wanted to bring up again. It ties in with what you've just said too, because D was talking about your manner of analyzing. (D2)

J. She disre . . . just a couple of statements she made, she managed to just about knock the props out (E2) . . . and I think she was very glad to see this . . . (H2) in a way. (S1) And I don't know what my response should have been. Afterward I thought well maybe I should have said, "you bitch!" you know . . . but I didn't . . . there have been a number of attempts, D, to pull you into the group or make you find out what you're like. You pushed them off. And a lot of your pushing off has been because you're purely pissed off at the group because sometimes you haven't been taken in. Caught up in a beautiful little world. . . . (H3)

D. Who has made attempts to draw me or anyone else into the group? (H2, W2)

J. What a nonsensical statement! (H3)

D. You made the statement. I asked a question. (H2, D1) (Group laughter). (E2)

J. You just asked the question. I'm just saying . . . O.K., what a nonsensical question. (S1)

D. I agree with you. (D1) (Pause)

* Something which struck me last time. Comments were being made about D and statements about not needing the group. (W1) There's a possibility that D may be going through right now outside some rather difficult things which cause her to defensively defend herself against them and be able to keep

going, to not at this time admit that she has terrific needs and so forth and therefore when she is not just necessarily well integrated into the group . . . (A2)

J. I think that this just . . . part of that may be true. (S1) But I think that she wants us to know that there are problems outside of the group or to think that there are problems outside of the group. I think that she has also decided people have questions. Say, well, you haven't shown too much response, you haven't shown you are affected by the statements which have come out and she's said, "You know I'm going to show them." So now we really don't know what her reactions are. (W2) But we have all sorts, we have a fantasy you know it's easy to build up a fantasy that this girl is sitting in here and silently pulling them into her great big bosom, you know. And I think that she wants to project this image, that she can take it all in, that she's suffering and she does feel. In other words, what she projects. It's easy to project any number of images into that. She has fostered the impression that she is a very feeling sort of person, even though she doesn't show it. (H3, E3)

*   There have been a number of reactions to D. I guess L and DN have been incredulous about the genuineness of her affect. . . . JD has always come to her defense . . . clearly the person D gets to most is J . . . (W2)

J. Doesn't seem fair to me, you know. (E2) Gee, I can sit there and I try to react in any number of ways. She's sitting in an unassailable position. (H2, S3)

D. J, well if our first little run-in hadn't meant so much to you as you indicated and felt last week, why is it that all through the year ever since that time, there has been this thing between us? (H2)

J. I've been trying to figure this out all year long. I think my reaction to you is overdetermined. I think . . . I don't know . . . I don't know. (S1) I just won't stand for it though. (D1) And if you're going to . . . admittedly I won't stand for you picking on me. O.K. You're getting to me but I won't take too much more of it you know. And even if it's in my imagination, I still won't take too much more of it. Just you know, stay away from me, bitch! (H3)

D. Well, I hadn't picked at you before last time. (D2, H2)

J. Oh come off it! (H3)

*   It's not always that D comes to you. You invite it. (W2)

J. Part of it might be a masochistic delight, O.K.? But I don't know. It might be that I . . . I don't know (S1) . . . maybe I like feeling like an ass (S3), or something like this. But I don't know. I'm saying that I don't know that many of my efforts which I think have been fairly valid in one or two statements, and I was concerned about what she thought about them. She managed to say, "Ha, you're being like a playing, grownup, little boy." And I'm incredibly sensitive in this spot. (E2)

Conclusion

We have presented an interaction scheme for scoring behavior in a number of different kinds of primary groups. The scheme is meant to be general in order to facilitate the study of important dimensions of interpersonal behavior within groups and, as such, to be useful both for understanding particular groups and for comparing groups of different kinds. The scheme is not designed, however, to preclude the use of other, more specific schemes.

The following chapters will show how many of the variables in the small group model can be measured with this scheme, and also how the small units used for scoring interaction can be combined into higher-order units to give more global measures of prevailing "group moods" and to facilitate the study of sequential shifts in the prevailing style of interaction on which the group is working. The following discussion will present a complementary scheme for content analysis; this is the other central method we have developed for the analysis of primary group data.

Categories for the analysis of content

Informal and formal approaches to content analysis
Much of the data used by the researcher to understand group processes consists of the contents of spoken or written communications. He listens to conversations between group members, interviews individuals, and reads diaries and documents produced by members. While doing all this, the researcher is constantly categorizing, comparing, noting repetitions and uniformities, as well as differences in what different members say. Much of what the researcher performs along these lines is informal, with little consciousness of the procedures involved. There are times, however, when he needs to proceed systematically to develop hypotheses and to test them in more rigorous ways than intuitive procedures allow. More formalized methods of content analysis have been developed to make this possible. They have two important values—they allow the researcher to clarify and test his own theories and they allow others to replicate his work or compare their own with it in a precise way. Thus if researcher A carries out a study of the dinner table conversations of middle class families, and researcher B of lower class families, they may make sounder, more credible statements about the social class differences in dinner table conversation if they can test these differences statistically rather than concluding : "It is our impression that lower class families talk more about X, Y, Z than do middle class families." We are not denigrating intuitive procedures; such procedures are an important part of a "clinical" understanding which is absolutely necessary for developing hypotheses. The point is, however, that intuitive understanding can *only* result in hypotheses. Unless these hypotheses are rigorously tested with quantifiable observations they remain hypotheses.

An outline follows of a formal method of content analysis which can be applied to conversational content, interviews, diaries, and other written documents relating to primary groups. The procedure is largely drawn from Stone, Dunphy, Smith, and Ogilvie, *The General Inquirer: A Computer Approach to Content Analysis.*[21] The particular units of analysis discussed here are not all taken directly from the book, but are modified for the particular processes of small group analysis. Nevertheless, a computer can carry out all the operations suggested here. On the other hand, all the operations can also be carried out by the investigator without a computer; the computer simply relieves the tedium of ensuring coding reliability and making counts on large amounts of data. It also makes the filing and retrieving of data fast and accurate.

While a computer is not a necessary part of our content analysis scheme, computer-based content analysis does present a useful model for the content analysis process even if done entirely by hand. The value of the computer model is that, to be programmed for the computer, the categories and method of analysis must be made explicit, and hence the whole process is replicable and open to scholarly criticism and debate. If categories and procedures remain in the mind of the researcher, cumulative theory-building by empirical testing is impossible.

What then is content analysis?
Content analysis is "any research technique for making inferences by systematically and objectively identifying characteristics within text." [22] As far as we are concerned, the term "text" loosely refers to any body of verbal data, from tape recordings of conversation to typed memoranda. The definition stresses that content analysis is a technique which operates by identifying specified characteristics in text. This implies that the investigator approaches the text with some concrete ideas of what variables he is looking for and that he employs a method which will identify instances of the variables within the text. He might, for instance, be interested in the extent to which the members of a work group show support, in their conversations, for union and management goals. He must, in this case, have a clear idea of what are the respective goals of management and of the union and also of how support and opposition can be expressed. Content analysis will then allow him to discover precisely when a union or management goal is referred to and whether the attitude expressed is pro or con in each case. He can then determine quantitatively the amount of attention devoted to union and management goals respectively and the level of support or opposition to each in the group or groups under study. We have stressed the use of explicit and replicable methods, for only such methods consistently achieve the reliable results which are the basis of scientific procedure.

Finally, why would anyone be interested in such a question as "the extent to which group members support or oppose the goals of management or union?" From the point of view of the researcher, the answer must be "because it has some theoretical implications." It may be, for example, that the researcher has predicted that, at a certain organizational level, there will be conflict about loyalties to corporate and union goals but that most issues will be resolved in favor of the union. This hypothesis may be derived from a proposition of organizational theory which predicts that informal primary groups composed of foremen organized on a lateral basis will experience conflicting loyalties when union and corporate loyalties demand divergent action and that, further, support for management in such cases will vary inversely with the number of years spent by the average foreman in the group at lower levels within the organization concerned. Measurement of relative support for union and management goals makes it possible to relate the variable "support for management" defined as

$$\frac{\# \text{ instances of expressed support for mgt. goals } + \# \text{instances of expressed opposition to union goals}}{\# \text{ instances of expressed support for union goals } + \# \text{instances of expressed opposition to mgt. goals}}$$

with the variable "years of service at lower levels in the organization."

Thus the definition emphasizes that content analysis must be undertaken with the aim of making inferences to theory. In the specific cases dealt with, it is possible to refute the proposition derived from theory—a process which has important implications for the theory if repeated often enough.

Using content analysis in studying primary groups
But of what general use is content analysis to the social scientist who is interested in small groups? What is the range of theoretical issues to which it has relevance? The answer to this question is that content analysis is the major method for analyzing and understanding the verbal subculture represented by the primary group. The scope extends from a relatively simple analysis of the main topical concerns of members to an analysis of the recurrent themes and even myths which they develop to give meaning to their actions. Used over time, content analysis can yield important insights into the evolution of primary group subcultures. Two studies which have directed attention to this latter issue will be reviewed as examples of what can be done with content analysis.

Both studies are analyses of content—group discussion and written reports by group members—produced over the course of a year by members of a self-analytic group course in the Department of Social Relations at Harvard University. Theodore Mills, the author of the first study, devised a systematic method of content analysis and used it to code the content of group discussion.[23] Mills formulates some of the basic issues which groups of this kind cannot avoid working on. For example : Is the orientation of members to the instructor to be dependent, rebellious, detached, or independent? Is orientation to a member's peers to be competitive, condescending, contentious, or collaborative? Are feelings of affection to find a legitimate and satisfactory channel of expression? Mills is able to demonstrate, by his content analysis, that (1) after a mock "revolt" against the instructor, affectively neutral references decrease, references to persons and events within the group increase, negative references to authority increase, and positive expressions rise to a new plateau; and (2) after a later attack on the entire enterprise of the group, negative expressions decrease, positive ones rise to a higher plateau, and other content categories show no substantial change. On the basis of these empirically derived results, Mills proceeds to develop a theory of the life cycle of self-analytic groups.

In a subsequent study, I used a more elaborate set of categories to analyze the content of weekly reports written by members of two sections of the same course.[24] My concern, like Mills', was to trace the cultural evolution of these small groups. Using a computer to score 83 content variables, I was able to show that (1) the two groups were more similar than different in the phases through which they passed and (2) that marked shifts in the topical concerns of group members could be characterized. These shifts were related to the behavior of some of the central group members who played symbolic roles in a process of dialectic debate through which group issues were initiated and resolved.

Procedures in undertaking content analysis

In carrying out content analyses such as these, the small group researcher identifies "specified characteristics" within text. In the case of the two researchers discussed above, each chose a number of content categories which seemed most relevant to his theoretical concerns. But can we generalize about the "specified characteristics" which might prove useful to the student of primary groups? There are certain categories of interest to most small group researchers, but first let us discuss the general classes of units which are important and then proceed to indicate in more detail some specific units most researchers of primary groups will need to include in any thorough scheme for content analysis.

Content units

Item: The most elementary content unit that the investigator may wish to identify is an "item." Item analysis is the identification of a specific sign which is invariate in form and has a stable referent. The researcher may wish, for example, to record the number of times Mr. Grenoble is referred to by the members of a group. Mr. Grenoble may be the work group supervisor and the researcher may wish to measure the amount of attention devoted to him by various group members. Mr. Grenoble's name is an "item" and a simple count of the number of times his name is mentioned is a simple measure of the concern for him expressed by the group members. As another example of item analysis, the researcher may want to note the number of times different family members refer to specific recreational activities. A list is made of every recreational activity engaged in by the family members—for example : tennis, golf, swimming, skiing—and a note made of how many spontaneous references to each is made by each family member.

Tag: More frequently employed than item analysis is "tag analysis." A tag is a class of items which can be regarded as representing alternate ways of expressing the same concept, where the concept can be represented by a single word or simple word combination. The researcher may be concerned, for example, with the relative number of references, not to a single specific recreational activity but to recreational activities versus work activities. In this case, two "tag categories" are created, one called *recreation* and the other called *work*. Each tag would then consist of a number of items as follows :

RECREATION	WORK
tennis	typing
golf	cooking
swimming	doing the washing
football	cleaning
skiing	dusting
hunting	repairing
fishing	writing
	studying

In this case instead of—or in addition to—recording the frequency of each item, the frequency of the use of the tag would be recorded. This enables a comparison to be made, for example, of the extent to which husbands and wives in the families under study orient themselves to recreational or work activities. Landis and Burt, for example, studied the personal conversations of men and women and found that men concentrated on "business affairs" while women concentrated on "person affairs" (gossip) and "clothes." [25]

Topic and symbol: The simplest form of tag analysis is the kind of analysis of topic outlined. While it allows the researcher to make some useful generalizations, these are likely to be no more startling than the conclusions of Landis and Burt. More significant in most cases are two kinds of tag analysis which are particularly crucial for primary group analysis, that is, symbol and image analysis.

A symbol is an item, topic, or set of related topics with strong emotional associations which may be different for different individuals or groups. The term was first introduced into content analysis by Lasswell and was popularized by the Hoover Institute Symbol Studies published in the

1950s.[26] These studies were carried out by a group associated with Lasswell, Lerner, and Pool. Altogether 19,553 editorials from the *New York Times, Isvestia, Le Temps* and the *Frankfurter Zeitung* from 1890 to 1945 were analyzed for trends in the degree of attention devoted to important political symbols. In Lasswell's view, a key symbol is a basic term of "the political myth" [27] and the symbols recorded in the content analysis were terms such as "democracy" and "nationalism."

The analysis of political symbols in newspaper editorials may seem removed from primary group analysis. Nevertheless, small groups also have their key symbols which form part of the unifying myths which give meaning to group life. One might cite, for example, the emphasis on "competition" in certain business groups or "solidarity" in some union groups. Also included under the term "symbol" are those symbolic *social* objects— people, groups, or collectivities—which have strong emotional associations for people in the group. To some extent, symbol analysis can be dealt with similarly to topic analysis. A symbol can be a tag. Mills, for example, makes what is a systematic taxonomy of social objects for coding small group conservations. The categories he arrives at, listed below, are essentially tag categories of the kind outlined.

Mills' Classification of Social Objects [28]

Internal to interacting group	External to interacting group
1. superior male	1. superior male
2. superior female	2. superior female
3. subordinate male	3. subordinate male
4. subordinate female	4. subordinate female
5. group itself as a collectivity	5. collectivities (various)

Mills' method (called Sign Process Analysis) thus classifies all social objects by their (1) locus—in or out of the group, (2) their sociological status, (3) sex, and (4) individual versus collective nature. Using this system, Mills is able to chart the way in which attention in the classroom group he studied moved from concern with external to internal figures, from individuals to groups, and from higher to lower status figures. This is only one aspect of Mills' Sign Process Analysis.

Topic and symbol analysis involve classifying words and idioms as appropriate instances of a limited number of areas of subject matter. When interest is in a wide range of topics or in making a more or less "complete" analysis of topical concerns, this involves creating a range of interrelated tags or, the construction of what has become to be called a "content analysis dictionary," that is, a classified system with tags as units, in which each tag consists of a finite number of items.

A content analysis dictionary is a concrete representation of the investigator's theory in relation to verbal content, and it specifies those semantic categories which he regards as theoretically important. Actually the term "dictionary" as it is used here is derived from computer usage, and a content analysis dictionary is more similar to a thesaurus than to a regular dictionary such as Webster's. Both a content analysis dictionary and a thesaurus arrange words and phrases of similar meanings under conceptual headings so that the meaning of any word can be summarized by listing the headings under which it occurs. For example, referring back to Mills' classification of social objects, the meaning of the term "our teacher" would be summarized by listing the headings under which it is classified : *internal, superior, male.* The term's meaning would be distinguished from that of "our national president" by the first tag, which is the only one which would differ from the definition of "our teacher" : *external, superior, male.*

It should be noted that the meaning given to a particular item like "teacher" or "president" may vary from one researcher to another. Another researcher, studying leisure time peer groups for instance, may define "teacher" as *external, adult, authority.* In devising his categories, the social scientist makes the kinds of classifications he believes will be of most use to him; those relevant to his theory and the hypotheses he wishes to test, and those of practical use in analyzing the kinds of documents in which he is interested. Because the purposes of researchers differ, so will their categories. On the other hand, similarities in research purpose indicate the necessity for and use of some standard, comparable categories.

Thus a content analysis dictionary is a cluster of categories linked by the fact that they represent different variables in the investigator's theory. A dictionary is a semantic classification indicating the relevance of particular items, tags, or tag contingencies to the investigator's theory. In its fullest form a dictionary lists all instances of words and phrases which are considered relevant to the theory and indicates the particular variables to which they are relevant. Such a complete formulation is most relevant where a computer is to be used. For the purposes of non-computer content analysis, it is only necessary to give category headings or tag names, a clear definition of each tag, and a large enough sample of the items to be included in each tag category to ensure reliability in coding.

The following is a typical outline of the definition of a tag category, in this case the category "kin."

Tag: kin.
Definition: this category includes the terms for all blood relatives and in-laws normally considered kin in U.S. society.
Sample items: mother, father, wife, husband, sons, daughter, cousin, aunt, mother-in-law, sister-in-law, but *not* cousin-in-law or second cousin.

A dictionary may consist of any number of content categories. The actual categories included will have entry words of kinds likely to be used

Figure 4.3: *Tag tally from the general inquirer*

GENERAL INQUIRER WORD TAG TALLY

DOCUMENT 1 FIRST ID 00130

	Raw Scores					Index Scores as Percent				
	Sub	Vrb	Obj	Ucl	Total	Sub	Vrb	Obj	Ucl	Total
SELF	219	1	42	123	385	4.8	.0	.9	2.7	8.5
SELVES	13		19	3	16	.3	.0	.0	.1	.4
OTHER	36	1		30	86	.8		.4	.7	1.9
MALE-ROLE	79		18	26	123	1.7	.0	.4	.6	2.7
FEMALE-ROLE	45		23	29	97	1.0	.0	.5	.6	2.1
NEUTER-ROLE	15		6	14	35	.3	.0	.1	.3	.8
JOB-ROLE	2		2	3	7	.0		.0	.1	.2
GROUPS										
SMALL-GROUP	2		2		4	.0		.0	.0	.1
LARGE-GROUP	6	1		9	16	.1		.0	.2	.4
PHYSICAL OBJECTS										
BODY-PART	11		5	4	20	.2	.0	.1	.0	.4
FOOD	1		1	1	3	.0	.0	.0	.0	.1
CLOTHING	1		8	6	15	.0	.0	.2	.1	.3
TOOL	11	2	5	10	28	.2	.0	.1	.2	.6
NATURAL-OBJ	24		9	8	41	.5	.0	.2	.2	.9
NON-SPC-OBJ	6	3	8	81	98	.1	.1	.2	1.8	2.2
PHYSICAL QUALIFIERS										
SENSORY-REF	8	5	7	4	13	.2	.0	.0	.1	.3
TIME-REF	15	14	17	174	201	.3	.1	.2	3.8	4.4
SPACE-REF	8	3	18	194	234	.2	.3	.4	4.3	5.2
QUAN-REF	20		21	146	190	.4	.1	.5	3.2	4.2
ENVIRONMENTS										
SOCIAL-PLACE	8	7	26	43	84	.2	.2	.6	.9	1.8
NATUR-WORLD	6	12	2	11	31	.1	.3	.0	.2	.7

LETTERS FROM JENNY.   SECTION ONE.

4541 WORDS   502 SENTENCES

	Raw Scores					Index Scores as Percent				
	Sub	Vrb	Obj	Ucl	Total	Sub	Vrb	Obj	Ucl	Total
AROUSAL	3	2	3	5	10	.1	.0	.0	.1	.2
URGE	2	16	3	10	31	.0	.4	.1	.2	.7
AFFECTION	4	5		10	22	.1	.1	.1	.2	.5
PLEASURE	8	2	2	3	15	.2	.2	.0	.1	.3
DISTRESS	18	17	1	4	40	.4	.4	.0	.1	.9
ANGER	2	3			5	.0	.1	.0	.0	.1
THOUGHT										
SENSE	5	15		11	26	.1	.1	.1	.2	.2
THINK		21	4	33	63		.5	.1	.7	1.4
IF	3	1	1	44	49	.1	.0	.0	1.0	1.1
EQUAL	2	7	1	7	17	.0	.2	.0	.2	.4
NOT	5	4	3	82	94	.1	.1	.1	1.8	2.1
CAUSE										
DEF-MECH				7	7	.0	.0	.0	.2	.2
EVALUATION										
GOOD	21	1	7	14	43	.5	.0	.2	.3	.9
BAD	11	5	1	3	14	.2	.1	.0	.1	.3
OUGHT				49	55	.0	.1	.0	1.1	1.2
SOCIAL-EMOTIONAL ACTIONS										
COMMUNICATE	2	22	6	34	64	.0	.5	.1	.7	1.4
APPROACH		34		7	41	.0	.7	.0	.2	.9
GUIDE	1	22	4	12	39	.0	.5	.1	.3	.9
CONTROL		5		3	8	.0	.1	.0	.1	.2
FOLLOW		4		1	5	.0	.1	.0	.0	.1
ATTACK	1	3	4	4	8	.0	.5	.1	.2	.8
AVOID	1	21		10	36	.0	.1	.0	.1	.2

124

CULTURE

	Raw Scores					Index Scores as Percent				
	Sub	Vrb	Obj	Ucl	Total	Sub	Vrb	Obj	Ucl	Total
IDEAL-VALUE	11	3	7	7	28	.2	.1	.2	.2	.6
DEVIATION	3	8		2	13	.1	.1		.1	.3
ACTION-NORM	5	3	11	17	36	.1	.1	.2	.4	.8
MESSAGE-FRM	21	4	64	23	112	.5	.1	1.4	.5	2.5
THOUGHT-FRM		2		7	9	.0	.0	.0	.2	.2

INSTITUTIONS

	Raw Scores					Index Scores as Percent				
	Sub	Vrb	Obj	Ucl	Total	Sub	Vrb	Obj	Ucl	Total
ACADEMIC	5	6	5	19	35	.1	.1	.1	.4	.8
ARTISTIC	4	2	7	3	16	.1	.1	.2	.1	.4
COMMUNITY	1	3	3	3	10	.0	.1	.1	.1	.2
ECONOMIC	22	19	37	31	109	.5	.4	.8	.7	2.4
FAMILY	8	5	12	16	41	.2	.1	.3	.4	.9
LEGAL	2	8	1	4	15	.1	.2	.0	.1	.3
MEDICAL	6	8		7	13	.1	.2	.0	.1	.3
MILITARY					1	.0	.0	.0	.0	.0
POLITICAL	6	3	1	7	19	.1	.1	.0	.2	.4
RECREATIONAL	8	2	3	8	20	.2	.0	.1	.2	.4
RELIGIOUS	2	2	2	4	9	.0	.0	.0	.1	.1
TECHNOLOGICAL	12	16		16	51	.3	.4	.2	.4	1.1

STATUS CONNOTATIONS

	Raw Scores					Index Scores as Percent				
	Sub	Vrb	Obj	Ucl	Total	Sub	Vrb	Obj	Ucl	Total
HIGHER-STAT	6		5	7	18	.1	.0	.1	.2	.4
PEER-STATUS	13		2	2	17	.3	.0	.0	.0	.4
LOWER-STATUS	7	1	7	4	19	.2	.0	.2	.1	.4

IMPERSONAL-ACTIONS

	Raw Scores					Index Scores as Percent				
	Sub	Vrb	Obj	Ucl	Total	Sub	Vrb	Obj	Ucl	Total
ATTEMPT	1	5	1	3	9	.0	.1	.0	.1	.2
GET		28	1	5	34	.0	.6	.0	.1	.7
POSSESS	1	48	1	38	88	.0	1.1	.0	.8	1.9
EXPEL	1	9		1	12	.0	.2	.0	.0	.3
WORK	1	30		17	48	.2	.7	.0	.4	1.1
MOVE	8	22		9	39	.2	.5	.0	.2	.9

PSYCHOLOGICAL THEMES

	Raw Scores					Index Scores as Percent				
	Sub	Vrb	Obj	Ucl	Total	Sub	Vrb	Obj	Ucl	Total
OVERSTATE	22	6	15	117	160	.2	.1	.3	2.6	3.5
UNDERSTATE	10	2	8	70	90	.2	.0	.2	1.5	2.0
SIGN-STRONG	13	56	3	12	84	.3	1.2	.1	.3	1.8
SIGN-WEAK	20	24	7	10	57	.4	.5	.1	.4	1.3
SIGN-ACCEPT	11	54	7	18	90	.2	1.2	.2	.4	2.0
SIGN-REJECT	12	43	4	30	89	.3	.9	.1	.7	2.0
MALE-THEME	6	1	2	4	13	.1	.0	.0	.1	.3
FEMALE-THEME	29	8	22	29	88	.6	.2	.3	.6	1.9
SEX-THEME	13	10	15	17	55	.3	.2	.3	.4	1.2
SIGN-ASCEND	19	23	6	60	108	.4	.5	.1	1.3	2.4
SIGN-AUTH	8	2	2	16	28	.2	.0	.0	.4	.6
DANGER-THEME	2	1	3	7	13	.0	.0	.1	.2	.3
DEATH-THEME	12	24	5	18	59	.3	.5	.1	.4	1.3

by members of the groups under study. The number of categories and the kinds of categories will be dependent on the investigator's theories. If there is a category "kin," for example, this will be because a researcher wishes to test some hypothesis, perhaps about the extent to which the members in these groups are concerned with "kin" versus "non-kin" persons. Or a researcher might be studying adolescent peer groups and posit that, as the mean age of teenage groups increases, references to kin figures decline in proportion to non-kin figures.This then might indicate the lessening salience of the family as a reference group for the maturing adolescent.

A dictionary may be used to trace such trends, or make comparisons between groups, over a large range of variables. The simplest use of a dictionary is to measure the amount of attention, in different documents or conversations, devoted to the categories in the dictionary. The application of the dictionary to a body of text results in simple frequency counts of the number of times the words in each category of the dictionary are used in each document. Such a summary of a document is called a "tag tally" —it is simply a tally of the frequency with which each tag was applied to a particular document. Figure 4.3 shows a tag tally consisting of 83 variables or tags which resulted from the use of a computer program (*The General Inquirer*).

Note that as well as raw scores being presented, "index scores" are presented. The documents and conversations we wish to compare, for the frequency with which different content variables are used, are often of different lengths (where length is measured by the number of words in the document). In this case, simple frequencies are not a useful basis for comparison, and the frequency for each tag is converted into a percentage of the total number of words in the document. These converted scores are referred to as index scores and are a better basis for comparison than raw scores where documents are of unequal lengths. By applying a content analysis dictionary to different documents, the contents of the documents can be reduced to frequency counts on important content variables. Converting these frequencies to index scores makes it possible to compare the amount of attention devoted to these variables by the authors of the documents. Researchers are able to say, for example, that indeed as teenagers grow older their group conversations show a sharply decreasing rate of references to kin persons and a rising rate of references to non-kin persons. Similar statements may also be made about the attention devoted to a wide range of other content variables and appropriate inferences made about the theoretical meaning of these trends. However, this is still one of the simplest kinds of content analysis—the systematic classification of symbols considered as discrete and unrelated categories.

Attitude: A dictionary can be more than a simple classification of symbols. Content analysis can be considerably more sophisticated than a systematic method for arriving at simple counts of symbol freqency over a number of documents. When undertaking a symbol analysis, many researchers will want to investigate the nature of the symbol in more detail than just measuring the number of references to it. The researcher may want, first, to measure the *intensity* of the emotional involvement with the symbol. Osgood's Evaluative Assertion Analysis is probably the best known content analysis system which measures intensity of attitude. Attitudinal intensity is measured on a six point scale : extremely favorable, quite favorable, slightly favorable, slightly unfavorable, quite unfavorable, extremely unfavorable. Osgood makes some observations which indicate the specific classes of signs which convey intensity to the listener or reader :

In general, strong intensity ($+3$) is carried by the verb "to be" (X *is* a Y), the verb "to have" (X *does not have* Y), and most unqualified simple verbs when used in the present tense (X *loves* Y); moderate intensity is carried by verbs implying imminent, partial, probably, increasing, etc., association or disassociation (X plans to or is trying to do Y), by tenses other than the present (X has favored Y), and by most modal auxiliary forms (X used to help Y); weak intensity is carried by connectors which imply only possible or hypothetical relation between actor and complement (X may commit, might agree with, ought to join Y). Indexing adverbs are also useful guides, for example, absolutely, definitely, positively ($+3$), normally, ordinarily, usually ($+2$), slightly, occasionally and somewhat ($+1$).[29]

The researcher will often want to go even further than the scoring of emotional intensity and record also the valence or direction of the attitude toward the symbol : whether the speaker or writer is for, against, or neutral to the symbol. This kind of analysis involves a more complex form of content analysis. Here we go beyond simple counts on single variables to counts on conjunctions between variables, what are sometimes referred to as contingency relationships. An item, topic, or symbolic social object is identified but scored differently according to its relationship to an accompanying attitudinal unit.

For example, Baldwin, using a content analysis system referred to as "personal structure analysis," studied the contiguities of certain topics and social objects with attitudinal categories in a series of letters written by the same person, "Jenny." [30] It was found that Jenny's letters were concerned with 15 main subjects such as Ross (her son), women, men, her family, herself, money, death, health. Her attitudes to each of these symbols were then analyzed as favorable, unfavorable, or neutral. It was found, for instance, that Jenny's attitudes to other women were consistently unfavorable.

The same basic method has been applied to small group analysis by Mills in his Sign Process Analysis.[31] In this method, the classification of objects discussed above is followed by a final operation where the scorer decides whether the cultural standard evoked by the statement was positive, negative, or neutral. Mills traced changes in the affective attitude of group members to the internal and external system over the course of a year (*see* fig. 4.4).

Figure 4.4: Results from Mills' sign process analysis

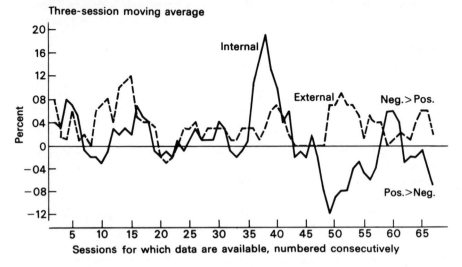

Preponderance of negative over positive affect regarding the internal system compared with preponderance of negative over positive affect regarding the external situation

Source: Reprinted from Theodore M. Mills, *Group Transformation: An Analysis of a Learning Group.* © 1964. Reprinted by permission of Prentice-Hall, Inc., Englewood Cliffs, New Jersey.

Mills uses this information to develop a theory of the relationship of the psychological processes to projection and displacement in group development.

Image: The researcher can go further in his symbol analysis than the description of the attitudinal valence and intensity of emotional involvement with particular symbols. He may also be interested in describing the chief characteristics attributed to the symbol, the major ways in which the members typify it. This is usually referred to as the *image* of the object. Image analysis is essentially an analysis of the major traits ascribed to particular objects and a comparison of the traits they share in common with, or which distinguish them from, each other.

For instance, I studied the role images of central members in two self-analytic groups.[32] In both groups, five distinct roles were distinguished, and each role was similar in the two groups and had a good deal of consistency

over time. The five roles were varied : instructor—the only formally designated role—, aggressor, scapegoat, seducer, and idol.

The role of aggressor, for example, was played by an individual in
each group who consistently seized opportunities to create rifts in group
relationships, reacted strongly against the introduction of personal material,
particularly when it was of a sexual nature, and seized on apparent points
of weakness and vulnerability in others in order to ridicule and belittle
them. The content categories *attack, military,* and *sign-reject* were most
strongly used in describing the occupants of this particular role. These
tags were used to characterize words which signified aggression. Moreover, in describing the actions of the aggressor, group members also used
the tag *danger-theme* which was applied to words indicating threat or
danger and also the tag *distress* attached to words indicating guilt and
anxiety. Similarly *overstate* words were used a great deal; these are words
which add emphasis—such as tremendous, very—and which were used
here to refer to the extreme nature and extreme effects of the aggressor's
actions. These and other tags clearly indicated that the image of the
aggressor, as the name indicates, was one in which aggression and interpersonal rejection were central and where emotional involvement, particularly anxiety and guilt, ran high.

Theme: To go beyond tag or topic analysis to a fuller exploration of a
symbol involves the researcher in a higher-order contingency analysis.
One common form of contingency analysis extends the idea of image
analysis further than so far described. A more adequate image analysis
takes sentence structure into account to develop an analysis of theme. A
simple theme occurring in the conversation of a delinquent gang might be
"cops are thugs." This theme might be identified by a simple contingency
analysis of two tag categories, "police" and "aggression."

POLICE	AGGRESSION
cop	hit
cops	punch
police	rough
policeman	manhandle
policemen	attack
	karate

The theme would occur wherever there was a sentence in which any
item from the "police" list coincided with any item from the "aggression"
list. Instances of the theme might be :

> They were a bunch of *rough cops.*
> The *cops manhandled* my friends.
> Jim was *hit by* a *police* lieutenant.

One would need, however, to exclude such sentences as "Jim *hit* a *cop.*"

Generally speaking, a theme can be defined as an assertion which links one of a class of active verbs with a noun or class of nouns as either subject or object—*cop hit, supervisor fired,* Bill *helped me.* More static assertions which primarily involve nouns and modifiers are referred to as images. However, as the example above (*rough cops*) indicates, this cannot be regarded as a hard and fast division.

Thematic scoring requires the researcher to take into account not only a contingency relationship between tags, but also the sequence or order in which the tags appear. Generally speaking, the order represents specific syntactical relationships. One of the advantages of the *General Inquirer* system is that it can scan large bodies of data very quickly for themes like the following :

> *self: reject: female role*
> examples: *I hate women.*
> > *I despise* the *girl.*
> > *I* really *disliked Mary* intensely. (female)

Simple sequence scoring of this kind can result in some problems. The following sentence, for example, has the opposite meaning to those above, but would be retrieved by the computer as the same as those above :

> *I hated* to see *her* go.

The human coder will immediately see the inappropriateness of the retrieval and can eliminate instances like this.

Myth: In thematic scoring tag and sequence analysis are used within sentence units. However, the analysis of story, plot, and myth requires units larger than the sentence. The analysis of group myths is very important, and one of the most difficult processes the researcher can tackle. By a myth we mean an idealized, universalized plot involving symbols and/or symbolic persons. For example, I might quote one version of a myth which recurred in a delinquent gang I studied in Sydney, Australia. This myth recreated what might be referred to as the Robin Hood myth—the outlaw who redresses injustice inflicted on the oppressed by the oppressors :

This teenager was working for a fellow who ran that paper shop—see? Well, the fellow who ran that shop was short payin' him. When he'd get his envelope there wasn't the right pay in it. Well, he left and his mates got together one night and they milked the gas from a car and got all his Sunday papers, piled them in a heap, threw the gas on them and set 'em alight. The cops got them for it and they were all in together, but it showed him that teenagers won't be pushed around.[33]

Similar stories with much the same punch line or "moral" were frequently related in the group.

The term "myth" does not imply that the story does not have a basis in reality, only that it has been simplified, idealized, and modified for the implicit purpose of giving meaning to group action. Stories and myths consist of people, places, and an action sequence which links the people and places in a situation that is usually referred to as a plot. Researchers are often concerned to discern the common elements in different versions of the same story which is retold by several people with some variation, or between a number of "unrelated" fantasies introduced into a group over a period of time.

In such a case an image analysis of the central persons in the story is usually made. It may be sufficient, for example, to designate the hero and the villain. Then the actions which these persons perform on each other and on others are categorized. Finally, the plot is characterized by studying whether certain sequences of action tend to recur. The analysis of myth will be treated in some detail later in this book when we deal with the measurement of cultural variables.

The content analysis program

It is not sufficient to identify the basic units to be used in a program of content analysis. An effective and replicable content analysis procedure must also include a "program," that is, "a set of rules for organizing the data, applying categories, determining contingencies, and arranging the results for inspection and further statistical tests. The program is essentially a set of consecutive procedures for processing data." [34]

Mills, for example, in explaining sign process analysis, includes a ten page section on program, which he refers to as "the scoring operations." Mills describes how the coder breaks up the flow of conversation into units, identifies and categorizes the objects being referred to, the assertions being made about the objects, and whether the assertion is positive, negative, or neutral.[35]

Given a procedure as explicit as this, it is possible to achieve inter-coder reliability; other researchers can collect and code data in a comparable way so that direct comparison of results is possible.

Specific content categories for the analysis of primary group data

In general terms the requirements for conducting an effective content analysis have been outlined. But now a crucial question emerges: Can we specify in advance of a particular study what content categories should be used? Just as we argued for the usefulness of a set of general categories for scoring interactions in primary groups, we argue for a set of general categories for scoring content. We are *not* arguing that the categories advanced here are the only categories which can be usefully employed in studying groups. Particularly in the area of content, the investigator will wish to develop a range of categories appropriate to the subculture of the particular groups he is studying. Nevertheless, it seems reasonable to advance a core of basic content variables which can be used in a wide range of studies because they relate to continuing theoretical concerns of the small group researcher, and to continuity in small groups themselves. For while primary groups of different kinds exhibit widely differing topical concerns, they also exhibit some common concerns. They are, for instance, all concerned to some extent with particular persons, with interpersonal behavior, and with values and goals. A suggested set of categories for common areas such as these makes good sense and also allows for cumulative and comparable research. What we are proposing here could be referred to as a core dictionary for the analysis of primary group materials.

The concrete categories are listed in table 4.2.

Table 4.2: Content categories and sample entries

A   *Classification of objects*

   I   *Social objects*

     (a)   INGROUP   whether the object is inside or outside the group, or alternatively, specification of the particular group or groups of which he (it) is a member.
Example. Jim Burns = special investment group (SIG); trust investment committee (TIC); trust committee (TC).

     (b)   SEX   whether the object is male or female in the case of a person; is sex specific or neuter (sex of incumbent not culturally determined) if a role; or has a male membership, female membership, or mixed membership if a collectivity. Thus there are four categories: male, female, neuter, mixed.

     (c)   TYPE   whether the object is a person, a role, a small group, a collectivity, or a classificatory group (class). Thus there are five categories: person, role, group, collectivity, class.

     (d)   STATUS   which status rank the person occupies given the calibration of status being used in the study. The object may be assigned superior, peer, or subordinate status taking the average group member as a point of reference; or assigned a numerical status value according to formal rank in the organization or other appropriate criteria.

     (e)   AGE   assigned only if the object is a person. Numerical age may be assigned, or a number indicating the age range into which the subject falls.

     (f)   INSTITUTIONAL REFERENT   whether the object is associated with academic, military, economic and technological, artistic, kin, legal, medical, political, recreational, or religious sectors of society. Omitted for ingroup persons as the institutional referment of the group is presumably assumed in the study.

PRONOUNS:

self	I, me, mine, my, myself.
selves	we, us, our, ours, ourselves.
direct other	you, you, your, yours, yourselves.
male other	he, he, him, his, himself.
female other	she, she, her, hers, herself.
plural other	they, they, them, their, theirs, themselves.
non-personal pronoun, it, its.	

In transcripts, insert the pronoun referent in parenthesis: he (Tom Jones) said . . . then the referent is coded as above.

II *Non-Social Objects*

Natural objects: tree, fish, grass.
Natural places: ocean, beach, forest.
Social places: restaurant, street.
Physical artifacts: food, clothing, tools
Cultural (non-physical) objects:

  (a) ideal values: truth, beauty, justice.
  (b) deviations: immorality, falsehood, vice.
  (c) cognitive abstractions: assumptions, descriptions, deductions.

B *Classification of Qualifiers*

(a)	TIME—	past	old, ancient, last night.
		present	now, at present, currently.
		future	coming, tomorrow, future.
		unit	hour, minute, day, month.
(b)	SPACE—	near/together	close, beside, near.
		far/apart	distant, separate, removed.
		up	high, lofty, up.
		down	down, below, deep.
		unit	inch, mile, acre.
(c)	QUANTITY—	many/large	large, immense, multiple.
		few/small	few, little, tiny.
		metrics	one, two, hundred.
(d)	SENSORY—	touch	rough, smooth, sharp.
		sight	blue, shiny, dull.
		taste	sweet, bitter, sour.
		smell	acrid, stinking.
		aural	loud, quiet, staccato.
(e)	INTENSITY—	emphasis	tremendous, great, startling.
		underemphasis	somewhat, perhaps, rather.
(f)	RELATIONAL—		quick*est*, near*er*, loud*est*.
(g)	EVALUATION—	good	fine, O.K., excellent.
		bad	shoddy, poor, stupid.
		ought	should, ought, must.

C *Categories for Actions and Processes*

I. *Personal and Interpersonal Processes*
    (a) THINK   think, wonder, ponder.
    (b) SENSE   feel, sense, react.
    (c) COMMUNICATE   talk, speak, write.
    (d) DOMINATE—guide   command, direct, teach.
    (e) SUBMIT—follow   conform, imitate, obey.
    (f) WORK—cooperate   cooperate, contribute.
    (g) EXPRESS—   happy, laugh, cry.
    (h) RESIST—avoid   resign, retreat, deny.
    (i) LOVE—befriend   thank, embrace, welcome.
    (j) HATE—attack   resent, exploit, condemn.

II. *Impersonal Processes*
    (a) CHANGE—develop, evolve, change.
    (b) STASIS—continue, remain, level.
    (c) BEGIN—begin, start, get under way.
    (d) INCREASE—rise, surpass, reach, grow.
    (e) FUNCTION—operate, function.
    (f) DECLINE—decrease, end, drop, fall, diminish.

We will begin first with the classificatian of objects. The basic division here is social, non-social, and cultural. Social objects consist in all those persons, roles, groups, or collectivities which are referred to by the group members. Each one of these social objects is classified according to categories I(a) through (f). The result may be illustrated by a hypothetical example : the target group is an industrial work group and at their midday lunch break conversation, the social object "doctor" is referred to. This could then be coded as follows :

DOCTOR = Outgroup + Neuter + Person + Superior + Adult + Medical

(*Note* : if it were Doctor Tom Marshall, Plant Physician, who was being referred to, *neuter* would change to *male*.)

Another example : Tom Jones is a member of a high school peer group— and is referred to by one of the group members. This could be coded as follows :

TOM JONES = Ingroup + Male + Person + Peer + Adolescent

(*Note* : in the case of an ingroup person, we do not bother to record that the group is an academic and/or recreational group, unless of course we are making a comparative study of these different kinds of groups.)

The classification of social objects in this way enables the most prominent types of social objects with whom the group members as a whole, or as individuals, are most concerned to be sorted out quickly. The investigator may wish, of course, to add other categories of specific importance for his study. He may be interested, for example, in studying military combat teams and wish to make a much more differentiated set of categories for military roles. If 90% of the social objects discussed are military, a narrower set of categories may reveal different roles, units, or individuals within the military who gain differential importance to particular combat units.

Categories for pronouns are included, even though pronouns are always identified with their referent which is coded as are other social objects. Pronouns are a useful indicator of group identification. One can, for instance, take all sentences in which the pronoun tag *"selves"* is used and list the referents associated with the items in that class. One may compare with these referents in the sentences tagged *"other-they."* This can give interesting insights into the ingroup-outgroup division in the minds of the group members.

Non-social objects will be divided into very different categories according to the specific study. However, a minimal breakdown between the "natural" and the "cultural" and between things, places, and abstractions is suggested. Within these broad divisions the investigator will want to make finer categories. In the case of social places, for example, a family researcher might distinguish six general categories : home, work, school, organized recreation place, informal recreation place, other.

Cultural objects should probably include the category of physical artifacts. The term "cultural" is reserved for those objects which are intellectual abstractions. Cultural objects are divided into two categories of values : one dealing with ideal values—things positively valued—and deviations—things devalued or negatively valued. The final category is for cognitive abstractions. Here again, these general categories represent only the most basic divisions. The individual researcher will probably wish to list, for example, all those abstract concepts, apart from values, used in a group and then construct categories to approximate the way in which group members divide up their conceptual world.

The categories for qualifiers refer both to nouns and verbs and, in some cases, particularly the evaluation tags, to images and themes. The categories are self-explanatory and are particularly useful for image and action analysis when used in conjunction with nouns and verbs, respectively.

The categories for actions and processes are divided into two general classes of (1) personal and interpersonal processes, and (2) nonpersonal processes. Personal and interpersonal processes involve two categories for what are primarily inner personal processes : *think* and *sense*. There is a category for communication words which imply communication in a general sense but do not specify its precise interpersonal meaning. Other more specific communication terms are broken down into categories which approximate those used for interaction scoring. "Dominate-guide," for example, consists of words which imply action of a kind which would be scored dominance or guidance if observed directly. This parallelism between the interaction and content schemes is deliberate and we hope useful in allowing a study of the relation between the behavior people exhibit and the behavior they talk about.

Not all verbs deal with personal and interpersonal processes, and a number of categories referring primarily to status and change are included. The action and process categories allow us to summarize the main categories of action discussed in a group and, hence, to perform an "action analysis."

These are the basic categories for content analysis. They are neither indispensable nor the ultimate or only content categories the researcher can use. They should be regarded rather as a core of categories which the investigator would do well to consider, at least, to accept if they are relevant to his theories, and to expand and modify as his research interests dictate.

Before we leave the analysis of content, however, there is one higher-order content unit which we were not able to discuss until some of the concrete categories were outlined. This is the analysis of values, norms, and goals—a closer specification of the method of analyzing evaluation.

Five categories are relevant to the process of valuation. These are *good, bad, ought, ideal values,* and *deviations.* All the items in these categories act as cues to the investigator that the process of valuation is in operation. Sentences tagged with these categories can be sorted out and analyzed in detail to determine what values, norms, and goals are being expressed. The crucial question here is: "What is being evaluated?" in the case of the categories *good, bad* and *ought,* the researcher looks for the conjunction of value categories and particular categories or items of objects, actions, and perhaps themes. For example:

I think we *ought* to have a *meeting* to decide what we're gonna do about this.

Here there is a value placed upon group deliberation as a way of reaching decisions about action. If someone responds: "No. I think John should decide it himself," there is a counterposition of two opposed themes. Theme 1 is: *value, group, decision.* Theme 2 is: *value, individual, decision.*

The categories *good* and *bad* are usually simpler. The statement, for example, "delinquents are bad" is an instance of the theme: *devalue delinquents.* Ideal values and deviations essentially contain the contingency *value object* or *value action* implied within them. The term "courage," an example of an *ideal value,* does not need a value marker to indicate that it is valued. These categories are the basis from which a thorough-going value analysis is made. This higher-order content analysis scheme will be illustrated subsequently in this book when values are discussed in more detail.

The content analysis categories in fig. 4.5 can now be summarized.

Figure 4.5: Types of content analysis

MAJOR CATEGORY DIVISIONS—HIGHER-ORDER ANALYSIS

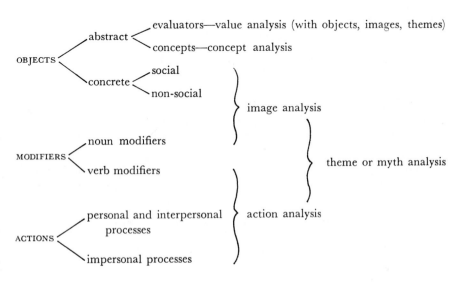

Fig. 4.5 indicates the way in which content analysis begins with tag-type categories consisting of ordered lists of signs which can be meaningfully characterized by a common head or tag. From these categories higher level analyses are built up by specifying particular kinds of contingency relationships—contingencies of classes of noun modifiers and social objects, for example, in the case of an image analysis of social objects. Unfortunately, the ways in which an investigator proceeds to make some of the other higher-order contingency analyses is not yet completely clear—the use of higher-order contingencies in content analysis is still in its infancy. Nevertheless, such analyses can be profitably attempted and no doubt the principles on which they can best be done will become clearer. Later in this book, we shall discuss in more detail each of these types of analysis under the appropriate variable headings.

Notes

[1] *See:* Philip J. Stone, Dexter C. Dunphy, Marshall S. Smith, and Daniel M. Ogilvie, *The General Inquirer* (Cambridge, Mass.: M.I.T. Press, 1966), chap. 4, "The Construction of Categories."

[2] Walter B. Miller, Hildred Geertz, and Henry S. Cutter, "Aggression in a Boys' Street Corner Group," *Psychiatry,* vol. 24 (November 1961): 283–98.

[3] Robert F. Bales, *Interaction Process Analysis* (Cambridge, Mass.: Addison-Wesley, 1951), p. 37.

[4] Bernard Steinzor, "The Development and Evaluation of a Measure of Social Interaction," *Human Relations,* vol. 12, no. 2 (1949): 109.

[5] Hans H. Strupp, *Psychotherapists in Action* (New York: Grune and Stratten, 1960). This system is also summarized in Edgar F. Borgatta and Betty Crowther, *A Workbook for the Study of Social Interaction* (Chicago: Rand McNally, 1965).

[6] Nell A. Flanders, *Teacher Influence, Pupil Attitudes, and Achievement* (U.S. Office of Education, Cooperative Research Project no. 397, 1960, mimeo).

[7] Richard Mann, *Interpersonal Styles and Group Development: An Analysis of the Leader-Member Relationship* (New York: Wiley, 1967), 60–1.

[8] Ibid.

[9] Ibid., p. 63–4.

[10] Donald M. Medley and Harold E. Meizel, "A Technique for Measuring Classroom Behavior," *Journal of Educational Psychology,* vol. 49 (April 1958): 86–92.

[11] Timothy Leary, *Interpersonal Diagnosis of Personality* (New York: Ronald Press, 1957).

[12] Ibid.

[13] Ruth W. Washburn and Josephine R. Hilgard, "A Quantitative Clinical Method of Recording the Social Behavior of Young Children," *Journal of Genetic Psychology,* vol. 45 (1934): 390–405.

[14] Ibid.

[15] *See,* for a wide variety of such methods: Nathaniel Gage, ed., *A Handbook of Research Teaching* (Chicago: Rand McNally, 1963).

[16] W. W. Lewis, J. M. Newell, and John Withall, "An Analysis of Classroom Patterns of Communication," *Psychological Reports,* vol. 9, no. 21 (October 1961): 211–19; W. W. Lewis and J. M. Newell, "Analysis of Classroom Interaction through Communication Behaviors" (Madison: University of Wisconsin, n.d., mimeo).

[17] Arthur S. Couch and L. F. Carter, "A Factorial Study of the Rated Behavior of Group Members," paper read at the Eastern Sociological Association Annual Meeting, March, 1952.

[18] Robert F. Bales, "Some Uniformities of Behavior in Small Social Systems," in *Readings in Social Psychology,* Guy E. Swanson, Theodore Newcomb and Eugene Hartley (New York: Holt, Rinehart and Winston, 1952), pp. 146–59.

[19] Dexter C. Dunphy, "Social Change in Self-Analytic Groups" (Ph.D. diss., Harvard University, 1964).

[20] Robert F. Bales, "Interaction Process Analysis," in *International Encyclopedia of the Social Sciences,* ed. Alvin Johnson (New York: Macmillan and Free Press, 1968).

[21] Philip J. Stone, Dexter C. Dunphy, Daniel M. Ogilvie, and Marshall S. Smith, *The General Inquirer: A Computer Approach to Content Analysis* (Cambridge, Mass.: M.I.T. Press, 1966).

[22] Ibid., p. 5.

[23] Theodore Mills, *Group Transformation: Analysis of a Learning Group* (Englewood Cliffs, N.J.: Prentice-Hall, 1964).

[24] Dexter C. Dunphy, "Phases, Roles and Myths in Self-Analytic Groups," *Journal of Applied Behavioral Science,* vol. 4, no. 2 (1968): 195–225; for a summary *see:* Dexter C. Dunphy, "Social Change in Self-Analytic Groups," in Stone, et al., *The General Inquirer,* pp. 287–340.

25 M. H. Landis and H. E. Burtt, "A Study of Conversation," *Journal of Comparative Psychology,* vol. 4 (February 1924): 81–9.

26 Harold Lasswell and Nathan Leites, *Language of Politics* (Cambridge, Mass.: M.I.T. Press, 1949).

27 Ibid., p. 13.

28 Mills, *Group Transformation,* p. 21.

29 Charles E. Osgood, "Evaluative Assertion Analysis," *Litera,* vol. 3: 47–102; summarized in Ithiel de Sola Pool, ed., *Trends in Content Analysis* (Urbana, Ill.: Illinois University Press, 1959).

30 Alfred L. Baldwin, "Personal Structure Analysis," *Journal of Abnormal and Social Psychology,* vol. 37 (1942): 163–83.

31 Ibid.

32 Dexter C. Dunphy, *Cliques, Crowds and Gangs* (Melbourne: Cheshire Publishing, 1969).

33 Ibid.

34 Stone, et al., *The General Inquirer,* p. 39.

35 Mills, *Group Transformation,* pp. 20–30.

part II

THE KEY VARIABLES AND THEIR MEASUREMENT

In chapter 3 we discussed a conceptual model and gave an overview of the main classes of variables we propose including in our model of the primary group as a social system. In chapter 4 the principle quantitative methods which can be employed to measure such variables were outlined. Part 2 introduces the particular variables we propose to measure and each variable is operationally defined.

At this point the reader may wish to turn back to figure 3.1 on page XX which gives an overview of the theoretical model. We will now fill out the detail within each of the boxes or cells in the diagram by presenting the specific variables within each class. The variables will be introduced systematically, proceeding across each row from the top to the bottom. This is not an arbitrary choice. The model has been set up to follow what would be, generally speaking, a natural order for the field investigator who is openly conducting research as a participant-observer. The model is defined in operational terms; not only are the variables described so that the researcher can readily measure them, but also the order in which they can be measured is also indicated. The researcher would normally begin by observing what people do (row 1), who communicates with whom about what (row 2), how the group is divided into differentiated and stratified subgroups and roles (rows 3 and 4), how resources are processed through the system (row 5), and finally, the way in which the system as a whole is integrated (row 6).

In any particular research, the exigencies of the situation may lead the researcher to depart from this general sequence. Research activity in real life must be responsive to the opportunities and problems which occur rather than being rigidly organized.

We have chosen to be very specific about each variable. In addition to describing its measurement, a brief overview of previous research relating to the variable is often given, along with some of the more interesting examples of its use in empirical research, and sometimes some of the more important generalizations resulting from research to date. In each case we show how the variable can be measured, sometimes giving alternate or complementary methods. Our aim has been to provide an exposition of the model detailed enough to be useful in practice, but sufficiently terse for the reader to mainain a sense of the totality of the emerging model.

chapter 5

Planning and implementing a research strategy *

Introduction

In this book, field work refers to the observation and analysis of the primary group in its natural setting. This involves finding a group—or groups—and maintaining an acceptable role in it for as long as is necessary to understand how it operates and what it means to its members. There are often problems associated with each stage of identifying a group, gaining access to it, and establishing sufficient rapport with group members to begin collecting data. This chapter describes how to establish an appropriate researcher role, how to adapt the role to particular circumstances that may arise in early contacts with the group, and how to begin gathering data on some of the more global characteristics of the group.

Choosing an appropriate type of research role

Buford Junker [1] suggests that there are four basic options for the field researcher which lie along a continuum from complete participation in the group to detached observation of it. Junker's approach has merit and these basic role options will be reviewed giving an evaluation of some advantages and disadvantages of each approach.

The complete participant
The role of complete participant conceals observer activity. The researcher

* David Frazer has made a major contribution to this chapter.

becomes a full member of the group he is investigating and hopes to share its most guarded secrets. The role is frequently adopted to investigate groups which make a sharp distinction between outsiders, the information which is presented to them, and group members. Where strict barriers are set up against outside penetration, the researcher's only choice may be to look for another group or to become a fully-fledged member of the group while concealing any suggestion of research. Groups which refuse any overt investigation can only be investigated covertly.

An example of this type of approach to field work can be found in *When Prophecy Fails* by Festinger, Riecken, and Schachter.[2] The book records the study of a small group of people who were convinced that the world was about to be destroyed and that only they had been given special warning of the impending disaster. In the event of the catastrophe they would be assembled in one place and would be removed safely by the "Guardians." The researchers had to adopt the complete participant approach because of the group's attitude to nonbelievers. In spite of some difficulties, five observers infiltrated the group and were accepted as "true believers."

Needless to say, the observers of this group faced some severe methodological and practical difficulties. They noted that "in the first place, it is clear that we are unable to rely on the standard array of technical tools of social psychology. Our material is largely qualitative rather than quantitative and even simple tabulations of what we observed would be difficult."[3] In order to conceal their research objectives, they had to forego any notetaking, use of questionnaires, or even probing questions which might have aroused suspicion. At times they had to resort to the standby technique of the complete participant—excusing oneself from the group to go to the restroom to make notes on something important.

The complete participant role is sometimes adopted in studying groups which are not particularly secretive. The researcher may feel that by identifying closely with the group under study he can gain a greater depth of understanding of their way of life, their cognitive perceptions, and emotional reactions. He may also feel that, by adopting such a role, he can expect to gain greater acceptance and, therefore, be in a position to see the group processes more clearly. In a remarkable case of "total immersion," William Caudill became a patient for two months in a private psychiatric ward to study the dynamics of patient groupings and culture from the inside.[4] He recorded, however, the problems of ethics, personal strain, and fear of harming other patients' therapy as factors limiting the advantages of this role. Donald Roy's investigation of quota restriction provides an example of the adoption of this role for a combination of all the reasons advanced here.[5] By working as a radial drill operator in a machine shop for eleven months, he was able to gain acceptance as a regular work group member, but he also experienced difficulty in data recording. Occasionally he would make surreptitious notes on the job, but mostly he set down notes from memory at the end of each day.

Sometimes the complete participant role may be the only method available, but it presents some major disadvantages which go beyond the difficulties of systematic data gathering. The researcher's freedom to observe the group from the point of view of an outsider often becomes very limited as the study progresses. His membership role tends to bias his observations of the relationships between the primary group and the larger social system. Maintaining an "objective" viewpoint can place considerable strain on the observer by severely limiting his own self-expression and yet, the more he attempts to express himself as a group member, the more he runs the risk of "over-identification" with the point of view of those in the group. In addition, the social scientist usually emerges from his disguise when the study is completed, often revealing his identity through publication. He can expect at this point to be regarded by the group as a spy or traitor, especially if his association has been secretive. Having been accepted as a *bona fide* member of the group, he should hardly be surprised by reactions of outrage when his deception is revealed. He must also be prepared to cope with other ethical issues when it comes to reporting material he has gathered in this guise.[6] The invasion of privacy is becoming not only a social but a legal issue, and as this trend increases, the possibility of using the role of complete participant may diminish substantially. Therefore this role is only appropriate in a minority of research situations, should be used sparingly, and with a clear recognition of the ethical issues involved as well as the limitations it places on the application of systematic quantitative measures.

The complete observer
In this role the researcher observes the group but does not participate. The role of complete observer is most often assumed by researchers studying classroom groups and other groups meeting under laboratory conditions. One-way viewing screens and sound facilities are frequently used to minimize personal contact between the researcher and the group under observation. These conditions can rarely be adopted in field settings although they can be approximated when the observer adopts the role of a casual bystander. All the observational methods discussed in this book are appropriate for use with this role, but interview and questionnaire methods have to be abandoned if the role is strictly interpreted to mean no contact at all between the researcher and his subjects.

One can question the rationale behind this role and whether the assumptions underlying the rationale are valid. The role is usually adopted because it is assumed that such a role interferes least with the group's natural processes. While this seems reasonable enough, in fact an unknown and "faceless" observer can have more impact on a group than one who is known, and particularly known to be committed to the group by inter-personal relationships with group members. The unknown observer fre-quently becomes a repository for the anxieties and fears of group members who begin to see him as one who "knows all," is "really pulling the strings," is "a malevolent influence on the group." As a result group be-havior can become overcontrolled and unspontaneous.

Another argument sometimes advanced is that such a role preserves the researcher from emotional involvement in the group and preserves the objectivity of the observer. Anyone who has seen the acting out that fre-quently occurs, even among experienced observers, behind one-way screens will be quick to disagree with such a naïve assumption.

It is obvious that the complete participant/complete observer dicho-tomy represents two contradictory and irreconcilable points of view on the involvement of the researcher. On the one hand, complete immersion in a group and identification with it leads to ready acceptance and an ability to see the world through the eyes of group members (although it does lead to a loss of the objectivity and detachment needed to put events and their meanings into a wider social perspective). On the other hand, the neutrali-ty that seems to offer the latter advantages has real pragmatic disadvan-tages. Too much neutrality can lead to the ending of relationships, to suspicion and lack of trust, to a drying up of the intimate sources of information about the meaning of group action to those who participate in it. Rosalie Wax describes some research she undertook in an American segregation center for Japanese Americans during the Second World War. In this situation she had to walk a tightrope between sympathetic identifi-cation and neutrality :

One of the most challenging and intriguing field situations is the investigation of conflict between factions. The two major factions of the Tule Lake Segregation Center were a group of pro-Japanese fanatics who employed Fascist techniques, and a group of liberals, some of whom, interestingly enough, were gamblers and *sake* bootleggers. I am genuinely proud of having remained on excellent terms with the leaders of both these factions, some of whom even told me their plans "so that I could watch and write down what happened."

These leaders so greatly needed an admiring and respectful audience that they were willing to hold long conversations with me, sometime before they trusted me to keep information from the administration or from their Japanese American rivals for power. However, in order to get certain information, it was necessary that I obtain their trust. Although this took time, it was not particularly difficult. I told them that I would not repeat what they told me. If, like the Center's vice king, the informant was particularly cautious, I told him to watch me and see whether I kept my word. After six months of checking up on me, even the vice king became a fluent informant, plying me with distilled *sake* which loosened his tongue but did not make my notetaking particularly accurate. The leaders of both factions knew I was consulting their rivals, and, as the conflict grew more intense, they denounced each other to me at length and in detail. They never, however, asked me for information about their rivals, nor did I volunteer any, preferring to maintain the attitude of one who was willing to be convinced that the person with whom I was talking was on the side of right and justice. In short, I assumed that both sides had some justification for what they were doing and always remained open to conviction.

Recently I heard a field worker studying a political pressure group complain of difficulties with leaders. He reported that when they questioned him about his sentiments he replied that he was neutral. I think he was making an error. Leaders of a social movement gain nothing by expressing their views before a neutral or ostentatiously fair-minded audience, determined at the outset not to take sides. If there is no chance whatever that the listener may change his mind, the leader is wasting his time.

I do not advise that an interviewer pretend to adopt views of which he does not approve. He will, however, do well to remember that a coquette is in a much better situation to learn about men than a nun.[7]

In accepting the idea that a role of complete neutrality is usually inappropriate to field work, we cannot simply dismiss the issue. What is needed is to increase our awareness of the particular ways in which the researcher's participations affect the development of group norms, the resolution of conflict, the intensifying of belief. If there are pressures on the researcher to conform to some group norms and to react to events, how does his conformity and reaction affect the flow of events? The researcher is, of course, involved in social interchanges with group members, and the relationships of exchange and reciprocity into which he is entering should be examined. Why do these people permit him to study them at all? What do they seek in return for his invasion of their privacy? What information are they most likely to give and to withhold?

The novice researcher sometimes abandons all detachment, trying frantically to become just another group member. But he loses one of the most valuable resources he possesses which can be traded for information about the group : his relative detachment from particular pressure groups, his unique ways of viewing situations and relationships which are all too familiar to his subjects, and the simple fact that he represents a culture or sub-culture different from their own. Paradoxically, the researcher who rushes to become "just another group member," may find that he has lost his outside status and that consequently his value to group members has radically diminished. Thus the active, identifying participant sacrifices detachment for the sake of greater control over the situation observed and greater intuitive understanding of participants. He hangs on the edge of over-rapport. The passive, neutral observer may see things from a broader perspective but may miss important, confidential information and incur the suspicion of his subject group. There is no simple answer to this dilemma, but some combination of both participation in group activity and explicit observation of it is generally the most fruitful approach to the analysis of the primary group as an ongoing social system. For this reason, two fruitful variants on the roles already discussed will be presented.

The participant-as-observer

This role conceals most of the researcher's observer activities but they are not kept completely hidden. Observer activities are subordinated to participation a good deal of the time, but the observer takes on a more insistent role as a researcher to avert the gaps in data gathering and recording which are part of the complete participant role. At one end of the scale—the almost complete participant—can be placed such approaches as Melville Dalton's role, described in *Men Who Manage*.[8] Dalton's only explicit acknowledgement of his research aim was to tell people at his plant that he was interested in "all kinds of personnel problems." As a regular employee in a staff position he had some official legitimation for his continued efforts to investigate cliques, power struggles, and personnel conflicts. The freedom with which he was able to gather data testifies to his skill and to people's tendency to accept vague explanations of what one is doing when there is a relationship of trust. Without creating undue suspicion of his activities, Dalton was even able to read back interviews reconstructed after the fact to intimates who checked them for accuracy. His research illustrates how the researcher can remain active and be considered primarily as a participant and yet openly investigate such delicate matters as cliques and their interrelationships. Nevertheless because he never thoroughly acknowledged the full character of his research, he faced some of the same problems as the complete participant in recording data.

The role assumed by William Whyte in investigating adult gangs in an Italian slum represents the midpoint of this role.[9] While Whyte openly acknowledged that he was writing a book about the area, he was introduced to others as "one of Doc's friends." People reacted to him and evaluated him mainly in this way. Most of his data recording was done from memory or in the presence of intimates such as Doc himself.

At the other end of this role, and even merging at times with the observer-as-participant role, are the roles typically taken by researchers in community studies.[10] In such cases people often spend as much time in participating in various activities of the community as they do in observing, interviewing, or taking notes. But the shift to explicit techniques is marked. Notes are taken openly and questionnaires and explicit observational techniques are used. Ezra Vogel's book, *Japan's New Middle Class*,[11] provides an example of a flexible role ranging from the observer-as-participant to the participant-as-observer. For more than a year Vogel and his wife studied six Japanese families who had agreed to cooperate in the research. The families agreed to one visit a week for a year and so the Vogels were able to find ample time for joining in social activities as well as using formal methods of collecting data. In any conflict between developing good relations and gathering information, the former was given priority. The researchers accumulated some 600 hours of scheduled visits in people's homes for the purpose of research, the time being devoted mainly to interviewing and discussion.

The observer-as-participant

This role makes the observer activity publicly known and known in detail at the outset. Research goals and research activities are stressed rather than played down and the researcher spends a major part of his time in his role as social scientist. Thus the participant aspects of his role become subordinated to the observer aspects. Such a role may cut the researcher off from some of the group's more carefully guarded secrets but it does not necessarily do so. If the researcher is able to develop a relationship of trust, confidential information is quite frequently divulged. However, it is usually given with maximum constraints upon reporting, in other words, this role faces the strongest explicit expectations constraining the researcher to maintain in his reporting the group's distinction between private and public information. Such constraints are applied because group members sense that there may be insufficient personal ties to prevent confidential information being divulged.

Melford Spiro's *Children of the Kibbutz* is an example of how this role can be used very effectively.[12] The Spiros lived in the kibbutz for a year as social researchers. While they worked alongside kibbutz members in the fields for part of the day, most of their time was spent in open observation or interviews concerning the age-levels in the educational system. Their activities were consistently open and their status as social scientists explicitly maintained throughout the study. For the most part, the role they adopted in studying the various school classes was that of the unobtrusive, non-participating observer.

An evaluation of research roles

In this book, the "participant-observer" means the range of role activities that include both the participant-as-observer and the observer-as-participant. The optimum role for field work lies in this range unless special circumstances dictate otherwise. Certainly a major modification of the methods advanced here as central to group study would be necessary if the researcher adopts the role of complete observer or of complete participant. The preference for the role of participant-observer is dictated by a desire for an optimum solution to the dilemmas facing the researcher who attempts to gather scientifically and publish acceptable data on the primary group considered as a whole. The role also has the advantage of allowing the researcher to include in his repertoire a range of stances and activities which is wide enough to adapt to developments in his subject group. His problem can be seen as analogous to the swings of work and expressivity occurring in task groups. At times he must meet especially insistent demands for building rapport through participation; at other times, when rapport problems recede, he can concentrate on achieving research goals more directly.[13]

The participant-observer role enables the researcher to move freely enough within and outside the primary group to gain comprehensive information on the group and its environment. Yet, because the role does not cut him off from his subjects, it can be used to verify and clarify motives and norms imputed to members on the basis of observation. It allows him to respond in a human way to those in the group and yet still retain the objectivity needed for effective analysis. While we cannot specify exactly what the field researcher should do in all situations, there are some specific suggestions which can be helpful, such as the instructions given by Sherif and Sherif to their field workers. To gain acceptance and to develop rapport, the field researcher should :

1. Insure by word and deed that group members are aware of his lack of authority in the situations where they were together.
2. Appear in word and deed as . . . [one] who is interested in them, wishes them well, and may be helpful on occasions.
3. Avoid any signs of dislike or disapproval of any member, on the one hand, or signs of favoritism on the other.
4. Avoid suggesting or initiating activities for the group *unless* such activities are deliberately planned as part of the research design.
5. Be helpful in activities initiated by group members without display of skills which put the observer in a rivalry situation with group members.[14]

Rules such as these are aimed to help the researcher gain acceptance as a participant without competing with other members for attention and prestige in the group.

Of course no amount of deliberation on roles and keeping of rules will alone ensure the success of a study. A good deal of the success of any field study depends on the character of the field researcher himself. If he is spontaneous and responsive in his reactions to others and respects them, he can afford to make some blunders in carrying out the research because mistakes will only serve to make him seem more human and approachable. If he is basically cold, hostile, or contemptuous with his subjects, any mistake will be counted against him and cooperation and trust will rapidly diminish. Because primary groups depend ultimately on personal relationships, acceptance, even as a researcher, depends finally on the quality of personal relationship developed with group members.

Moving in on the situation

Defining the kind of group to be studied

Having defined the kind of research role that seems most suited to primary groups, the research strategy can be further refined by a consideration of the kind of group to be studied. From the point of view of gaining access, establishing rapport, and gathering data, primary groups can be classified in two dimensions : (1) the degree to which the group's decision processes are internal to the group, that is, the group's autonomy, and (2) the degree to which its norms are largely self-generated or given by the larger social context, that is, the informal or formal nature of the group. Placing these dimensions in conjunction yields the typology shown in figure 5.1 and permits us to classify particular kinds of group into it in a way which is helpful in guiding the researcher.

By an *autonomous* group we mean that the primary source of authority concerning group action is internal to the group itself. In the case of the nuclear family, for example, decisions fundamental to the life and operation of the family are made by members of the family, particularly the parents. Similarly, in adolescent peer groups, decisions as to where to go, when to meet, and what to do are made by the group members themselves rather than referred to an outside authority. The opposite is true, however, in classroom groups and military units where the group is subject to a chain of command. Such groups tend to be *non-autonomous*.

The term *formal* applies to those groups where behavior in the group is governed to a significant extent by norms external to the group, whether those norms are norms of a larger unit or traditional societal norms. In an *informal* group, by contrast, behavior in the group is governed by norms indigenous to the group itself. For example, leisure time groups or therapy groups have much more freedom to define their own norms for behavior than do families or industrial work groups. This does not deny the fact that the norms of even the most informal groups are affected to some extent by the nature of the social environment.

The usefulness of this classification relates both to the directions it suggests for data collection and to issues of gaining and maintaining entry to groups of the kinds indicated. The culture of those groups which are autonomous-informal is influenced relatively more by the personal characteristics of members than in those groups which are non-autonomous formal. Environmental characteristics are relatively more important in the latter groups. Similarly, in autonomous groups, issues of solidarity assume paramount importance in the group culture, while in non-autonomous groups, instrumental issues are more important.

The classification suggests particular adaptations the researcher must make in his role if he is to get the maximum information from the particular kind of group he is studying. Specifically :

1. Getting preliminary information is usually much easier for non-autonomous groups. In such cases there are often official records or people higher up in the hierarchy who can provide a significant amount of information on the nature and functioning of the groups selected for study.

2. Moving in on the group and establishing rapport is more crucial in autonomous groups. While higher authorities can provide a researcher with legitimate reasons for becoming part of a non-autonomous group, he often has to establish his own reasons for access and win his own way into an autonomous group. Often this means discovering the informal leaders and winning their confidence so they can help legitimize the researcher's presence and hence the study. When the informal leader can be won over, he will cross many of the researcher's hurdles for him. It is usually harder to gain access to an autonomous group but, once it is done, the problem of maintaining rapport often takes care of itself. It is easier to gain access to a non-autonomous group, but the problem of rapport may persist for a longer period because an outsider has authorized the researcher's presence. Organizational studies often report problems of rapport arising because the researcher was suspected of being a spy under the sponsorship of higher management.[15]

3. Problems of data gathering are different according to the type of group. Non-autonomous groups can usually be found in designated places at specified times during the day. The observer does not have to spend hours looking here and there or waiting for hours for the group to turn up, as is frequently the case with autonomous groups. Because of the physical mobility of the autonomous informal group, the use of technical paraphernalia and scoring techniques is much more difficult. Equipment can be set up and used readily with non-autonomous groups because they usually meet in one or a small number of locales.

Identifying groups and defining their boundaries
While some researchers will have specific groups in mind for study, others will come to the task with only an idea of the kind of group they wish to observe. For the researcher in the latter position, the first task is to locate particular groups of the kind in which he is interested. Students of autonomous informal groups frequently find themselves in this position. They have an interest in gangs or peer groups, for example, and an idea of the geographical area in which they wish to work. But how are informal groups of this type to be located? The Sherif and Sherif study presents a useful strategy for locating autonomous informal groups. The Sherifs instructed their field workers to:

Choose one or several locales in the area as the initial base of operations: for example, a park, soda fountain, empty lot, playground, "hangout," agency, or recreation center. Observe the interactions between boys between the ages of 13 and

18 years. Investigate these locales at different times of the day, but regularly. . . . By returning regularly at different times to a location where you have observed boys interacting, the probability is increased that the same boys will be observed again. Once a recurrent association is spotted in one place, it should be followed to other locations. All observations at this phase of the study are from "outside" or "at a distance". . . . When a number of boys, 13–18 years old, have been observed interacting together during at least four observation periods within approximately two weeks, this cluster is a potential group for study.

The aim of the selection procedure is to locate a pattern of regular association among at least six or seven individuals, possibly with a "fringe" of less frequent interaction with other boys.[16]

Another method which I have used is to begin with the more formal settings of youth clubs and to use these settings to establish initial relationships with some young people in the area. One can then move out of the more formal settings into other community situations where these youngsters meet. The more formal setting is used to gain entry into the informal youth association patterns in the area. Undoubtedly this approach is more adaptable to middle class peer groups, whereas that used by Sherif and Sherif is more appropriate in lower class settings.

The identification of autonomous formal groups such as families presents few problems because the basic household unit is clearly defined and observable. Similarly, non-autonomous informal groups such as therapy groups may be readily identified through contacting medical and welfare agencies. The identification of non-autonomous formal groups is usually simple also because executives of the organizations involved can readily point out task-related groups. In formal settings there are, however, informal associations which are not indicated on organization charts. The cabal, discussed at some length in chapter 2, is a particularly clear example of this. Another example is the informal structure of peer relations in a high school population. There the total population is readily identified, but the particular pattern of associations within it may be quite difficult to determine. With a large population such as this, sociometric methods may be used to establish a quick, rough mapping of friendship patterns. A number of methods have been devised to take large numbers of sociometric choices and summarize them quickly and efficiently to point up the clusters of choices which represent mutual interrelationships.[17] Generally speaking, the existence of a formal setting will facilitate the use of a more formal method of research such as a printed questionnaire or direct interview.

Problems of timing role changes and novel interventions
The researcher should maintain flexibility in his role repertoire and concentrate alternately on building and maintaining rapport and data gathering. Once the researcher has identified his group and established himself

in it, he is faced with the question of *timing*. How do you know when a change in behavior is appropriate? When is it appropriate to undertake a new kind of intervention in order to gather data of a different kind?

Understanding what a research relationship involves for the researcher and for group members can help the researcher decide more effectively what his role should be at any given time. Joseph Gusfield brought this issue into focus :

A great deal of understanding of the field-work process can be gained by conceiving of it as frequently involving a reciprocal exchange between two persons—a research worker who wants to get data, and a respondent who has certain gratifications as his aim. Both participate in a social act governed by a normative structure that implies rules of behavior. The key question in this analysis is: What is each giving and what is each getting in return? [18]

As Rosalie Wax points out, there are two crucial questions for the field worker to ask himself :

Why should anybody in this group bother to talk to me? Why should this man take time out from his work, gambling, or pleasant loafing to answer my questions? I suggest that as the field worker discovers the correct answers he will improve not only his technique in obtaining information but also his ability to evaluate it. I suggest, moreover, that the correct answers to these questions will tend to show that whether an informant likes, hates, or just doesn't give a hoot about the field worker, he will talk because he and the field worker are making an exchange, are consciously or unconsciously giving each other something they both desire or need.[19]

The relationship between the investigator and his group is always one of reciprocity, and this relationship needs to be understood and utilized in order to secure and maintain a good relationship. Group members are often looking for a source of support for what they are doing. They will use the researcher as a sounding board to seek opinions about what to do in ambiguous situations. Bott stresses that the most general reason why families entered into research was that they wished "to evaluate themselves in comparison with other families or with families in general." [20] On occasion, Bott or her associates were put on the spot by being directly asked for advice on child care. These couples were seeking direction as to what a good marriage is and what good parents do. Gusfield gives another example of this desire for support. One of the WCTU executives let off steam to Gusfield in an interview on an issue which she said others in the organization disagreed about with her. It later came to light that she was in a serious conflict about that very matter with other executives, a conflict so deep that her job was threatened. Gusfield concludes about the disclosure: "She didn't tell these things but apparently used the interview to seek sympathetic alliance and justification." [21]

People with problems find solace in a sympathetic ear and the investigator may find himself talking to such people, especially in the early stages of a study. Often the people who open up first are those with gripes or criticisms. This gives a biased view unless care is exercised to widen the sample. Blau gives an example of this process, stressing the important effect of his changing value to group members :

It is my impression that the best informants in the early weeks tended to be officials who occupied marginal positions in the work group or the organization. Being not fully integrated among colleagues or somewhat alienated from the bureaucratic system may have made these officials more critical of their social environment, less restrained by feelings of loyalty from sharing their criticism with an outsider, and more interested in the approval of the observer than were those who received much social support and approval within the organization.

The marginal position of the observer in the bureaucratic field situation complements the marginal position of the informants, and this entails a danger. The observer may be tempted to rely too much on officials who make themselves easily accessible to him at the outset. If he yields to this temptation, he will obtain a distorted picture of the organization and the group structure. Moreover, if he becomes identified with deviant individuals or cliques, his ability to establish rapport with the majority and his effectiveness as an impartial observer will be impeded.

. . . During the later phases of the field work, my best informants were no longer largely officials who occupied marginal positions but included some of the most competent and highly respected ones. I think what happened was that once I became accepted as a social scientist, my prestige rose, increasing the value of my approval and respect for respondents. As long as my respect was not worth much, only the marginal officials who commanded little respect in the organization were interested in earning it, but later, when my respect came to be worth more, other officials too became interested in earning it.[22]

Blau points to another exchange : that of the ego enhancer. After his prestige rose in the agency, his respect became a more valued commodity to earn. Consequently, even the high status members of the agency courted him for his respect. It is also probable that his status rose partly because he had become a repository of much valuable information of the type which is not readily communicated upward. This is the kind of information that executives find it hard to obtain.

Not all the uses to which the investigator is put for the gratifications of his subjects are comfortable. Wax writes of the problems of personal antipathy and ethics she felt when informants tried to exploit her in order to obtain gifts or favors from the Relocation Center administration. The pro-Japanese fanatics tried to use her as a spy on administrative activities and sometimes requested dangerous favors.[23]

Such pressures often occur early in a study and represent attempts on the part of group members to test the limits of their relationship with the researcher. Spergel gives other instances from his experience with gangs, mentioning incidents where gang members tried to bait or frighten him. He took these to be attempts to test whether or not he was a "right guy" and to test his areas of personal strength and weakness.[24] The researcher is wise to react to such situations by firmly defining the relationship in a way that is comfortable to him. He should insist on receiving the kind of personal respect from group members which he is willing to accord to them. Most groups are ready to recognize such a fair exchange when it is brought to their attention.

Regardless of the specific elements in the exchange, the fundamental question always is : When does the investigator have sufficient resources to increase his rights to a wider range of information about the group? These resources include not just his exchange value in terms of relieving boredom, satisfying curiosity, giving support, lending a sympathetic ear to gripes, enhancing someone's ego, or giving friendship, but also the level of trust which has developed in the respondents. Looking at the research activity through time, the investigator may perceive times in which his position is inflated in terms of his ability to move freely in gaining information and times in which his value and the respondent's trust are severely deflated. Robert K. Bain writes of his difficulty in a study of a factory to maintain interaction with both the management and the workers. He experienced a time of deflation or "cooling off" with the workers he was attempting to investigate :

After completing the map of the floor of the plant, I spent a great deal of time in the receptionist's office (which adjoined the office of the superintendent and plant manager) gathering from the files personal data and job history concerning the employees. This was supplemented with information concerning previous work experience in the plant gathered by informal interviews with the workers themselves. However, I was spending most of my time in the office.

I began to notice a slight "cooling off" on the part of some of the workers. Perhaps I had become a bit too closely identified with the front office and officials, or perhaps it was merely felt that I was too close to their ears. As soon as I fully realized this, I changed my tactics and spent much more time out on the floor, continuing to talk informally with the workers, sometimes asking questions, often just passing the time of day.

. . . When the time came to start the sociometric study (which was about a month after I entered the plant), I felt that I still did not have enough rapport with the workers for such a study. Moreover, there were indications that some of them were getting tired of being questioned. Apparently I had not originally been explicit enough about the probable length of the research, and many had thought that it wold not take more than a few weeks or a month at the most. They were beginning, I suspect, to wonder just what I was doing that should take so long a time. . . . The solution . . . to this problem was so obvious that I don't know why I didn't think of it before. The solution was to do some work for a change.

I spent the next couple of weeks working on first one job and then another, with both white and colored workers, male and female.[25]

Bain's sensing that an appropriate level of rapport is required before certain exploration for information can be undertaken is basic to research strategy. Until the necessary foundation, in the form of reciprocity and trust, has been laid, the subject group will find very objectionable certain forms of data-recording and certain questions. Blau writes of how his impatience to collect data led him into a blunder when his subjects still were suspicious that he was a spy from another government agency:

I took every opportunity to become acquainted with these agents, asking them about their work and going to lunch with little groups, and slowly began to establish some rapport. But I soon became impatient with the slow progress I was making and decided that I could use my time more economically, since I was sitting in this room and watching what was going on anyway, by making the quantitative record of the social interaction among agents that I had planned. I proceeded to start this record of all social contacts in the department within a week from the day I had been introduced to its members. This was a serious mistake.

I had just begun to overcome the suspicion and resistance aroused by my entry, and now I employed a technique of observation that the agents found very objectionable and that increased their resistance to the study again. Of course, I explained that I simply wanted to get a systematic record of the social contacts among officials, but this did not meet the objections of the agents. Even those who apparently believed my explanations considered such a record ridiculous and emphasized that I could not gain an understanding of the agent's job by sitting in the office but must go into the field, where the most importat work was being done. Others suspected that I really tried to check on how much time they wasted, as exemplified by the mocking comment one whispered to me when he left the room: "I'm going to the washroom; will be back in two minutes." The continual observation to which keeping such a record subjects respondents makes them self-conscious and is irritating. I evidently should have waited until my rapport was much better before using this technique (as I did, of course, in the second study).[26]

Other cases of haste could be cited. What they usually reveal is that the investigator is using a method of data-gathering that is objectionable or requesting information that will not be given because the respondents do not yet trust the investigator sufficiently, or because the investigator is not seen as having highly enough desired exchange resources to make it worth while cooperating with him.

Gathering preliminary data on global patterns

Global patterns

The general research strategy adopted in a study of a primary group will depend upon the kind of research role undertaken and the kind of primary group under study. This does not mean there are no general patterns which apply to most studies. The following chapters setting forth the model's variables are arranged in the most general pattern of investigation once an open participant observer stance has been chosen. The areas of investigation that are either too sensitive for earlier stages of research, or which depend on earlier stages of research for their own development, have been placed toward the end. Those areas of investigation which can usually be looked at immediately have been placed at the beginning for this reason. An analysis of the global patterns of the primary group is placed first.

In the early days of research it is necessary to sacrifice data-gathering on all but the most non-threatening matters to the primacy of building trust and working out exchange relationships. Global measures are the kinds of matters on which information gathering can begin immediately. Inquiries concerning them gives the participant-observer an air of sympathetic interest and allows him to begin building a systematic picture of the group without feeding the anxieties of individual members about his probing into intimate, controversial, or sacred matters. Information gathering of this kind also places the informant in the role of expert, which is satisfying and also reduces anxiety.

The researcher is well advised to keep a systematic set of field notes, outlining his observations and reactions at the time they occur. The outline given by Sherif and Sherif to their field researchers is clear and helpful :

Observation reports—Outline

1. Date and exact hours of observation.
2. A rough diagram or map of the places where observations were made.
3. Description of and approximate number of persons (including non-members) present at the start of each observation.
4. Changes in the participants and circumstances of these changes (arrivals and departures).
5. Activities or topics of discussion throughout the observation period.
6. Description and details on behavioral events relevant to the focus of the phase of the study at the time (e.g., status differentiation) in terms of specific words and actions of the participating individuals, designated by name or symbol (before observer learns names).
7. Separately indented comments, giving the observer's impressions, evaluations, or "hunches" labeled as such, or his comparison of the observation with an event or action previously reported.[27]   .

To this we would add as point eight : The inclusion of a brief description of the researcher's role on the occasion; what he did and said, and whether or not he participated actively in the events described.

The "shape" of the group

In his initial data gathering attempts, the investigator normally sets out to establish the general parameters of the group before proceeding to a detailed examination of its elements and their interrelationships. These general parameters are the *global pattern* of the group, and figure 5.1 outlines its chief characteristics. Beginning with the structure of the group, the first problem is to define the group boundary and the absolute member size of the group. It has already been noted in chapter 3 that boundaries of open systems are relative rather than absolute. Consequently, it is sometimes difficult to establish a definite boundary, particularly in the early stages of a study when a representative variety of group settings has not been observed. In many formal groups, a formal membership list or organization chart provides the required information. In other groups, no such formal definitions are available, although the group may be defined by a geographical boundary. This is the case, for example, when all occu-

Figure 5.1: Global pattern variables

ADAPTIVE	STRUCTURE	GROUP COMPOSITION	PROCESS
1. Significant external social objects: persons, groups, and institutions. 2. Group image as perceived by external social objects.	Absolute size and life span	Member homogeneity (i.e., similarity of members' age, sex, social class, ethnicity, membership in other groups, including kinship, period of membership in this group)	Turnover (i.e., recruitment, and graduation, desertion, and expulsion rates)
Enumeration of group setting (geographical/social milieu)	Enumeration of basic activities	Differential participation in settings and activities. (i.e., who does, does not participate in each and amount of time spent in both settings and activities in man–hours)—*See* matrix	Fluctuation in "attendance" in group settings (mean, variation, range); sequences of movement through settings and activities (i.e., the temporal rhythms of group process)

pants of a particular room belong to a group, or when the members are the only people who "hang out" on a particular street corner. In other groups, "belonging" is a relative matter. Some individuals are regarded as central to the group, in that everyone agrees that they belong to it, while others are fringe or marginal members about whose membership there may be no real agreement. Membership in groups has both an interactive and subjective basis, but in his initial definitions of membership the investigator will wish to determine the credible candidates for membership, that is, all those who are regarded by themselves or some others as belonging or who act as though they belong to the group. Subsequently, when more adequate criteria are available, adjustments of the membership list may be made. In establishing his initial membership list, the investigator talks with persons in or in touch with the setting until he feels that he has determined the group's peripheral boundary as clearly as possible. His basic questions are : "Who says he belongs to this group? Who is said by others to belong to this group?" If the researcher can gain the confidence of one or two of the central group members, he can often have them check the tentative list with him. They are usually quick to indicate those whom they feel have been omitted or mistakenly included and they often articulate some of the important criteria for membership.

Establishing the current social boundaries of the group needs to be complemented with establishing the temporal boundaries of the group : its lifespan. How long has the group been in existence and how long do its members expect it to continue? Formal groups, such as school classes, are usually set up for stated time periods while informal groups often form, flourish, and distintegrate in an unplanned and spontaneous fashion.

Having defined these basic structural parameters, the researcher proceeds to define their qualitive aspects in more detail. If there are twenty members in the group, then information can be gathered about the homogeneity of those ascribed and achieved characteristics most likely to influence the group life. Either by questionnaire or interview, the researcher proceeds to establish the age, sex, social class, religion, ethnic group, membership in other groups, including kinship groups, and length of time the individual has been a member of the group. Other factors which are often relevant in formal settings are pay, seniority, supervisor rating, and job classification. The relative importance of these factors as bases of differentiation in the group will need to be examined later in the study.

The process aspect of size consists in selection or recruitment and desertion, graduation, or expulsion rates for the group. In this regard, there can be marked differences between groups of the same size. A group of men may meet regularly at a bowling alley for many years, while an annual summer camp group may have high turnover. The ratio of recruitment rate to the combined rate of expulsion, desertion and/or graduation is referred to as the membership turnover. Where turnover is a crucial factor in determining the character of the group, it can be studied in detail for the particular membership characteristics referred to above. For example, a trend to recruit older members or more members of one sex may eventually create significant changes in the group's social structure.

Finally, the major sources of social contact in the group's external system must be determined: what persons, groups, or institutions in the environment exercise a major influence on the group or are significantly influenced by it. In a gang, for example, this may be a friendly social worker, the local police, the boys' families, and an older gang. The researcher will also want to know what image of the group is held by these external persons and groups, and it is useful, therefore, to interview them and obtain descriptions of the group from their point of view.

The size of the group, the distinctive characteristics of its members, the rate of turnover, and the significant social objects in the environment are the first line of global characteristics to be determined.

Having determined the general form of the group, such questions arise as: Where does the group operate? What do the group members do? And, when do they do these things?

Settings and activities

The investigator needs to categorize the key settings in which a group operates. This is a simple matter where the group is only constituted in a single place. A particular industrial work group, for example, may simply exist as a group in a single situation—on an assembly line. On the other hand, an adolescent peer group may meet in a variety of settings— various homes, street corners, stores, beaches, and so on. Each of these situations may confront the group with different social expectations and involve different activities. The major settings may be determined initially by interviews and/or diaries; however, where possible, actual observation should confirm and verify what is reported as the study proceeds.

Having determined the settings which afford a backdrop for group action, the investigator needs to determine the main activity or activities performed by group members in each setting. Once again, this may be determined initially by interviews or diaries, but subsequently the researcher will need to verify his findings by observation. The same methods can be used to assess the differential participation of group members in different settings and activities. The researcher will want to know who does and who does not participate in each, and the amount of time spent in both settings and activities in man-hours. The results of this inquiry can be formulated and summarized in the *activities and setting matrix* (Fig. 5.2).

From this matrix the number of settings, activities, and differential rates of participation can readily be determined. The matrix, in this case, indicates that some activities (a, b, c,) are performed in all settings, while some (d, f, g, i) are only performed in a single setting. The total time

Figure 5.2: Activities and settings matrix

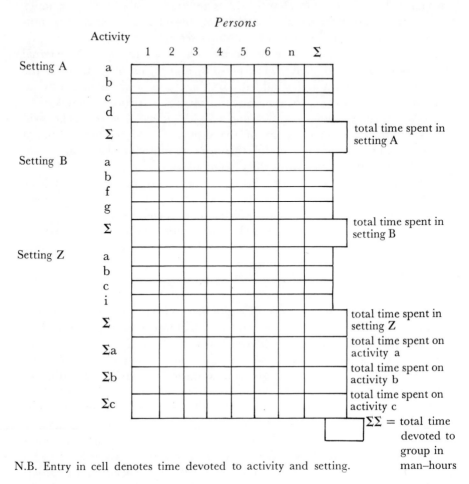

N.B. Entry in cell denotes time devoted to activity and setting.

Additional information

Time spent in activities but not in the group context

devoted to each activity, to each setting, and to the group as a whole in man-hours can also be seen. In addition, the researcher should collect information about the amount of time spent by each individual in the setting or activity apart from the group context. A person may, for example, belong to a group whose members go skating, although he frequently skates by himself or with others not in the group. It is important in determining the meaning of the group for him that it not be viewed as the sole purveyor of skating activity.

The activities and settings matrix is a simple way of organizing basic data about a group and, in particular, an excellent way of making gross comparisons between one group and another. In addition, noting sequences of settings and activities over time is a way of determining the natural rhythm or tempo of group processes. In adolescent groups, for example, it is common to find small sub-groups meeting in informal settings during weekdays, but gathering for total group meetings in more formal settings on weekends. This pattern of alternating dispersion and collection is a basic rhythm of adolescent social life and gives a clue to the different functions performed by cliques and crowds.[28]

Such an analysis of basic activities can also lead to a clearer understanding of reciprocal role relationships in primary groups. In a study of the task differentiation of husband and wife in family activities, Herbst made a penetrating analysis of the relationship of basic family activities to the roles of spouses. The basic family activities were divided into household duties, child control and care, social activities, and economic activities. A sample of ten- to twelve-year-old children were questioned about the extent to which their parents participated in activities under specific headings: ironing, table manners, mow lawn, pay for holidays. Analysis of the data showed that household duties could be further subdivided into duties performed largely by wives alone—wife's household duties—and duties usually performed by the husband alone—husband's household duties. This gave six basic categories of family activity. Herbst arranged these six areas so that he could predict the order in which the husband would take up or relinquish family activities. As Herbst describes it: "Given the number of regions in which the husband participates in the family's activities, one can predict in which of the six regions he will or will not participate. The prediction will be correct in 83 percent of all cases, and not be out by more than one region in the remaining cases." [29]

Herbst made the same kind of analysis for the wife and for the children of various ages and both sexes, discovering that for each major role a definite but different pattern existed.

It is not only the temporal sequence of activities which is important, but also the spatial arrangement of activities. A map of the spatial settings in which the group operates and the major physical objects—buildings, parks, machinery, etc.—which influence the physical patterning of group activities can also yield insights into group structure. This is particularly the case where the group itself is responsible in part for the design of its own environment. The placement of symbolic physical objects and the actual spaces of time separating various activities and contact between individuals often reflects features of the group's social structure. These features take on meaning, however, as the researcher turns to the direct observation of the group and the actual patterning of social activities.

Notes

[1] Buford H. Junker, *Field Work* (Chicago: University of Chicago Press, 1960), pp. 35–9.

[2] Leon Festinger, Henry W. Riecken, and Stanley Schachter, *When Prophecy Fails* (Minneapolis: University of Minnesota Press; New York: Harper Torchbooks, 1956).

[3] Ibid., p. 249.

[4] William Caudill, Frederick C. Redlich, Helen R. Gilmore, and Eugene B. Brody, "Social Structure and Interaction Processes in a Psychiatric Ward," *The American Journal of Orthopsychiatry,* vol. 22 (1952): 314–34; William Caudill, *The Psychiatric Hospital as a Small Society* (Cambridge, Mass.: Harvard University Press, 1958).

[5] Donald Roy, "Quota Restriction and Goldbricking in a Machine Shop," *American Journal of Sociology,* vol. 57 (1952): 427–42.

[6] For other examples of the complete participant role, *see:* John H. Griffin, *Black Like Me* (Boston: Houghton Mifflin, 1961); Mortimer A. Sullivan, Ralph C. Queen, and Stewart A. Patrick, "Participant Observation as Employed in the Study of a Military Training Program," *American Sociological Review,* vol. 23 (1958): 660–67.

[7] Rosalie H. Wax, "Reciprocity in Field Work," in *Human Organization Research,* eds. Richard N. Adams and Jack J. Preiss (Homewood, Ill.: Dorsey Press, 1960), pp. 96–7.

[8] Melville Dalton, *Men Who Manage* (New York: Wiley, 1959), p. 277, *see* the methodological appendix for techniques used; further details are to be found in Dalton, "Preconceptions and Methods" in *Sociologists at Work,* ed. P. H. Hammond (New York: Basic Books, 1964), chap. 3, pp. 50–95.

[9] William Foote Whyte, *Street Corner Society,* 2d ed. (Chicago: University of Chicago Press, 1955), *see* particularly the methodological appendix.

[10] *See:* August B. Hollingshead, *Elmtown's Youth* (New York: Wiley, 1949), pp. 11–45; John R. Seely, Alexander Sim, and Elizabeth W. Loosely, *Crestwood Heights* (New York: Basic Books, 1956), pp. 12–25, 425–31.

[11] Ezra Vogel, *Japan's New Middle Class* (Berkeley, Calif.: University of California Press, 1963), pp. 271–84.

[12] Melford E. Spiro, *Children of the Kibbutz* (New York: Schocken Books, 1965).

[13] W. Richard Scott, "Field Methods in the Study of Organizations" in *Handbook of Organizations,* ed. James G. March (Chicago: Rand McNally, 1965), p. 266.

[14] Muzafer Sherif and Carolyn Sherif, *Reference Groups* (New York: Harper and Row, 1964).

[15] Peter Blau, *The Dynamics of Bureaucracy,* rev. ed. (Chicago: University of Chicago Press, 1963), pp. 277–78; Joseph Gusfield, "Fieldwork Reciprocities in Studying a Social Movement" in *Human Organization Research,* pp. 100–01; Robert K. Bain, "The Researcher's Role: A Case Study," in *Human Organizations Research,* p. 149.

[16] Sherif and Sherif, *Reference Groups,* pp. 115–16.

[17] Albert E. Beaton, "An Inter-battery Factor Analytic Approach to Clique Analysis," *Sociometry,* vol. 29, no. 2 (June 1966): 135–45; James S. Coleman and Duncan MacRae, "Electronic Data Processing of Sociometric Data for Groups up to

1,000 in Size," *American Sociological Review*, vol. 25 (1960): 722/27; Murran Glanzer and Robert Glaser, "Techniques for the Study of Group Structure and Behavior," *Psychological Bulletin*, vol. 56, no. 5 (Sept. 1959): 317–32; Charles H. Hubbell, "An Input-Output Approach to Clique Identification," *Sociometry*, vol. 28, no. 4 (Dec. 1965): 377–99; Duncan MacRae, "Direct Factor Analysis of Sociometric Data," *Sociometry*, vol. 23 (Dev. 1960): 360–71; Anatol Rapoport and William J. Horvath, "A Study of a Large Sociogram," *Behavioral Science*, vol. 6, no. 4 (1961): 279–91; Seymour Spilerman, "Structural Analysis and the Generation of Sociograms," *Behavioral Science*, vol. 2 (July 1966): 321–18; Benjamin Wright and Mary Evitts, "Direct Factor Analysis in Sociometry," *Sociometry*, vol. 24 (March 1961): 82–98.

[18] Gusfield, "Fieldwork Reciprocities," p. 99.

[19] Wax, "Reciprocity in Field Work," p. 92.

[20] Elizabeth Bott, *Family and Social Network* (London: Tavistock Publications, 1957), p. 40.

[21] Gusfield, "Fieldwork Reciprocities," p. 105.

[22] Blau, *The Dynamics of Bureaucracy*, pp. 282–83.

[23] Wax, "Reciprocity in Field Work," p. 95.

[24] Irving Spergel, *Racketville, Slumtown, Haulburg* (Chicago: University of Chicago Press, 1964), p. 193.

[25] Bain, "The Researcher's Role," p. 145.

[26] Blau, *The Dynamics of Bureaucracy*, pp. 279–80.

[27] Sherif and Sherif, *Reference Groups*, p. 122.

[28] Dexter C. Dunphy, *Cliques, Crowds and Gangs* (Melbourne: Cheshire Publishing Pty., 1969), p. 60.

[29] P. G. Herbst, "Task Differentiation of Husband and Wife in Family Activities" in *A Modern Introduction to the Family*, Norman W. Bell and Ezra F. Vogel (Glencoe, Ill.: Free Press, 1960); p. 345; *see also:* P. G. Herbst, "The Measurement of Family Relationships," *Human Relations*, vol. 5, no. 1 (1952): 3–35.

chapter 6

Identifying, Coding, and Interpreting Interaction Patterns

Introduction

Let us imagine ourselves as having made initial contact with the members of a primary group and gained their permission to be present when the group gathers as a whole. After we have been observing the group members for a while, we begin to discern that some people habitually join each other to participate in particular activities, seek each other out to exchange confidences, address remarks to each other, and so on. On the other hand, there are others who largely ignore or avoid each other. As we become more curious about such regularities in behavior, we begin to form some idea of who communicates with whom and how often. We also become aware that the communications take place in different forms: through face-to-face conversation, over the phone, or by memorandum. As we get to know the members of the group better, we often have the opportunity to hear members describe "what they said to Joe about such and such" and so we begin to learn also what is the typical content of such communications.

These are processes we go through intuitively in any group we join for the first time, and they are similar to processes adopted by the social scientist as he begins to study a new group. As social scientists, our first attempts at understanding group structure and processes center around determining the relatively stable interaction patterns between group members. That is, we want to know who communicates with whom, the frequency with which such communications take place, the forms taken by communication and, ultimately, the typical content of such communications. Such stable patterns of communication in small groups are usually referred to as "the communication network." Determining the communication network is usually the first task of the researcher. An understanding of differentiated positions and sub-groups within the social structure, of the emergence and maintenance of group norms, and many other facets of group life depends upon the prior identification and description of the communication network. The stable aspects of the communication network form the basis of the social structure of the group. A series of systematic steps can be taken by the investigator to establish, as accurately and efficiently as possible, what the basic communication network is and what information is carried in it.

Laboratory studies of small groups have often examined the effects of different kinds of communication networks on other small group variables, such as group productivity and member satisfaction. Such studies usually enforce a particular geometric pattern of interaction, such as the communication networks illustrated in Figure 6.1. Studies of the effects of position

Figure 6.1: Communication networks

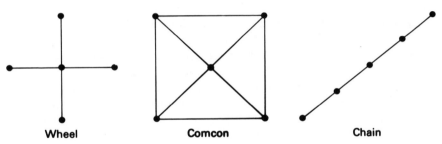

Wheel　　　　　　　**Comcon**　　　　　　　**Chain**

and role in such situations indicate that the effectiveness of task completion, or productivity, is markedly affected by the pattern of communication. Similarly, individual satisfaction is markedly affected by the relative centrality of a person in the communication network.[1] However, geometric communication patterns of the kinds studied in these small groups seldom exist in primary groups. Instead, communication patterns are generally more complex. Nevertheless, the field researcher is interested in determining the communication pattern, even if it is more complex, in describing it accurately, and in assessing the consequences in terms of satisfaction and the achievement of group goals. Therefore, the question for the field researcher is : How can he best go about determining and describing the duration, direction, and content of communication within the group, and between the group and significant groups and individuals in the environment?

There are two levels of interest in communication. One level is charting, mapping, or otherwise measuring the "flow" of communication. The other level is specifying the nature of the messages that are carried from one part of the system to the other, that is, performing an analysis of the *content* of the flow. Included in the term communication are both symbolic non-verbal interaction—conversation, gestures, etc.—between people and also the exchange of goods.

In an interesting discussion of communication in organizations, Guetzkow distinguishes : (a) the combination of organizational components involved in the communication, (b) whether the process is simultaneous or serial, and (c) whether the form of the communication is transitory or stable.[2] These same distinctions seem useful for understanding communication flow in primary groups. For instance, in regard to (a) we want to know how many individuals are involved in a full communication cycle. Sometimes there will be simply a dyadic relationship with one individual talking to another. Sometimes the total membership of the group will be engaged in general interaction.

The *timing* of communication is also important. When all individuals in a group are present at the same time, all have simultaneous access to the messages being transmitted. However, this is not so when individuals communicate serially with each other, as when A calls B on the telephone, B mentions the information he has received from A the next day, B forgets to tell C, and so on. When group members communicate in this serial manner, the messages travel irregularly through the group, reaching different people at different times and, in some cases, never being received by some members. Communication flow of this kind affects and is affected by the coordination of the group and the status of individual members.

The form taken by a message is also important. Some messages may be given fairly permanent form, such as a letter or memorandum. A written communication is more permanent and generally less open to misinterpretation, but may easily be ignored or set aside for a period. It can, however, be stored and retrieved intact. Verbal communication makes immediate demands on the hearer's attention, but is not usually stored, generally cannot be retrieved intact, and is usually more open to misinterpretation than a written message.

Studying communication networks

Charting the short-term, within group, face-to-face communication patterns

The social situation which is usually most accessible to the researcher is the immediate, face-to-face interaction between group members gathered in a particular situation. Such a situation is analogous to the face-to-face

Persons to whom acts are directed

Persons initiating acts		JOE		BILL		MARY		SUSAN		GROUP		TOTAL PARTICIPATION	
		Raw score	Percent of total acts initiated	Raw score	Percent of total acts initiated	Raw score	Percent of total acts initiated	Raw score	Percent of total acts initiated	Raw score	Percent of total acts initiated	Raw score	Percent of total acts initiated
JOE	D												
	S												
	W												
	E												
	A												
	H												
	Σ												
BILL	D												
	S												
	W												
	E												
	A												
	H												
	Σ												
MARY	D												
	S												
	W												
	E												
	A												
	H												
	Σ												
SUSAN	D												
	S												
	W												
	E												
	A												
	H												
	Σ												
Total acts received													

Figure 6.2: Interaction Matrix for a four person group

discussion group frequently studied under laboratory conditions and, therefore, methods similar to those developed for laboratory study are appropriate. Specific instances of such situations in real life are the family dinner
table discussion, the chatting of a work group during its lunch break, the
board meeting, or discussion of a topic in a classroom.

The interaction matrix.   In studying communication in such situations,
the researcher generally works with a set of interaction categories such as
those presented in chapter 4. The researcher notes the initiator of each act
and the person to whom the act is directed, and then categorizes the act
into one of the interaction categories. This summary transcript of the
interaction can then be used to compile an interaction matrix. This is
simply a tabulation of the number of acts in each category which are
addressed by each individual in the group to each other individual, and to
the group as a whole, with appropriate subtotals and totals (*see* fig. 6.2 for
the layout of such a matrix).

The first thing which can be derived from the interaction matrix is
who talks to whom and how much. People can then be ranked in terms
of their total participation, and it can quickly be seen which individuals do
not interact with each other at all. Each major category of behavior (dominance, hostility, etc.) càn be studied and the exchanges between members

Figure 6.3: Rates of affectively negative interaction in a management meeting

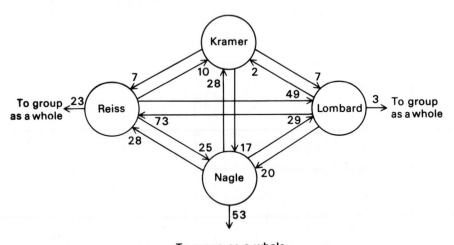

To group as a whole

From: Paul Lawrence and Dexter C. Dunphy, "Commentary on the Midway
Foods Case" (Boston: Harvard University, Graduate School of Business Administration, n.d.).

of behavior of just one type will be noticeable. It is sometimes useful to convert part or all of the matrix into a diagram in order to visualize relationships more easily. For example, in studying a management meeting which was marked by a great deal of conflict, I took the negativity rates from the interaction matrix and plotted them as shown in figure 6.3. The figure illustrates that Reiss is literally bombarded with negative acts, a response to the deviant role he was playing in this session. A chart similar to this can be made for interaction in any category or for total communication rates.

In the interaction matrix, the total interaction rates are broken down by category, so the interaction profiles for different individuals in the group can be compared, either by comparing the raw frequencies in the table or, better still, the percentage (of total acts initiated) which is devoted, for example, by Joe and Bill to dominant behavior. Each individual's interaction profile can be compared with the interaction profile of the group as a whole to see who departs most from the "average" picture of the group. The interaction profile is an important ingredient in characterizing an individual's role in a group. In a way that is directly comparable, the average percent of acts in each category forms a group interaction profile which facilitates the comparison of groups on the basic character of interaction occurring in them.

Higher-order interaction units for sequential analysis.   Interaction analysis is useful for giving an overall characterization of interaction in a group or for describing a person's characteristic interactive style. It is also a way of studying changes in interaction patterns over time and of locating persistent or recurrent regularities in group processes usually referred to as "phases." The simplest way of doing this, and the method which has typically been used in laboratory studies, is to divide the total period studied into a number of equal time periods and to compile an interaction matrix for each time period. These matrixes can then be used to trace systematic trends in interaction over time.

Bales, for instance, using interaction process analysis, has shown that when an hour's session of a problem solving group is divided into three equal time periods, the predominant types of activity shift from one phase to another in a systematic manner. The rate of acts of information decreases steadily from initial to final phase, while the rate of acts of suggestion rises. Acts of opinion increase in the middle phase and then fall off again. Both positive and negative reactions increase in rate from the initial to the final phase, with the positive reactions increasing more rapidly in the final phase. In phase one, members are collecting information, in phase two, evaluating the information, and in phase three, pressing for a decision with a concomitant increase in support for some members and rejection of others. Bales summarizes the results as follows :

Groups tend to move their interactions from a relative emphasis upon problems of orientation, to problems of evaluation, and subsequently to problems of control and concurrent with these transitions the relative frequency of both negative reactions and positive reactions tends to increase.[3]

Studies have also been made of the phases through which problem solving groups move over a series of six or eight meetings. Empirical evidence exists for a generalized phase pattern here, too.[4]

Investigators studying phase movements within sessions and across sessions have generally defined phases as equal time periods and then studied shifts, from one time period to another, in the emphasis on inter-action categories. While this method has an appealing simplicity and often yields useful and theoretically interesting results, it can disguise very important regularities in group processes. Actually, what the researcher is doing is to create larger units than the basic units of interaction analysis which present too confused and irregular a sequential pattern to be easily assimilated. The investigator, therefore, tries to isolate *general* trends in the data; but actually the decision faced by the investigator at this level is the same in trying to establish a lower order unit for interaction analysis, that is, whether to choose a "natural" or a "mechanical" unit. A natural unit is related to the forms of language rather than imposed from outside as are mechanical time divisions.

A unit is needed which is related to the meaning the interaction has for participants. But the question arises : What could be considered a meaningful unit at this higher level? The answer to this question lies close to what is sometimes referred to as a "change of mood" in the group. (This is not to be confused with a change of topic which is similar, but which takes place at the level of content.) A change of group mood is a marked shift in the predominant interactive style currently prevailing in the group. This is also referred to as a change in the group "atmosphere." For example, a change of mood occurs when a group that has been working consistently in a task-oriented fashion suddenly moves into a phase marked by a drop in task activity and a sharp increase in hostility. Such a change may well be lost in a system of tracing trends over time which relies on equal time divisions. The time division may come in the middle of a hostile exchange, thus dividing the hostility rate between two adjacent phases. Similarly, where bursts of hostility are repeated intermittently, being related systematically to work-oriented behavior, such a sequential relationship will not be revealed where phases are defined as equal time periods. No one summary method can show everything about the interaction process it represents, but there is a need for a summary method which reveals natural sequences in interaction.

What we propose for sequential analysis is a consistent criterion that will reliably measure major switches in group mood, regardless of how often such switches occur and the lengths of time for which the moods persist. The criterion locates persisting changes in the type of interaction categories being employed in group discussion and is performed on the string of interaction scores which result from scoring group interaction in the way suggested. The researcher should proceed as follows :

As interaction in the group begins, a count is kept for each category of its frequency of occurrence (including intensity) and also of total frequency over all categories. A dominant mood is established when one category attains a frequency of 10, has been contributed to by at least *two* speakers, and also captures one-third of the total frequency to that point. When a dominant mood is established, the counts on all categories are switched back to zero, including the total. With the next act, the procedure begins again, but dominant mood should be regarded as continuing until another mood is established.

The procedure may be explained in the following way : (1) A dominant mood should reach a frequency of at least 10 because a mood should not be regarded as dominant simply because, for example, the first two of three acts in a group session have been devoted to expressivity. In other words, this somewhat arbitrary criterion allows scores to stabilize a little before a decision is made on their significance. (2) Contributions should be made by at least two speakers so that the researcher can be sure the switch in moods is an interpersonal phenomenon. If one group member chooses to monopolize the conversation and is consistently dominant, this may tell more about him than about the group. If he is joined in his dominance by another, however, there is an interpersonal phenomenon—a joint bid to define group interaction in a particular way. (3) The category should reach at least one-third of the total acts to that point because the researcher needs to define units which are marked off within the flow of communication by a relatively high degree of internal consistency. The units should be *predominantly* concerned with a particular kind of behavior and because there are six poles of behavior, where one pole captures one-third of the acts in a sequence, it assumes considerable significance in the group.

This method can be illustrated by applying it to the segment of interaction used earlier in the microscopic scoring procedure (*see* page 114 chap. 4). Figure 6.4 shows the scores for the six categories transcribed, so they can be read sequentially from left to right. Figure 6.5 shows the same scores totalled in the way suggested above.

It will be seen (fig. 6.5) that the interaction begins with a work-oriented phase which establishes itself after twenty acts. At this point the progressive total for work is 11, and as 11/20 is greater than one-third, a work phase is established. (Reference to the transcript indicates that more than two speakers have contributed to the work total.) All running totals are then switched back to zero and the count begins again. This time a

Figure 6.4: Sequential transcription of interaction scores

D	1	2	1 1	1	3 1	1 2	1 3				
S	3	1	1	3	3 1	2	2	3 2			
A	1		2			3					
H	2 2 1	1 2 1	3 2 3	2	3	3	2 2	2 3			
W	2 1	2	2	1	2	2	3	2			
E	2	2 2	2	2	2	2					

Figure 6.5: Sequential transformation of interaction scores showing switches in group mood

```
D   1                                   2                       1
S                      3           1          1            1
A          1
H                                  2    5   7 (10)  2
W   2   4 5     6 8 9      (11) 1              3
E                    2    4         2                  2
Σ   2 3 5 6 7 8 10 11 13 16 18(20) 1 2 4 6 8 9 12 16(19) 2 4 5 6
              WORK                           HOSTILITY


D                          2   || 2
S       2          5   6        || 1 4
A   2
H          5      7 9  (12) 2 5
W 1      3    5                 2
E        5    7                       2
Σ 7 9 10 12 18 20 22 27 29 30 31(34) 4 7 9 10 13 15   .   .   .   .
       HOSTILITY (Cont.)                   HOSTILITY
```

switch of mood occurs after nineteen acts. At this point the score for hostility is 10, and, as $10/19 > 1/3$ and more than two speakers have contributed hostile remarks, a dominant mood of hostility replaces the work mood established in the previous phase. The running totals are switched back to zero and counting begins again. This time another mood is not established for thirty-four acts, but once again a mood of hostility is established $(12/34 > 1/3)$.

These macroscopic units can be used to perform a sequence analysis which reveals structural consistencies in the dynamic processes of the groups under study. It is of considerable interest to find, for example, that in a particular therapy group a dominant mood of expression is followed nine times out of ten by a dominant mood of hostility. Such a result presents the researcher with a major behavioral regularity which demands explanation and facilitates prediction. Sequences of this kind are not necessarily dependent on the temporal framework of group sessions, and may vary a good deal in length. As a result, they are easily overlooked when phases are defined in terms of mechanical units. But how are such sequences to be detected? An "input-output matrix" is a simple but effective way of doing this. Such a matrix is shown below (fig. 6.6). It is simply a six by six matrix similar to the who-to-whom interaction matrix shown earlier. In this case, however, not people but categories are listed along the sides of the matrix. What is scored in the matrix is the sequence of switches of mood in the group. In the sample transcript just scored, for example, the

Figure 6.6: Input-output matrix for sequence analysis

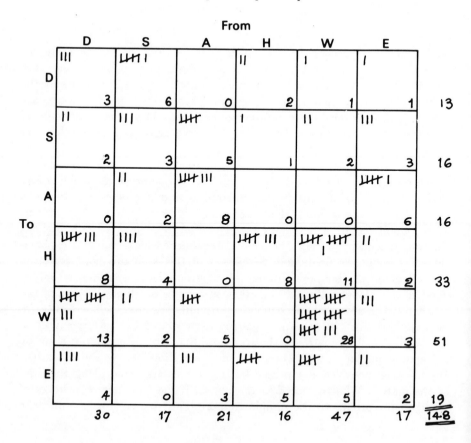

Figure 6.7: Completed input-output matrix

researcher would begin by noting that interaction changes from work to hostility. Work is located on the vertical coordinate and hostility on the horizontal coordinate by entering a check mark in the corresponding box as shown in figure 6.6. As hostility is followed by hostility, the procedure is repeated by locating a check mark in the appropriate cell as shown by the X in figure 6.6. Figure 6.7 shows an input-output matrix completed for a series of sessions, and it can be seen very readily what are the typical sequences of mood in the group.

It will be seen that dominance is most often followed by work, although hostility is also a frequent sequence; that work is most often followed by more work, although also fairly frequently by hostility; that hostility is most frequently followed by further hostility, although expressivity is also a fair possibility; expressivity is followed most often by affection, which in turn tends to reinforce itself or run off into submission or work. Submission tends to recreate dominance or hostility. The most probable sequences can be diagrammed as in figure 6.8.

Figure 6.8: Most probable sequences of group mood

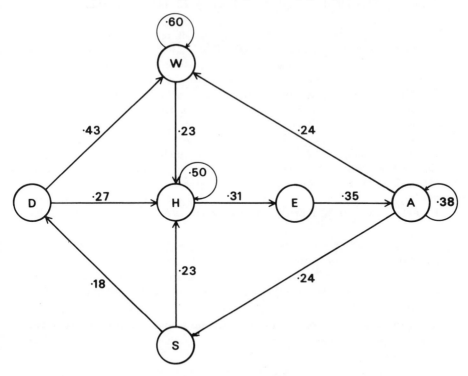

Predictions about the direction of group movement at any one time can be made with much better than chance probabilities. The diagram also lays bare the favored paths of interaction in a particular group. But if such an analysis is continued, with a closer look at who initiates moves in one or other direction, important insights will be gained into both key roles in the group and possible ways of influencing group action to control the situation.

Charting longer-term, sequential interaction patterns

The charting of communication taking place when group members are not assembled in the same place poses greater problems for the researcher. In the laboratory situation, the researcher often establishes and controls both the communication network and the form taken by messages in order to make systematic monitoring a practical possibility. The field researcher seldom has such control. While he can often manage to be present when the whole group, or a substantial section of it, assembles in one place, he cannot be in several locations at one time.

Sometimes it is possible to find a vantage point where a large proportion of interactions taking place are observable even though the actual content of the communication may not be accessible. This is often the case in organizational settings. Blau describes his method in such a situation:

To obtain quantitative indices of interactions, all contacts that any member of Department Y had with anyone in the office during 30.5 hours of observations were recorded. Neither the length of the exchange nor its content were given consideration in this count. The total number of interactions observed was 2,189. On the average, an official had 8.3 contacts per hour; 5.1 of these were associations with other agents in the department. These interactions included greetings and brief private conversations as well as consultations and other official business.

Four simple indices can be derived from this record: (1) the total number of contacts an individual had per hour; (2) the number of contacts an individual originated per hour; (3) the number of contacts an individual received per hour, that is, those contacts of his that the other participant in the exchange originated; and, (4) the proportion of an individual's total contacts that he originated, which provides an index of his initiative in social interactions.[5]

Blau found that the higher the supervisor's ratings of agent competence, the higher the number of contacts the agent would have. However, agents rated as highly competent did not initiate more contacts, they *received* more from those who were less proficient. A study such as Blau's indicates that the scoring of simple interaction frequencies and initiation rates can be a useful source of information about the group structure; it is not always possible, or even necessary, to have a detailed interaction analysis of a situation where conversations can be actually overheard.

Such a vantage point may be used to study sub-group formation, particularly where members are engaging in different freely chosen activities. Cliques are clusters of persons within the group who communicate more frequently with each other and identify more strongly with each other than with the remaining members in the group. Cliques are often directly visible to the researcher by the physical arrangement of their members and by the differentiated activities in which they engage.

Zaleznik and Moment point out that : "In groups in a relatively fixed setting, records of recurrent activities and participating members will confirm the existence of subgroupings." [6] They illustrate a method which can be used to locate such groupings by quoting from Zaleznik's *Worker Satisfaction and Development:*

Figure 6.9: Cliques in a machine shop

Activity matrix

	Card-playing subgroup		Helping and lending tools	Conversation	
	Coffee A	Bid whist*		Coffee B	Conversation
Steve	x	x			
Marc	x	x	x		
Larry	x	x	x		
Luke	x	x	x		
Paul	x	x	x		
Nick	x	x	x		
Hal		x	x		
Bruce		x	x		
Ron			x		
Jim			x	x	x
Vito			x	x	x
George				x	x
Charlie					x
Axel					
Foreman					

*No distinction is made between "players" and "observers"

Reproduced from : Abraham Zaleznik, *Worker Satisfaction and Development* (Boston : Harvard University, Division of Research, Graduate School of Business Administration, 1956), p. 78.

The group under study consisted of 14 workers in a machine shop. There were several recurrent activities with fairly fixed memberships. The activity matrix taken from this study illustrates how subgroups may be identified [*see* Fig. 6.9]. The five recurrent activities are listed in the columns, and members in the rows. An X in the cell designates a member's participation in a particular activity. The matrix arrangement is reached by trial and error, the aim being to arrange rows and columns to indicate the clusters or subgroups. The matrix indicated the existence of two main sub-groups in the machine shop. These sub-groups are blocked in on the matrix for the purpose of emphasis. The sub-group consisting of Steve, Marc, Larry, Luke, Paul, Nick, Hal, and Bruce was organized around coffee drinking or card playing activities during rest periods. The members of this sub-group had several values in common. They were the younger members of the shop and generally had relatively low job status. The members of the conversation sub-group—Jim, Vito, George, and Charlie—were older and had higher job status as compared with the other sub-group.

The matrix also shows the link between the sub-groups. The activity of helping and lending tools involved more members than any other activity and included members of both sub-groups.[7]

Another method for collecting information about interaction over time is to make systematic time samples of member behavior. In this case, the researcher does not try to gather all interaction occurring in a particular time period, but instead takes systematic samples of interaction. He might, for example, record the interaction of A with others for five minutes every hour. Obviously, this method presumes that the investigator can penetrate the communication network at a sufficient number of strategic points to be able to gather a representative sample of interaction.

For instance, Horsfall and Arensberg studied four teams in the bottoming room of a shoe factory; they took fifteen-minute samples of interaction over several months. They were interested in the relationship between interaction rates within teams and team productivity and found that less interaction occurred in the more productive teams.[8] A similar system was used by Homans in studying a group of working girls—interaction was sampled every fifteen minutes.[9] Time sampling has the dual advantages of reducing the amount of data to be gathered and processed while also allowing the researcher to gather information on a range of group interaction.

However, there are many communication situations to be found where even this limited kind of observation is not possible. Even when there are a number of researchers working together, they cannot always predict when and where communication between members will take place, and often it would not be appropriate for a researcher to be present even if the situation could be predicted—the field researcher who manages to predict and be present at the fond goodnight of a teenage couple is unlikely to be appreciated, to say the least!

One way which has been used to overcome this problem is to enlist the aid of group members as record keepers for the purposes of research. For example, in a study of adolescent peer groups,[10] I had the members of these groups keep "concurrent diaries" over a two-week period. These diaries were filled out on standard forms issued to all group members (see fig. 6.10). The diagram listed only contacts with group members over the two-week period. The concurrent diary method has the advantage of presenting a picture of the total interaction in a group over a sizeable period. Another advantage is that it allows for a reliability check. If A

Figure 6.10: Concurrent diary format

Day: Tuesday, May 1				Person: D. J.	
Time	Place	Contact initiated by:	Contact directed to:	Others present:	We talked about . . .

mentions that he called B, then B should also record the contact in this diary. Any discrepancies can be investigated and the researcher can feel sure he has a fairly accurate assessment of interaction over the period, provided he has the cooperation of his subjects.

The interaction data recorded in concurrent diaries can be arranged and summarized in an interaction matrix of the same kind as that discussed above. This opens the possibility of studying the similarity between interaction patterns in the total group setting and interaction patterns when the group is not gathered as a whole. Blau, for example, in the study of the agency mentioned above, compared the participation of agents in departmental meetings and their interaction in the normal day-to-day business of the department. He found that all but one of the six agents who received many contacts throughout the day, in contrast to only two of the nine others, participated three or more times during the formal meeting. He was thus able to demonstrate a consistency in status over the two settings.[11]

The reputed interaction network

A more frequently used, but probably less reliable, method than the concurrent diary is "member recall." A group member is asked to recall the persons with whom he engaged in certain activities in the past week or two and sometimes to estimate the number of times, or the amount of time spent in each activity. Information gained in this way can be entered in an interaction matrix and treated in the same fashion as other data. Lombard, in his study of interpersonal relations in a department store, was particularly interested in the way in which sales output norms were established and maintained through group interaction.[12] He, therefore, asked the girls in the clothing department, "With whom did you compare books last week?" Figure 6.11 shows in pictorial form the interactions which occurred, and in particular indicates the centrality of salesgirls S_5 and S_3 in this pattern.

It is possible to make use of the relative "unreliability" of such reports as these, that is, to use the discrepancies which usually occur between observed and reported action. Blau interviewed all members of the group of agents he was studying at their homes.[13] He gave each agent a set of cards, with each card bearing the names of colleagues in the group. The agent was asked to sort the names into two piles—those with whom he

Figure 6.11: Salesgirls' recalled interactions in checking books

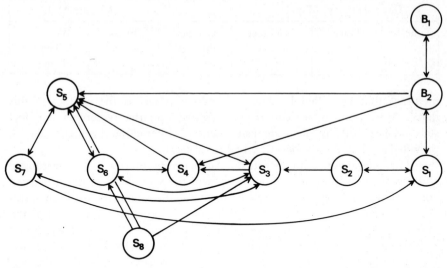

(Based on responses to the question: With whom did you compare books last week?)
Reproduced from: George Lombard, *Behavior in a Selling Group* (Boston: Harvard University, Division of Research, Graduate School of Business Administration, 1955), p. 67.

had spent a lunch period and those with whom he had never spent a lunch period. Blau found discrepancies of 39 percent between reports of the different agents on their contacts and concluded that such interview responses do not provide a reliable index of social contacts. He went on to use the discrepancies as a measure of social status. He found that the most expert agents exerted more social attraction than others, that is to say, they were more often named as associates by others whom they themselves did not name as associates. It seemed that even occasional contacts with the expert officer were remembered by others as significant, while the disproportionate number of contacts experienced by the expert officer made it more probable that he would forget encounters with those of significantly lower status.

The structures which can be traced as a result of such study are, however, not necessarily visible to any one person in the group and, to the extent that the structures are perceived, they may be perceived and interpreted differently by different members. Those aspects of the communication structure which are perceived or held to exist by group members can be referred to as "the reputed interaction network." Data from which the reputed interaction network can be ascertained can be obtained by asking each individual in the group to fill in, on an interaction matrix form, those relationships which he knows enough about to estimate: **for often talks (writes, etc.) to; *sometimes talks or writes to; O never talks or writes to;

blank equals don't know. These entries can be tallied and treated in the same way as observed interaction scores and compared with them. In particular, where observed interactions exist, but are not reported by an individual, sub-group, or by most group members, this is an important indication of the fact that such communications are not visible to the individual, the sub-group, or the general group membership. The reputational method locates groups as they exist in the minds of members, and such group structures are sometimes influenced by the needs and wishes of members.

The typical sociometric questions such as "who would you most like to work with?" or "who do you like the most?" are another way of locating cliques within primary groups. Here, however, the questions are phrased in such a way as to explicitly require the distortion of reality to match the wishes and needs of members. The resulting matrixes and sociograms are then reflections of the reference groups of individual members rather than of membership groups. Mutual choices, in this case, represent desired patterns of association rather than actual association patterns. This should be self-evident, but unfortunately in sociometric literature such patterns are frequently interpreted as indicating real associational patterns.

Charting the external communication network

Communications between members of the same primary group are not the only relationships with which we are concerned for there are usually important channels of communication between the primary group and its environment. The primary group is an open system and is involved in transactions with its environment. These transactions are of particular importance since they mediate larger social influences to the group and, in turn, allow the group to react to external pressures and, in some cases, modify them. We have dealt with the problem of identifying those persons, groups, and social agencies outside the group, which are most significant to it. Here we are concerned with charting the channels and content of communication between them and the group.

One of the most serious and effective attempts at studying the external communication networks of primary groups is Bott's study of family networks.[14] Bott and others made an intensive study of twenty normal families living in various districts of London. Within each family they concentrated on the relationships between husband and wife and, in particular, on the degree to which the activities in which they engaged were undertaken individually or together. They distinguished two very different patterns of marital relationship. The "segregated conjugal role relationship" occurs where husband and wife have relatively small proportion of joint activities. The "joint conjugal role relationship," on the other hand, occurs when the proportion of complementary and independent activities is relatively small and the proportion of joint activities is relatively large. One interesting aspect of the study is that the particular kind of marital relationship chosen in a family was found to be directly related to the particular pattern of the external communication network of the family, rather than to other internal factors. Bott gives a very clear definition of the external network :

In an organized group, the component individuals make up a larger social whole with common aims, interdependent roles, and a distinctive sub-culture. In network formation, on the other hand, only some, not all, of the component individuals have social relationships with friends, neighbors, and relatives who may be designated as A, B, C, D, E, F . . . N. One will find that some but not all of these external persons know one another. They do not form an organized group in the sense defined above. B might know A and C but none of the others; D might know F without knowing A, B, or E. Furthermore, all of these persons will have friends, neighbors and relatives of their own who are not known by family X. In a network the component external units do not make up a larger social whole; they are not surrounded by a common boundary.[15]

Bott was able to characterize family networks as close-knit or loose-knit according to whether there were many or few relationships among the component units of the network. She was then able to show that, as far as her twenty families were concerned, the degree of segregation of conjugal roles varied directly with the connectedness of the family's social network.

My study of adolescent peer groups in Sydney suburban areas, also examined the social environment of the groups.[16] In this study, I was able to demonstrate a tendency for adolescent neighborhood groups to form lateral relationships with other adolescent groups of the same age and vertical relationships with groups of older adolescents. The effective socialization of the individual adolescent was affected by his position within such a hierarchy because the transmission of values and social skills from older to younger adolescents was facilitated by the existence of such a hierarchy. This study illustrates the fact that the external network of a primary group may not consist entirely of relationships with individuals but also with groups. Sometimes parts or all of the external network may be completely inter-connected, in which case a group is formed, so that this group, rather than a collection of individuals, becomes the object related to.

External group relationships may be formal as well as informal. The work group in an organization, for example, has certain customary, even required, lines of communication, and the interconnectedness of the organizational environment is often deliberately organized and maintained. In this case it is desirable to record which interactions are required by the formal system and which are voluntarily initiated.

The external network may be studied by any or all of the methods outlined so far. It is sometimes possible to obtain a record of face-to-face interaction, although sampling is usually a necessity. The resulting data may be summarized in the form of an interaction matrix, with both group members and external persons and groups listed. A combination of diary and sampling of face-to-face interaction is particularly useful, for it can give both a general view of the overall relationships of the group to its environment and also the particular character of the most crucial relationships.

Content analysis of the main lines of communication

Summarizing content

There are two main aspects to studying the content of messages transmitted via communication networks. There is first the problem of summarizing or coding message contents, and second the problem of tracing changes in message contents as they are transmitted through the system. The first problem has been traditionally handled by one or another form of "content analysis," while the second has been the primary focus of attention in what is generally known as "communication theory."

It is possible to use the system of content analysis outlined previously in chapter 4 to monitor all or some of the interaction channels illustrated in the interaction matrix. There are two kinds of verbal data which can be appropriately used for analysis. The first is a recording or transcript of communication between group members. The second is a report of the content of communication by each group member. Where the investigator is able to be present and gather a transcript or summary of group interaction, this will be his prime source of data. However, even where the investigator is able to be present, there are certain advantages in processing group member reports of interaction as well as the researcher's coding of the interaction itself. Quantitative content analysis generally proceeds from categories regarded as important by the investigators and intensity is determined primarily by frequency : the more "important" topic, attitude, etc., is the one which is most repeated. Sometimes, however, a simple statement may carry extraordinary weight, and what the investigator sees as important from his viewpoint may not be seen as so important by the group members. However, if members are asked to summarize an extended meeting or communication sequence, they will concentrate attention on those aspects of it which are important to them and the fact that a series of reports are gathered ensures that important aspects of the communication will be emphasized in quantitative terms.

The simplest method for monitoring and summarizing communication content is to use the tag tally described in chapter 4. Where the aim is to make a comprehensive coverage of communication content rather than to study one particular aspect—such as values—in detail, the tag tally of a wide range of content variables is most appropriate. It is, in fact, directly comparable to the use of the interaction matrix. While the interaction matrix summarizes group interjection, the tag tally summarizes the content of interaction.

The researcher might, for instance, want to compare the content of communication in a number of heterosexual adolescent groups when (1) only boys are present, (2) only girls are present, and (3) when girls and boys are present. Transcripts or tapes of interaction under these circumstances would be gathered, the interaction for the content categories relevant to the hypotheses in mind coded, and the coded data summarized with tag tallies for each group under three situations. Systematic comparison of these tag tallies will reveal whether there are significant differences between the settings and in which categories the differences are most pronounced.

One of the chief uses of content analysis in the study of primary groups is to determine the main topics, attitudes, and so on which repeatedly occur in communication from one part of the group to another. Of course, it is usually not possible or practicable to study all communication in such detail except for very limited time periods. The researcher will usually make some kind of sampling of communication. Sampling can be done in two main ways; the researcher may endeavor to obtain a sample which is representative—or as nearly representative as possible—of all communication in all channels in the system, or he may decide to study only those channels which are of central importance in the system. A similar procedure to that recommended for interaction seems best. The investigator makes a detailed study of the content of interaction in a number of "typical" or "normal" face-to-face meetings of the whole group and, if possible, samples some of the chief lines of serial communication at key points. In addition, it is useful if members write reports or give brief oral accounts after each session of the contents of communication within the session.

Transformation of message contents in transmission
It is not enough to be able to summarize who says what to whom in a system of communication. The effectiveness with which messages are transmitted through the system and what additions and subtractions occur in the process is also important. A familiar childhood game begins with a number of children arranged in a circle. A brief story is inserted into this communication net at a specific place in the circle. Person A then recounts the story to B, who recounts it to C, and so on around the circle. When the story returns to A, the two versions are compared and the final version is generally found to be an amusing distortion of the first version. This is a fairly accurate model of what happens in any human system of communication where there is an attempt to pass information around the system in

a serial fashion. Systems differ, however, in the extent to which they are concerned with accurate transmission of messages and in the extent to which messages are transformed in transmission.

Messages can be changed in transmission in a number of ways. One simple way is through *omission*. We frequently hear the exclamation, "Oh, I was just speaking to X and I forgot to tell him. . . ." Another common way in which a message may be changed is through *distortion*. Rumor is a classic example of the distortion of information as it is passed along in serial fashion. Both omissions and distortions in communication can be readily identified if samples of communication concerning the same messages are taken at different points in the communication network, and content analyzed.

Transformation of messages can be studied quantitatively by taking tag tallies of documents (memoranda) or conversations in a series. The tag scores in the series can be plotted to show trends in data loss or changes in emphasis in the message contents. For example, in a study of informal relations in a housing project, Festinger and his colleagues actually manipulated the input of information into the informal system so that they could study rumor transmission.[17] Two similar rumors were introduced into two courts of the housing project and then within forty-eight hours each resident was interviewed to check on the spread of the rumors through informal channels. A number of issues can be studied in this way. First, it is possible to check the structure of the actual channels used by asking each resident about his informants. Second, the process of transformation can be studied in the way indicated, by noting significant additions or subtractions in the information as this informant is now able to represent it to the interviewer. Third, it is possible to estimate the relative interest value of different information by tracing the speed with which the information is transmitted through the communication network. It is interesting that some groups are sufficiently conscious of their patterns of communication to formalize them in the interests of efficiency. In a study of a Jewish adolescent peer group in Sydney by Hammerman and Cormie, for example, it was found that informal sub-groups had organized normal communication paths into an efficient serial communication network.[18] Within a couple of hours, any significant item of information could be transmitted through the entire group if an initial phone call was made to the key person in the network.

Notes

[1] *See:* Harold J. Leavitt, "Some Effects of Certain Communication Patterns on Group Performance," *Journal of Abnormal and Social Psychology,* vol. 46 (1951), pp. 38–50.

[2] Harold Guetzkow, "Communications in Organizations" in *Handbook of Organizations,* ed. James March (Chicago: Rand McNally, 1965), chap. 12.

[3] Robert F. Bales, "Some Uniformities of Behavior in Small Social Systems," in *Readings in Social Psychology,* eds. Guy E. Swanson, Theodore H. Newcomb, and Eugene L. Hartley (New York: Henry Holt and Co., 1952), pp. 146–59.

[4] Christopher Heinicke and Robert F. Bales, "Developmental Trends in the Structure of Small Groups," Sociometry, vol. 16, no. 1 (1953): 7–38; Hugh Philp and Dexter C. Dunphy, "Developmental Trends in Small Groups," *Sociometry,* vol. 22 (1959): 162–74.

[5] Peter Blau, *The Dynamics of Bureaucracy* (Chicago: University of Chicago Press, 1963), pp. 144–45.

[6] Abraham Zaleznik and David Moment, *The Dynamics of Interpersonal Behavior* (New York: John Wiley, 1964), p. 77.

[7] Abraham Zaleznik, *Worker Satisfaction and Development* (Boston: Harvard University, Division of Research, Graduate School of Business Administration, 1956), pp. 77–8.

[8] A. B. Horsfall and Conrad M. Arensberg, "Teamwork and Productivity in a Shoe Factory," *Human Organization,* vol. 8, no. 1 (1949): 13–25.

[9] George C. Homans, "The Cash Posters: A Study of a Group of Working Girls," *American Sociological Review,* vol. 19 (Dec. 1954): 724–33.

[10] Dexter C. Dunphy, *Clique, Crowds and Gangs* (Melbourne: Cheshire Publishing Pty., 1969), pp.

[11] Peter Blau, *The Dynamics of Bureaucracy,* p. 154.

[12] George Lombard, *Behavior in a Selling Group* (Boston: Harvard University, Division of Research, Graduate School of Business Administration, 1955), p. 67.

[13] Peter Blau, *The Dynamics of Bureaucracy,* pp. 151–52.

[14] Elizabeth Bott, *Family and Social Network* (London: Tavistock Publications, 1957).

[15] Ibid., pp. 58–9.

[16] Dexter C. Dunphy, *Cliques, Crowds and Gangs.*

[17] Leon Festinger, Stanley Schachter, and Kurt Back, *Social Pressures in Informal Groups* (Stanford, Calif.: Stanford University Press, 1963).

[18] Mary Cormie and Toby Hammerman, "Harcarmel—An Adolescent Group in Habonim Jewish Youth Movement" (Sydney: University of New South Wales, 1968).

chapter 7

The differentiation
of group structures and norms

Introduction

The central concepts of social structure are—position, role, and norm. Each of these concepts subsumes a variety of subsidiary concepts which have been found useful in developing descriptive models of social systems. While there has been considerable confusion in the past in the use of these central and related terms, it is fair to say that recent works have brought the terms a long way toward conceptual clarity and empirical definition. Within the limits set by a handbook such as this, we shall proceed to explicate these three clusters of concepts, indicating how they may be used to illuminate behavior in primary groups.

The term "social structure" indicates that the social scientist tries to characterize consistencies in the behavior of people involved in a group, organization, or society by making an analogy to physical structures. Social scientists have been directly influenced by the kinds of models developed in more established sciences such as biology, which, for example, is concerned with "skeletal structure," and physics which, is concerned with "atomic structure." But apart from this, social scientists are also influenced by the fact that most people involved in groups or organizations naturally construct simple models of a social structure in order to find their way through social situations. They identify positions ("a man in his position should know better than that") and they identify roles ("you're the secretary so you are supposed to keep minutes of these meetings"). The social scientist makes similar models, but attempts to operate more systematically and with greater precision and sophistication.

The part of the social system model being developed here identifies people as occupying certain *positions* in a network of social relationships, identifies the *norms* or rules which guide or govern their behavior toward each other, and then looks at their actual *role behavior* to see how they interpret these rules. The term *position* will be defined as "the location of actors in a system of social relationships." [1] The term *position* is neutral and implies neither high nor low status nor a formal role, but simply a point in the developing model. The term position does, however, imply a space of some kind and, in particular, the existence of other positions by which this one can be located. As in a geographical map, one position is identified by its relationship to others. Thus Lake Chocorua, where I am writing this chapter, is in New Hampshire *between the towns of Tamworth and Conway.* Such directions are of little use unless one recognizes some of the positions referred to. In social systems, as in maps, positions come to be referred to by identifying names, such as "manager," "teacher," "leader," "member," and so on. But the full specification of a position can only be made in relational terms, that is, by specifying the reciprocal relationships between a given position in the system and the others to which it is related. Thus the position of "teacher" is only fully specified when a roster of other roles are identified, such as : pupil, superintendent, janitor; and when the rules governing the relationships of these positions are specified, along with the kinds of concrete interactions which occur. Gross uses the term "focal position" to refer to the particular position being focused upon by the investigator for detailed study, and the term "counter position" for each other position to which it is related. Merton supplies the term "role set" to designate "the complement of role relationships which persons have by virtue of occupying a particular social status." [2] This terminology will be used here, and when each position in a group has been analyzed in this detailed way, and the descriptions have been collected and interrelated, a very important element of our system model will have been constructed.

But questions might well arise : "Why are there positions at all? and isn't a group simply a collection of individuals?" The answer to the second question is, very simply, "no." One important aspect of the social organization of groups which persist over any considerable time is the fact that positions and roles are differentiated from each other. The members of a group develop a common culture and certain common expectations about how different members will and should behave. Because of personality differences and questions of efficiency and convenience, group members institute, sometimes deliberately, sometimes not, a division of labor in the group. Different individuals are given or assume different responsibilities in the performance of collaborative and complementary activities. So there is always a differentiation of functions within a system, and it follows that there must accordingly be an allocation of specific functions to different persons or sets of persons within the group. In analyzing the group as a social system, the most significant unit of social structure is not the individual or self, but the position and the associated role or roles performed by the individual who occupies the position. As a group member the individual may act in ways which he would not do voluntarily or spontaneously in other situations or other groups. He may behave in a particular way because the group demands that he do so, either rewarding him for the performance or threatening to punish him for failure to perform in the expected way.

For instance, I personally dislike grading examination papers and would avoid this behavior if it were not expected of me by virtue of my position as professor. Similarly, most students dislike writing examinations. There is, therefore, little in our personalities that would lead my students and myself to engage in the reciprocal examiner-examinee relationship. It is an outgrowth of the social system rather than our individual personalities.

A role is expressed in terms of persisting regularities in the behavior of members. Some of these regularities will be common to all members of a group by virtue of their membership. These regularities form the basis for the *membership role*. Other regularities will occur in the behavior of only some of the members of the system, and these form the basis of *differentiated roles*. Not all regularities in the personal behavior of individual members are aspects of a role. A role must be defined in behavioral terms : it is what a person *does,* but only what he does by virtue of his position. If the chairman of a social club consistently polishes his glasses through meetings, this is likely to be a personal idiosyncracy rather than a role requirement. A role is the organized sector of a person's social orientation which constitutes and defines his participation in the interaction process. Some regularities in an individual's action are simply expressive of the individual's personality and not a response to the expectations of others. Hence, in identifying and defining a role, we must not only identify regularities in behavior but also discover from members in the system which of these regularities occur in response to their expectations. Those which do can be regarded as the components of the person's role.

Identifying differentiated positions and roles

In some groups, particularly those within organizations, it is easy to identify major differentiated roles in the system since they are institutionalized. Such roles usually have names, for example the foreman in an industrial work group, the chairman of a board of directors, the husband in the family. Roles of this kind are referred to as *formal roles*. On the other hand, even within formal organizations, informal roles exist side by side with formal ones, and, in many primary groups, all differentiated roles are informal. In this case it becomes more difficult to identify roles.

Whether or not a role is formally identified and named by the members of the system, it is normally *identified* by some examination of members' perceptions. An example is provided by a key study made by Slater, in which he indicated that even informal roles exist by virtue of the expectations of members.[3]

Role identification in the fully developed sense rests on the existence of a culture common to members of the system. The expectations members have as to the specialized roles each will perform are only a part of the common culture, but they constitute an important part of it. Possession of a common culture, in turn, implies some degree of *consensus*. There are degrees of consensus. All, or only some of the members of the system may have similar expectations, but yet not "know" that they are similar. And so on, with many degrees of complication.

The existence of consensus of whatever degree, of course, does not imply that all members are necessarily expected to behave alike on the overt level. Indeed, when role differentiation develops, the consensual expectation is precisely that the overt behavior of members will differ. The expectations are "common," "shared," "consensual," but the contents of the expected overt performances are "different," "contrasting," perhaps "complementary." This is one of the fundamental paradoxes that has occupied social theorists from the very beginning of serious thought about the nature of social systems, particularly in relation to the division of labor.[4]

Slater identifies major informal roles by having members rank themselves and all other members after each meeting according to ideas, guidance ability, and liking. He finds that the principal kind of differentiation which occurs is a "separation of the ranking of likes from the rankings on other measured characteristics." [5] He then identifies "idea specialist" and "best liked man" as the key roles in his groups and uses interaction data to construct composite interaction profiles for each of these specialists. He finds two sets of significant differences between the two role types in the behavior they typically exhibit and receive.

This demonstrates one characteristic approach used by the social scientist in studying roles. He uses member perceptions to identify role types, examines consistencies in the behavior of these role types, and draws conclusions as to the content of the role types and the functions they perform in maintaining the system. Another method is to identify distinctively different behavior patterns and determine whether these are undertaken in response to member expectations. Thus, when a role is identified, there are two different but complementary ways of looking at it. One way sees a person's role as made up of the expectations others have for his behavior, what they expect him to do because he occupies a particular position. This is the normative approach to the definition of roles because it generally stresses what the role occupant *ought* to do. Another way of characterizing roles is by looking at what the occupant of the role actually does, especially at the consistencies in his behavior toward the occupants of other positions. This is the behavioristic approach to role definition because it stresses what the role occupant *actually* does rather than what he ought to do. Both of these approaches seem not only valuable but also necessary complements to each other.

Roles as behavior—the enacted role

The term "enacted role" refers to the "role as expressed in behavior."

The most frequently used and most generally useful method of describing role behavior is by means of the *interaction profile,* a system of scoring interaction by which behavior is coded into a distinct number of categories. A summary is then made of the percentage of acts of each type initiated by the occupant(s) of a focal position, and this is regarded as the characteristic behavior of the role occupant. In order to be really meaningful, however, some comparison of the profile is needed. This comparison can either be with a mean for the total membership, or with profiles of occupants of other positions. The more profiles that can be gathered of different occupants of the same or similar focal positions, the more confidence the researcher can have in the specific behavior characteristic of that position. For example, if a researcher wished to characterize the behavior of U.S. general medical practitioners, he could feel more confident of an adequate characterization of that role if a representative sample of 1,000 G.P's was taken from the total population of G.P.'s and their interaction with patients was coded.

Even the comparison of simple frequencies of interaction for individual role incumbents can be useful in determining limits of variation in the performance of a particular role. For instance, Miller and Whyte studied teams of glass artisans.[6] They observed four shops in detail, noting for each man in the shop the number of situational interactions, interactions originated, and interactions responded to, both within and outside the shop. They contrast two men who had very distinctive interaction patterns: of twenty-three men in his shop, Carter had the highest number of interactions originated with his shop—160 in eight hours, or thirty per hour. He totalled 103 responses, tying for fourth place among all twenty-three men. His situational interactions were lowest of the four men with his work classification (jobs varied greatly in the extent to which they necessitated situational interaction). Carter made the most of the interaction possibilities provided by his work. By contrast, Pinelli, another worker in the same classification, presented an extreme contrast to Carter. He had the highest number of situational interactions (433) because of some specialized work he was doing, but for the eight hours, Pinelli had only 33 originations and 14 responses. Both of these workers occupied similar formal positions in the glass team, but their enacted roles showed considerable differences. Carter was an extremely active person socially and moved around freely within the constraints of the formal definition of his task and the physical situation. Pinelli was regarded as a disagreeable person who avoided contact with others and who was avoided as far as possible by other workers. Other glass workers' profiles fell between these two extremes.

The researcher is more often concerned with characterizing the basic similarities in the role performance of the incumbents of a particular position so that the role may be contrasted with the roles associated with other differentiated positions.

The widely reported experiment by White and Lippitt on leader behavior and member reaction in three social climates made extensive use of interaction profiles for this purpose.[7] Their work is an example of a field experiment with primary groups—research that is seldom undertaken. White and Lippitt organized four groups of ten-year-old boys into five clubs. The members of the clubs were roughly equated on personal and interpersonal behavior patterns and on socio-economic status. Four adult leaders were trained to proficiency in three leadership styles which they employed sequentially as they moved from one club to another at six-week intervals. Thus each club experienced each of the leadership styles under different leaders. All clubs met in the same place and engaged in similar activities. The behavior of the leaders and of the boys was observed during each meeting.

The three leadership styles have been referred to as autocratic (authoritarian, directive leadership), laissez-faire (leadership largely confined to providing expert information when requested), and democratic (policies and decisions arrived at by the group with active guidance of the leader). The leaders were briefed on the characteristics of these three role styles, and then their enacted roles were observed and quantitatively scored on the categories shown in figure 7.1. Figure 7.1 also contrasts the concrete behavior of the leaders. It is worth noting in this case that, with the possible exception of the democratic leadership styles, the leadership styles were not responsive to the members' expectations but to those of the experimenters. White and Lippitt also present profiles for the behavior received by three leadership role types (*see* fig. 7.2).

The results show that the democratic style was responded to by a much higher freqency of friendly, confiding behavior toward the leader, and of group-minded suggestions and, compared to the laissez-faire style, a much higher level of work-minded conversation. Two different kinds of group reactions occurred in the autocratic condition : aggressive and submissive. Some groups were extremely submissive. These two reactions are shown separately on the chart. Both responses had in common a small proportion of group-minded suggestions and a small amount of play-minded conversation.

A similar use of interaction was made by Slater. In the study men-

Figure 7.1: Comparison of behavior of average authoritarian, democratic, and laissez-faire leader

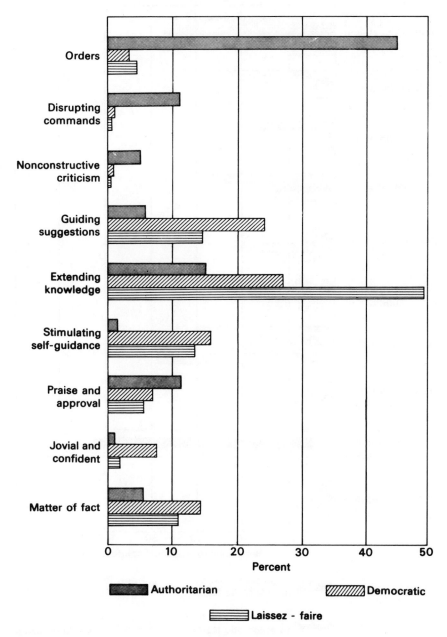

Reproduced from : Dorwin Cartwright and Alvin Zander, *Group Dynamics—Research and Theory* (Evanston, Ill.: Row, Peterson, 1953), p. 588.

Figure 7.2: Four patterns of child-to-leader relationship

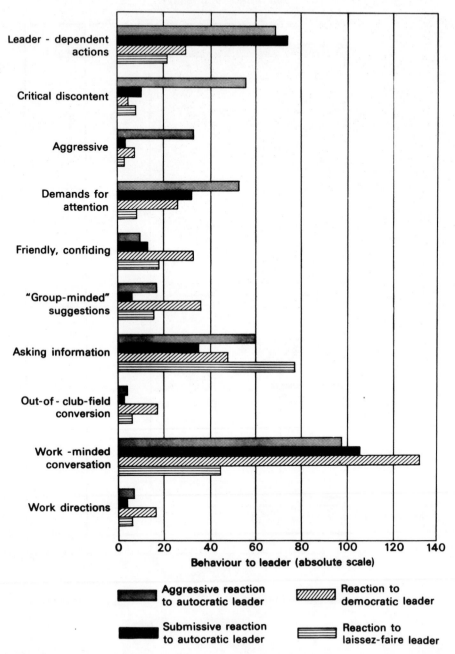

Reproduced from: Dorwin Cartwright and Alvin Zander, *Group Dynamics—Research and Theory* (Evanston, Ill.: Row, Peterson, 1953), p. 608.

tioned earlier in this chapter, Slater gives composite profiles of initiated activity for members of small groups named respectively as highest on guidance (or ideas) and on liking. The category system used was Interaction Process Analysis, and the scores for the two informal roles are shown in table 7.1.

Table 7.1: Comparison of initiation profiles for two group roles

		INITIATED	
INTERACTION CATEGORY		IDEA MEN	LIKED MEN
1.	Shows Solidarity	4.19	4.79
2.	Shows Tension Release	5.97	7.71
3.	Shows Agreement	14.60	14.97
4.	Gives Suggestion	8.66	5.68
5.	Gives Opinion	31.30	27.20
6.	Gives Orientation	17.90	17.91
7.	Asks Orientation	3.66	3.43
8.	Asks Opinion	2.39	2.73
9.	Asks Suggestion	.98	1.58
10.	Shows Disagreement	7.31	8.43
11.	Shows Tension Increase	1.97	3.67
12.	Shows Antagonism	1.07	1.90

Sample Size: 23 sessions

Significance levels of differences between roles   }   1 + 2 (.05 level)
categories 4 + 5 (.01 level)
10 + 11 + 12 (.05 level)

(Adapted from: P. Slater, "Role Differentiation in Small Groups" in *Family, Socialization and Interaction Process,* T. Parsons and R. F. Bales (London: Routledge and Kegan Paul, 1956), p. 279.

Slater summarizes these results by pointing out that "the idea man shows a concentration of activity in the task area, whereas the liked man shows a concentration in the socio-emotional types of activity, both positive and negative." [8] Thus, once roles have been identified, the behavior of the role occupants can be systematically compared, using the interaction profile.

However, in dealing with reciprocal role relationships, the researcher needs to characterize not only the regularities in the behavior of the role incumbent, but also regularities in the behavior of his role set. Consequently, it is useful to construct a profile of acts received by the incumbent of the focal position. In Slater's study, for example, the profiles of were obtained for acts *received* by the idea men and the liked men shown in Table 7.2.

Slater points out that the man in the liked position is higher in receiving solidarity and tension release and, although he shows more, does not receive significantly more negative reactions. The idea man receives more agreement. Slater's analysis demonstrates clearly that the two role types show

Table 7.2: Comparison of reactive profiles for two group roles

| | RECEIVED | |
INTERACTION CATEGORY	IDEA MEN	LIKED MEN
1. Shows Solidarity	2.90	3.68
2. Shows Tension Release	8.40	10.38
3. Shows Agreement	22.92	17.88
4. Gives Suggestion	6.14	6.36
5. Gives Opinion	26.28	28.86
6. Gives Orientation	15.24	13.73
7. Asks Orientation	2.78	3.01
8. Asks Opinion	2.00	1.98
9. Asks Suggestion	.72	.33
10. Shows Disagreement	9.50	10.21
11. Shows Tension Increase	1.30	1.37
12. Shows Antagonism	1.74	2.21

(Adapted from: Slater, ibid., p. 279.)   (1 + 2 significant at .05 level.)

significant and complementary differences between the types of overt behavior they tend to initiate and recieve. Further analysis also revealed an interdependence between the two roles themselves. When the mutual interaction of the pairs of idea men and liked men was examined, it was found that the two members interacted more with each other than other members, and agreed more with each other than with other members. This was particularly true of groups with a high level of consensus on the relative ranking of group members. It is evident that these are two mutually supportive positions : one specializing in goal achievement and the other in social-emotional, group maintaining behavior.

The studies by Lippitt and White and by Slater show that the inter-action profile, both proactive and reactive, is a useful way to characterize reciprocal role behavior between a focal position and either a single counter position or a total role set.

It is, however, not the only approach to the problem. In the previous chapter, a method for the sequential analysis of strings of interaction scores was traced which yielded a summary of regular patterns of group mood. Another procedure for analyzing role behavior is to take the sequence of group moods and search for consistencies in the initiation of such moods. Specialization in the induction of moods may be investigated by taking the point at which a mood is established and searching backward in the string of interaction measures to determine who contributed most acts to the creation of the mood through the previous phase.

Still another method which has been used to characterize roles is to specify in advance of a study, not a limited number of interaction categories, but a limited number of role types. The observer then attempts to assign individuals in the group to as many of these roles as seems appropriate. Examples of this approach are the work of Benne and Sheats [9] and Arsenian, Semrad, and Shapiro.[10] This view of role behavior can be called as the "role template" view. It assumes that there is a finite set or roster of roles which can be made operative in a small group situation, and that presumably group members carry the templates for these roles in their heads. While there is some evidence that this is true for some roles which continually recur in small groups (instrumental leader and sociocenter for example), there is no evidence that this is true for all roles. The diversity of roles which are played suggest that various kinds of behavior may be combined into different roles and that roles which consist of the same types of behavior may vary in the emphasis on some types of behavior. The diversity among roles is best preserved by recording microscopic behavior and using it to develop a detailed picture of the larger enacted role.

Roles as normative expectations—the transmitted role

Parsons defines a role as "the normatively regulated complex of behavior of one of the participants (of a system)." [11] To prevent confusion, while accepting his definition, the term "transmitted role" will be used. Parsons defines the role as it is transmitted to the role incumbent by the other members of the system. Norms govern and regulate role behavior. The concept has, however, been traditionally rather confused, partly because norms are often defined as *role expectations*. Expectations, however, can be of rather different kinds. Three kinds of expectations seem to be important in relation to the regularities in human behavior :

1. *Prescriptions and proscriptions:* Expectations which prescribe or proscribe certain kinds of action for the occupant of a role, for example, the secretary *must* keep the minutes of meetings and *not* forget to bring the minute book to meetings. These are obligatory norms.

2. *Preferences and aversions:* Expectations which indicate preferences for or against a certain kind of behavior while not prescribing or proscribing it, for example, "it is nice of the secretary to provide coffee, but you cannot really expect her to do it," and "I wish she wouldn't read the minutes so fast." These are preferential norms.

3. *Predictions:* Expectations which indicate that members predict or anticipate certain kinds of behavior on the basis of past experience with an individual. The behavior, however, is not part of the role as such; for instance, "Don't worry, I'm sure she'll remember to lock the door; she always has." These are predictive expectations. They are non-normative, and will be discussed further under the topic of role image. Here we are particularly concerned with normative expectations, that is with valued or sanctioned behavior. Obligatory and preferential norms are what govern

and guide role behavior, and the behavioral consistencies which match these norms are, therefore, considered to be the central characteristics of role behavior.

How does the researcher arrive at a description of the obligatory and preferential norms? He does so by identifying social positions and by gathering information on what other members expect of the occupant of a particular position. Bates and Cloyd deal directly with this point in their article, "Toward the Development of Operations for Defining Group Norms and Member Roles." [12] They point out that the characterization of norms depends on identifying behavior traits on which members of the group may have definite normative sentiments, establishing that these sentiments are shared by a significant portion of the group, and gathering evidence that members are aware that their attitudes are supported by agreement on the part of the other members of the group.

Bates and Cloyd use the term "norm" more in the sense that value is used in this book. The term norm seems better to apply to expectations for the behavior of occupants of differentiated rather than common roles. Nevertheless, the above steps can be applied just as well to norms relating to a particular position in a group as they can to the generalized membership role. The investigator can sometimes proceed directly by inspecting recorded lists of duties, if the role is a formal organized one, by interviewing members, and by asking them what the occupant must or must not do and what the member would and would not like him to do. The investigator may also follow discussions arising when conflict about role behavior occurs (as it frequently does), for this is one time when norms are most likely to be verbalized spontaneously by members. Having gathered a list of norms, the investigator, in some cases, may be able to submit a list or a questionnaire to members through a second wave of interviews to determine the extent of agreement within the group on the norms relating to specific positions and to rank norms in order of importance.

Let us now look more closely at some other concepts which are subsidiary to the concept of norm. Where a role is not clearly defined by generally accepted norms, role confusion or role ambiguity occurs. Role confusion exists when members are unsure about what a member should do by virtue of his role : where conflicting expectations exist, there is role conflict, that is, some group members may think a person should do something, while others think he should *not*. Role conflict exists when members hold contradictory norms for a role. Role confusion and role conflict are important sources of strain in a system and present an opportunity for change to occur within the system. Role confusion allows greater latitude for the person to transform the expectations of others for his position by clearly defining his own enacted role. Role conflict often results in the role incumbent being forced to conform to one of the conflicting sets of expectations from a subset of counter positions. It is inherently an unstable situation which demands solution by power manoevers or authoritative fiat. Norms may also vary in situational specificity. A manager of a small company, for example, may be expected to be distant, emotionally neutral, and dominant in some situations (board meetings, executive meetings, public ceremonies). He may be expected, on the other hand, to be personal, warm, and equalitarian at staff parties. The range of *applicability* of a norm over the major group situations is referred to as normative scope. It may be measured by the following ratio:

$$\text{Normative scope} = \frac{\text{no. situations in which norm applies}}{\text{total no. group situations}}$$

Norms may be measured along a few basic dimensions suggested by Gross. Gross speaks first of the "direction" of an expectation, that is, whether it is for or against behavior of a particular kind. This is also referred to by some as the valence of the norm. Given the direction of the norm, the next step is to estimate its intensity. As Gross suggests, any expectation can be placed on a continuum ranging from completely persuasive through preferential to mandatory. These intensity levels can be simply suggested in interviews or questionnaires by the words "may," "preferably should," "absolutely must," "may not," "preferably should not." Gross also deals with the problem of the classification of multiple expectations for a single focal position. He suggests one principle which is essentially structural: expectations should be classified first by "role sectors," that is, they should be divided into sets of expectations applied to the relationship of a focal position to a particular counter position.[13] He also suggests that expectations may be seen as rights and obligations. Obligations of the incumbent of a focal position are rights of the incumbent of a counter position and vice versa. Thirdly, he suggests (following Parsons) that expectations can hold for both behavior and attributes. The position of chairman, for example, may be reserved in a particular company for someone over forty and above five feet ten inches in height. Expectations of these kinds are for attributes rather than behavior.

Mediation roles

Differentiated roles can be divided into two kinds (internal and mediation) according to whether or not some members of a particular role set are *external* to the group membership. Where this occurs, the role is a mediation role because its function is to mediate between the group and the larger social system of which it is a part. Roles of this kind are very important as points of articulation between the group and its environment.

Because the group is an open system, it is involved in interchanges with its environment, and the interchanges occur mainly through mediation roles. Mediation roles are specialized roles involved in resource input and output and define the relationship of the group to significant external social objects.

The role of foreman in industrial work groups is an important mediation role. Walker, Guest, and Turner have made a detailed study and analysis of the foreman's role in industrial settings, and they present informative, concrete data on the foreman's pattern of interaction.[14] Table 7.3 summarizes the rates of interaction of one foreman on an assembly line with people within and outside his department.

Table 7.3: Foreman's interaction pattern

Nearly half of the foreman's time was spent in direct contact with other people. This involved verbal and non-verbal interaction (hand signals, nods, performing work together) with someone else. These interactions are summarized in the table.

CONTACT	NUMBER OF INCIDENTS	TOTAL MINUTES SPENT	PERCENT OF TOTAL TIME	AVERAGE TIME PER INCIDENT (MINS.)
OWN MEN:				
Regular operators ...	87	67	13.8	$\frac{3}{4}$
Utility man	14	10	2.1	$\frac{3}{4}$
Repair man	13	12	2.4	$\frac{3}{4}$
PEERS:				
Other foremen	23	33	6.9	$1\frac{1}{2}$
SUPERIORS:				
General foreman ...	7	28	5.8	4
Department supt. ...	3	15	3.0	5
General supt. or higher	0	0	0	0
SERVICE PERSONNEL:				
Maintenance	20	24	4.8	$1\frac{1}{4}$
Materials handling ...	5	5	1.1	1
Inspection	8	10	2.1	$1\frac{1}{4}$
Work standards	1	1	.2	1
OTHERS:				
Other hourly	6	4	.8	$\frac{3}{4}$
Observer	30	20	4.2	$\frac{3}{4}$
All others	11	10	2.1	1
NO CONTACT:	176	244	50.7	$1\frac{1}{2}$
TOTAL	404	483	100.0	

Source: Reprinted with permission from William F. Whyte, *Men at Work* (Homewood, Ill.: Richard D. Irwin, Inc. and The Dorsey Press, 1961), p. 192.

The table does not indicate how many individuals are in the foreman's role set, but it does indicate the range of counter positions with which he interacts. It also indicates the extreme brevity of the interaction time with each person. In addition, it is clear that only about 40 percent of the time he spends interacting with others is spent with his own men. The foreman in this case—which is fairly typical—moves mostly among people *outside* his department but within the organization. This allows him to act as an official channel for communication to and from his work group.

Figure 7.3: An adolescent clique's interaction pattern over two weeks

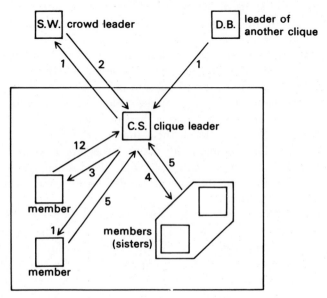

N.B. Numbers refer to the number of acts initiated by one member toward another; arrows indicate the direction of initiation.

My own study of clique and crowd interactions among adolescents pointed to the clique leader's role as the central mediating role for the clique.[15] Figure 7.3 shows a typical interaction pattern for a clique over a two-week period. The numbers in the figure indicate the number of interactions recorded in member's diaries over the period. This particular study showed how the social expectations of the more mature adolescents were mediated through the clique leaders to the members of the cliques. As a result, clique members were increasingly socialized into more mature social behavior.

These two examples of studies of mediation roles show simple interaction rates which were not broken down into the particular kinds of interaction exhibited in particular reciprocal role relationships. One would expect that the foreman's behavior toward his superiors, for example, would be markedly different from that shown toward his own men. Similarly, one would expect that the behavior of the clique leader toward the crowd leader and other clique leaders would vary from his behavior towards his followers in the clique. These studies would have been more informative if they had analyzed the character of behavior directed toward internal and external focal roles.

The role image

The above methods are designed to obtain the basic expectations of group members about the kinds of actions which are appropriate to a particular role and to provide an objective measure of how these expectations are responded to by the role incumbent.

These prescriptions and preferences are transmitted in various ways to the occupant of the role and influence his behavior. His actual behavior in the role, however, is not a simple one to one equivalent of these expectations. His personality fills out, modifies, adds to, even at times transgresses these norms. His enacted role is then perceived by the group members, and the common aspects of their images of his role behavior are his "role image." The common normative expectations define what he *should* do, the "enacted role" describes what the trained researcher perceives him to be doing, but the role image defines how members perceive the significance of the role for them.

One way of defining role image is to give members a list of behavioral traits and ask them to check off which traits apply to which group members. Table 7.4 shows such a check list derived from the interaction categories presented earlier. The group members check off the items which are weighted according to whether the person is seen as exhibiting the behavior frequently, fairly often, occasionally, or never. A person's role image, in this case, is an average profile of the list of behavioral traits, and it can be compared directly with the observer's ratings on the corresponding interaction categories.

The most thorough and informative approach to image analysis is through content analysis, for content analysis can yield a much more differentiated and qualitative analysis of the meaning of a role for group members. Content analysis in this case depends upon getting fairly free, that is, open-ended, descriptions of the role occupant by other group members or the occupants of the person's role set. These descriptions can be gathered formally, by requesting written or oral descriptions of the role occupant in response to such questions as : "Would you describe Mr. X or Mr. X's typical behavior?" or "Tell me about Mr. X." Alternatively, one may select from conversation or from member reports on group sessions those sentences which in fact describe the role incumbent under

Table 7.4: Check list for role image

Name of Scorer : ....

Name of Person Being Scored : ....

	Frequently	Fairly Often	Occasionally	Never
Commands or dominates others				
Gives advice or counsel to others				
Participates in decision-making				
Goes along with the decisions of others				
Is compliant, seeks help				
Submits to the direction of others				
Tries to persuade others to work for the group				
Actively pursues the task in hand				
Works reliably				
Is inattentive when the group is working				
Expresses feelings readily (e.g., jokes, laughs, shouts)				
Tells stories or relates incidents to amuse himself and the group				
Expresses affection for others				
Supports others				
Readily accepts others				
Ignores or avoids others				
Criticizes others				
Seems hostile and attacks others				

study. This informal approach has the advantage of providing a corpus of unguarded statements which group members might not wish to see committed to "the record." It has the disadvantage of rather unsystematic coverage—it may be, for example, that there is agreement among members about the significance of a person's role or some of his attributes, but that this is never discussed.

Content analysis of role image centers around :
1. Qualifying statements relating to the person himself or his role—these reveal attributes; for example, "He is *dirty* or *conscientious.*"
2. Actions performed by the role occupant; for example, "He is always dominating the group, telling people what to do."
3. Action qualifiers which modify the actions described; for example, "He interrupted her *rudely* at lunch yesterday."
4. Objects of his action; for example, "He really rewards his *workers* for conscientious performance."
5. Actions performed on him; for example, "His boss *asked* him to fly to Florida yesterday."

6. Persons or collectivities performing actions on him; for example, "his boss," in the previous example.

7. Normative expectations for actions or attributes; for example, "He *should* phone Mr. Smith when his boss asks him" or "He *ought* to dress more neatly."

Two examples of role image analysis may serve to convey what can be achieved by this method. Neither example carried out the analysis suggested above in its entirety, but both used content analysis of composite descriptions of role incumbents to characterize role enactment.

The first example is my study of informal roles in two self-analytic groups.[16] I asked the members of the groups to write weekly reports on group process, and from these reports selected sentences relating to each of the most frequently mentioned group members. All sentences referring to a particular person were regarded as a "group portrait" of that person's image. The stable elements of a person's image were extracted by analyzing the total description and extracting those tags on which the individual achieved first or second rank for at least three of the six equal time phases. The resulting tag profiles were then compared across groups in order to "match" similar informal roles. A good deal of correspondence was found between the images of informal roles in the two groups, and the content tags summarizing the corresponding roles are shown in table 7.5.

An example of what these tag profiles signified is contained in the description of one role, the "scapegoat :"

The two group members identified as playing this role were each the chief objects of aggressive attacks in their respective groups, and for extended periods of time they seemed to be the main focus of activity. The descriptions of the incumbents of this role are high on the tags that are also high in descriptions of the aggressor, notably *attack* and *sign-reject*. In this case, however, retrievals show . . . that the scapegoat is generally the object of attack rather than the initiator of attack. Consistent with this are high counts on *sign-weak*.

High counts on *self* reveal the personal involvement of group members, expressive of their frustration and anger about the behavior of the scapegoat. In addition, there is emphasis on tags implying normative control (*community, action-norm, guide, control, authority-theme*), and it is significant that four of these tags are also high for the instructor's role. This provides an important clue to the major reason for the scapegoating of this group member; he attempts to play an authoritative, task-oriented role (which the instructor refuses to assume) which creates emotional involvement and anger among group members. Afraid of attacking the instructor directly, the group members find a substitute who resembles him and act out the destruction of the instructor in phantasy form.

The scapegoat is an important role that emerges when groups are faced with major problems of status consensus. . . . Scapegoating the most anxious, dependent member is a way the members deny and handle their own fears about dependency needs.[17]

Instructor	Aggressor	Scapegoat	Seducer	Idol
Selves	Self	Self*	Other	Female-Role
Neuter-Role*	Other	Male-Role*	Sensory-Reference	Time-Reference
Job-Role*	Time-Reference	Action-Norm	Message-Form	If
Ideal-Value*	Spatial-Reference	Guide*	Equal*	Cause
Action-Norm	Quantity-Reference*	Control	Approach	Communicate
Message-Form	Arousal	Attack	Follow	Attempt
Ought*	Distress	Get	Work	Sex-Theme
Guide	Ought	Community	Get	Ascend-Theme
Control*	Attack*	Overstate	Community	
Academic*	Military*	Sign-Weak*	Legal*	
Family*	Recreational	Sign-Reject	Recreational	
Political	Overstate	Authority-Theme	Sex-Theme*	
Technological*	Sign-Reject*			
Higher-Status*	Danger-Theme			
Sign-Accept				
Authority-Theme				

* Tags on which both specialists were consistently high for four or more of the six phases.
N.B. The common characteristics listed are those tags for which both incumbents ranked first or second for at least three of the six phases.
(Reprinted from: Philip Stone, Dexter Dunphy, Marshall Smith, and Daniel Ogilvie, *The General Inquirer: A Computer Approach to Content Analysis* by permission of the M.I.T. Press, Cambridge, Mass., © 1966 by The Massachusetts Institute of Technology.)

Table 7.5: Summary of the characteristics of the common role images

207

Another study of images of informal roles is Kassarjian's study of twenty-five scientist engineers all working in the technical development center of a large industrial firm.[18] Kassarjian divided his scientists into four groups on the basis of their expressed values and job commitments.

Oriented scientists: value differentiations in favor of science and a job commitment to technical work.

Conflicted administrators: value differentiations in favor of science, but a job commitment to administration.

Oriented administrators: value differentiations in favor of business and a job commitment to administration.

Conflicted scientists: value differentiations in favor of business, but a job commitment to technical work.

Kassarjian gathered autobiographies from these scientists and content analyzed these to study the *self*-images of these various types. He made a more careful analysis of syntactic relationships than I did in the study reported above, and this is clearly shown, for example, in his summary of the common self-image of the *conflicted administrator:*

The conflicted administrator is next highest (to the oriented administrator) in presenting *self* as the subject or performer of action. The fact that his position on this designation (self as subject) improved over the general frequency of the tag self would indicate that he, too, perceives himself mainly as the perpetrator of actions. The conflicted administrator communicates with specific people—*male-role, female-role,* in *family,* and *organizational* settings. He presents his world as one in which he exercises a good measure of control, mostly by manipulating the constant change of influential dialogue. The conflicted administrator *approaches* people, positions and roles, and this activity is characterized by *affection* and *pleasure.* He also *guides*—mostly by organizing—community groups, church groups, project teams—the conflicted administrator *controls,* and is often himself *controlled;* in the former he exercises it over groups, and in the latter he is subjected to it by parents and superiors. He very often joins and participates (*follow*), hence once more placing himself in an interpersonal milieu. He *attempts* both in familial and organizational settings, often dealing with members of his family. And finally he also *moves,* and this usually signifies a betterment of his station in life.[19]

Thus content analysis is an important method in characterizing role image, either from the viewpoint of the actor's role set or from the viewpoint of the actor himself. Using content analysis systematically, the researcher can determine how the main characteristics of the actor and of his behavior are perceived by the actor himself and those who interact with him. Beyond this, these two sources of role image can be compared to measure the extent to which the role incumbent's self-image differs from the image perceived by members of his role set.

Processes of role differentiation
and role specialization

Unfortunately, very little concrete research has been undertaken on the processes through which roles become differentiated. For a long time speculation and research on role differentiation in small groups was focused on the emergence of "the group leader" and, in particular, on discovering whether there were personality characteristics common to all leaders. The failure to find correlations of a high order between personality variables and leadership led many to abandon the idea that personality is the prime determinant of emergent leadership. Instead, leadership was conceptualized as a set of group functions which might be performed by a number of members rather than a single member alone. This opened the way for a closer specification of different group role types which could be viewed in a dynamic rather than a static framework.

The most detailed study of the dynamics of role differentiation in small groups has been presented by Bales.[20] In a series of meetings of constructed laboratory groups of students, the member most chosen as "liked" was usually also chosen for "best ideas" and "guidance" in the first meeting. This coincidence of choice became less likely in later meetings. When observations for all four meetings were summarized, the member ranked highest on guidance and best ideas (highest initiator) was most actively disliked and ranked only third on a criterion of liking. It was also found that, where a person was capable of playing both the task leader and the social-emotional leader role, he usually gave up the task leader role in favor of being best-liked. In ten cases where the same person played both roles in the first meeting of an initially leaderless group, the best-ideas role was dropped nine times in favor of the best-liked role. In the remaining case, the individual concerned dropped both roles. Moreover, the conflict which typically characterizes the second session of such groups was shown to derive from a struggle for consensus about the relative position of central members in a status hierarchy. This struggle is successfully resolved, and equilibrium established in some cases by the differentiation of a "great man" leader who can offer both task leadership and group emotional support. Where such a leader is not available, two interdependent roles—leader and sociocenter—tend to emerge and perform these functions separately. Where consensus is not achieved, there appears to be a tendency for the emergence of a scapegoat role which functions to channel off negative affect from the system and so check the tendency to disequilibration.

Few studies have been made of role differentiation in long-term primary groups and obviously there is an important area of research here.

However, one study of role specialization in families is reported by Blood and Wolfe.[21] These authors used a small selection of family activities or tasks as an index of division of labor in the family. The eight tasks used in the study were:

1. Who repairs things around the house?
2. Who mows the lawn?
3. Who shovels the sidewalk?
4. Who keeps track of the money and the bills?
5. Who does the grocery shopping?
6. Who gets the husband's breakfast on work days?
7. Who straightens up the living room when company is coming?
8. Who does the evening dishes?

As the authors point out, major changes occur in the performance of these tasks by husband and wife, over the stages of the life cycle. The internal dynamics of family living, like the internal dynamics of any primary group which persists over long periods, produce role differentiation. Table 7.6 shows how the sharing of tasks changes over the family life cycle. The index of role "specialization" given in the table shows the proportion of tasks performed independently by either spouse. An index of eight, therefore, represents complete differentiation of labor, with no sharing of any task by husband and wife.

Blood and Wolfe point out that the differentiation proceeds as follows: "The honeymoon period of role experimentation involves more sharing of tasks than any later stage. For most couples, the honeymoon period is followed quickly by the retirement of the wife from work to housewifery, enabling her to begin specializing despite the newness of her

Table 7.6: Role specialization, by stage in family life cycle

MEAN ROLE SPECIALIZATION	STAGE IN FAMILY LIFE CYCLE			
Childrearing stages:	*Preschool*	*Preadolescent*	*Adolescent*	*Unlaunched*
	5.13	5.22	5.47	6.01
	(122)	(134)	(95)	(58)
Childless stages:	*Honeymoon*		*Postparental*	*Retired*
	4.77		5.82	6.00
	(18)		(83)	(9)
Childless couples:		6.22	4.71	5.13
		(9)	(28)	(8)

(Reproduced from: Robert O. Blood and Donald M. Wolfe, "Division of Labor in American Families," in *Role Theory, Concepts and Research,* eds., Bruce Biddle and Edwin Thomas [New York: John Wiley, 1966], p. 270.)

tasks. As the children become less of a burden and more of a resource, role differentiation between husband and wife increases at an accelerated pace, reaching its peak when the wife has fully trained children at her disposal, or the retired husband unlimited time to perform his own tasks." [22]

One can only hope that further studies of this kind will be made, not only for families, but also for other kinds of primary groups. It is important, however, to distinguish between two kinds of role development which occur in groups and which are sometimes confused : namely, role differentiation and role specialization. Role specialization occurs when an individual increasingly confines his behavior to one or more specific functions. Role specialization is demonstrated empirically by showing that an increasing proportion of an individual's behavior is devoted to a small number of interaction categories. Specifically role specialization occurs when the ratio :

$$\frac{\text{Number of acts initiated by the individual in one or more interaction categories}}{\text{Total acts initiated by individual in all categories}}$$

is greater at time 2 than at time 1, at time 3 than at time 2, and so on. On the other hand, role differentiation occurs when the ratio :

$$\frac{\text{Number of acts initiated by the individual in one or more interaction categories}}{\text{Total acts initiated by all group members in the same categories}}$$

is greater at the time 2 than time 1, at time 3 than time 2, and so on.

While these two processes (role specialization and role differentiation) often occur together, they are certainly analytically distinguishable, and may have different effects on the individual's status in the group. A person may adopt an increasingly specialized role, for example as "giver of affection". He has become more affectionate or supportive, but all the other members may follow his example. In this case, the group changes character. On the other hand, the group may increasingly rely on one member to provide affection and support and thus provide less of it themselves. In this case, role differentiation has occurred for while the same functions are being performed, the structure has changed. In addition, it should be noted that roles can become less specialized and less differentiated in some circumstances. There is nothing inevitable or irreversible about either of these two processes.

Notes

[1] Neal Gross, Ward S. Mason, and Alexander W. McEachern, *Explorations in Role Analysis* (New York : John Wiley, 1958), p. 48.

[2] Robert Merton, *Social Theory and Social Structure* (Glencoe, Ill. : Free Press, 1957).

3 Robert F. Bales and Philip Slater, "Role Differentiation in Small Decision-making Groups," in *Family, Socialization and Interaction Process,* Talcott Parsons and Robert F. Bales (London: Routledge and Kegan Paul, 1956), pp. 259–307.

4 Ibid., pp. 274–75.

5 Ibid., p. 277.

6 William F. Whyte, *Men at Work* (Homewood, Ill.: Irwin-Dorsey, 1961), chap. 10.

7 Ronald White and Ralph Lippitt, "Leader Behavior and Member Reaction in Three Social Climates," in *Group Dynamics—Research and Theory,* Dorwin Cartwright and Alvin Zander (Evanston, Ill.: Row, Peterson and Co., 1953), pp. 585–611.

8 Ibid., p. 280.

9 Kenneth Benne and Paul Sheats, "Functional Roles of Group Members," *Journal of Social Issues,* vol. 4, no. 2 (1948): pp. 41–9.

10 John Arsenian, Elvin Semrad, and David Shapiro, "An Analysis of Integral Functions in Small Groups," *International Journal of Group Psychotherapy,* vol. 12 (October 1962): 421–34.

11 Talcott Parsons, ed., *Theories of Society* (Glencoe, Ill.: Free Press, 1961), p. 42.

12 Alan P. Bates and Jerry S. Cloyd, "Toward the Development of Operations for Defining Group Norms and Member Roles," *Sociometry,* vol. 19 (1956): 26–39.

13 Gross et al., *Explorations in Role Analysis,* p. 62.

14 Charles R. Walker, Robert H. Guest, and Arthur N. Turner, *The Foreman on the Assembly Line* (Cambridge, Mass.: Harvard University Press, 1956).

15 Dexter C. Dunphy, *Cliques, Crowds and Gangs* (Melbourne: Cheshire Publishing Pty., 1969).

16 Dexter C. Dunphy, "Social Change in Self-Analytic Groups," in Philip J. Stone, Dexter C. Dunphy, Marshall S. Smith and Daniel M. Ogilvie, *The General Inquirer* (Cambridge, Mass.: M.I.T. Press, 1966), pp. 287–340; Dexter C. Dunphy "Phases, Roles and Myths in Self-Analytic Groups," *Journal of Applied Behavioral Science,* vol. 4, no. 2 (1968): 195–225.

17 Stone, et al., *The General Inquirer,* pp. 329–30.

18 J. B. Kassarjian, "Confrontation and Commitment" (D.B.A. thesis, Harvard University, Graduate School of Business Administration, 1966).

19 Ibid., pp. 170–71.

20 Robert F. Bales, "The Equilibrium Problem in Small Groups," in *Working Papers in the Theory of Action,* Talcott Parsons, Robert F. Bales, and Edward A. Shils (Glencoe, Ill.: Free Press, 1953), pp. 111–61.

21 Robert O. Blood and Donald M. Wolfe, "Division of Labor in American Families," in Role Theory: *Concepts and Research,* eds. Bruce Biddle and Edwin J. Thomas (New York: John Wiley, 1966), pp. 265–71.

22 Ibid., p. 271.

chapter 8

Resource allocation through evaluation

Introduction

As people interact in a group they gradually come to accept some patterns of meanings and certain personal relationships as more important than others. In particular, shared evaluative judgments arise which rank the relative importance of particular people and the positions they hold. These shared evaluative judgments become the bedrock on which the super-structure of a social order is built. The hierarchical ranking of group members, of positions, of styles of behavior, and even of such intangibles as ideas, makes behavior more predictable and simplifies choice and decision making.

Ranking or valuing is a basic component in any kind of social system. Even if a social system is considered only as a fair complex information processing system, there must be some way of evaluating inputs and some preferences for certain kinds of responses. Karl Deutsch has expressed this very clearly in terms of a cybernetic model:

The movements of messages through complex feedback networks may involve the problem of "value" or the "switchboard problem," that is, the problem of choice between different possibilities of routing different incoming messages through different channels or "associative trails" within the network. If many alternative channels are available for few messages, the functioning of the network may be hampered by indecision; if many messages have to compete for few channels, it may be hampered by "jamming."

The efficient functioning of any complex switchboard requires, therefore, some relatively stable operating rules, explicit or implied in the arrangements of the channels. These rules must decide the relative preferences and priorities in the reception, screening, and routing of all signals entering the network from outside or originating within it.[1]

But a social system is more than a communication system in which messages are transmitted. Resources of various kinds are also transmitted, consumed, accumulated, transformed, and exchanged with the group's environment. Group resources are all those valued personal qualities, personal, and interpersonal skills, and objects which are considered by members to be directly relevant to the continued existence of the group and the achievement of its goals. At least some of these resources are always in short supply, so decisions have to be made concerning how they shall be used and by whom. Social ranking in the group regulates the functioning of individuals by making differentials in the use and consumption of such group resources as money, office space, labor, social power, and affection legitimate. We will deal first with the ranking of positions in the primary group and then turn to the subject of understanding and measuring values themselves and tracing their effects on resource processing.

PART A: STATUS

Three sources of status

Ranking is inseparably connected with structural differentiation. Once differentiation takes place, group members begin to compare different positions and roles and judge them on their perceived merits and demerits. It is useful to follow our three-dimensional model of action and to distinguish between three kinds of differentiation which relate to social rank, that is, between task differentiation, power differentiation, and affectional differentiation.

Task differentiation deals with the allocation of differing jobs to various people so that the group may obtain its goals more effectively. In most primary groups some task or goal is highly valued and those who contribute substantially to its achievement are highly evaluated. Those who are more adept, more expert, have better ideas, or who can supply necessary resources are ranked more highly than others.

Power differentiation is related to the specialization of roles in the decision-making process. Some people emerge as more influential than others because they are able to motivate others and coordinate group action more effectively. To the extent that groups need at least minimal organization to function, the ability to control the behavior of members confers social rank and results in a hierarchical ranking on the dominance dimension.

Affectional differentiation is related to the needs of individuals to form emotional ties with people and is also influenced by the functional necessity for the number of such ties to be limited. In the midst of crowds and organizations one finds cliques and sub-groups. Sentiments develop wherever people spend extended periods of time together. The extent to which a person commands the affection of others also confers status.

In the case of task differentiation, an individual is ranked according to his contributions to the group in terms of goal achievement. In the case of power differentiation, he is ranked in terms of his general ability to control and coordinate the decisions and actions of group members. In the case of affectional differentiation, he is ranked according to the amount of personal affiliation or liking expressed for him by other group members. Status or rank on all three of these dimensions can be affected, of course, by factors independent of the group itself, for example, age, education, race, and family. Each of the three component dimensions of status will be discussed in more detail.

Power, influence, and authority as a source of status

The nature of power, influence and authority

In the definition of power and influence, a distinction between capability and actuality will be maintained. Power is defined in terms of the capacity to influence. Influence is power in action. This is similar to the distinction Robert Dahl makes between potential and actual influence:

The reasons why some individuals or groups acquire more influence than others over some scope of decisions are reducible to three:
1. Some actors have more political resources at their disposal than others.
2. Given the resources at their disposal, some actors use more of them to gain political influence.
3. Given the resources at their disposal, some actors use them more skilfully or effectively than others do.
Thus it is important to distinguish between the past or current influence of a particular actor within some scope of decisions, his probable future influence, and his *maximum potential influence* if he were to use *all* his existing political resources with optimum skill to acquire influence within that scope of decisions. An actor's current influence in any given scope always (or nearly always) falls short of his maximum potential influence.[2]

Cartwright also distinguishes between the potential and actual activity of modifying others' behavior through sanctions:

Whatever level of analysis is employed, it is clear that the number and type of agents, P_1, over whom a particular agent, O, exerts influence may vary greatly.

Thus, for example, a leader may have many, or only a few, followers; a union may exert influence on blue-collar workers but not on the members of the clerical staff. We shall refer to the set of agents, P1, over whom O exerts influence as *the domain of O's influence*. When we wish to refer to potential, rather than actual, influence we shall speak of the corresponding set as *the domain of O's power*. Whether P is conceived as an individual or an aggregate, it is clear that the influence of a given agent, O, may extend differentially to various states of P. Thus, for example, the financial vice-president of a company may virtually control its investment decisions but have no effect on its policies concerning unions; a foreman may control certain items of a worker's behavior without influencing the corresponding attitudes; and a union may determine a worker's attitudes toward a company without influencing his on-the-job behavior. The set of states of P subjected to influence by O is usually called the *range* (or scope) *of O's influence* with respect to P, and the set of P's states which O can influence is called the *range of O's power* with respect to P.[3]

Not all authors choose to distinguish between power and influence on this basis. There is also a strong tradition that separates power and influence on the basis of positive and negative sanctions. Parsons, for example, defines power in terms of the use of negative sanctions, whereas influence is conceived as entailing the use of positive sanctions.[4] We do not propose to adopt this distinction.

Part of the ambiguity and chaos observable in power analysis has resulted from a lack of specification. *Who* is influenced? On *what basis and issues* is he influenced? The distinction Cartwright makes between the domain and range, quoted above, will be employed here. Dahl lists the lack of these distinctions as one of the common errors encountered in the analysis of power and influence in political science:

1. Failing to distinguish clearly between participating in a decision, influencing a decision, and being affected by the consequences of a decision.
2. Failing to identify the scope or scopes within which an actor is said to be powerful.
3. Failing to distinguish different degrees of power, for example, by equating the proposition that power is distributed unequally in a political system with the proposition that the system is ruled by a ruling class.
4. Confusing an actor's past or present power with his potential power particularly by assuming that the greater the political resources an actor has access to, the greater his power must be.
5. Equating an actor's expected future power with his potential power, particularly by ignoring differences in incentives and skills.[5]

In some situations, the ability to influence or control others is strongly enhanced by the fact that power is specified in a contractual, legally binding form. Power which is institutionalized and made socially legitimate in this way is referred to as authority. Authority is a very important part of the operation of organizations but, of course, it also exists outside of organizations. In the family, for example, parents have legal authority to control the actions of their children up to a certain age.

Formal status refers to the specific right of certain positions to be given a high evaluation and rank and it affects power status most directly. Regardless of his personality, all group members recognize a company director as having a high status job. And because certain organizations are ranked more highly than others (for example, General Motors has more status than Joe's Roof and Tiling Co.), being president in one organization may have a higher status relative to the larger social context *and* to equivalent offices in the respective organizations. Part of the recognition of this right to a particular status inheres in the delegation of greater and lesser amounts of authority. Those with greater authority are ideally supposed to exercise a wider range of influence than those under them.

For a number of years theories of organization tended to conceive of the agent exerting influence as an office or position. Organizational control was exercised by authority vested in designated positions. Orders were supposedly followed without regard to personal considerations other than authority. This conception broke down rather early. Since there may be no correlation between positions and possession of valued personal attributes which reinforce and legitimate formal authority, anyone possessing these qualities may exercise influence. Because formal status is often unrelated to the personal abilities that merit esteem, and because no organization ever specifies all the kinds of relations that are to exist between office holders, an informal network of influence relations interpenetrates and complements the formal organizational specifications, Cartwright writes of this distinction :

One of the earliest and most influential of the revisionists was Barnard (1938) who advanced a distinction between the "authority of position" and the "authority of leadership." This distinction concerns the degree to which the success of an influence attempt is dependent upon the personal ability of the agent exerting influence; authority of position is independent of personal ability whereas authority of leadership rests on the superior ability of the agent regardless of the position he occupies. This general line of thought has been extended in various ways and now pervades the literature. A typical manifestation is the distinction proposed by Bass . . . between "personal power" and the "power of position." It is also reflected in the frequent designation of formal versus informal aspects of organizations.[6]

This means that where there is a formal ordering of positions, there may be other centres of power than those that are authorized. Outside an organization context this distinction is usually expressed as that between the reputed (ideal) and the real. In an investigation, then, interest can center on :

1. The formal designation of power relations.
2. The reputed power relations.
3. The observed power relations.

In a nonorganizational context the first of these interests disappears.

Measuring power and influences

Specifically then, the investigator analyzing power and influence must attempt to measure the following for each group member, or for the most central members :

A. *The individual's power base;* that is, the resources he possesses for influencing others.

1. His formal authority—areas of group life and people in the group over which he has been granted formal, legitimate control.

2. His informal power base—his possession of a strategic position in the communication network, access to information, possession of valued resources which give him non-legitimated but potentially effective control.

3. His reputed power base—how much influence others *think* the person could exercise if he tried.

Within each of these areas there needs to be clear specification of :

(a) the domain of power, that is, the particular *persons* over whom control can be exercised; and

(b) the range of power, that is, the kinds of *issues* over which the person can exercise influence.

B. *The individual's exercise of power;* that is, "influence."

1. His exercise of authority—the extent to which he uses the authority he possesses.

2. His observed influence—the observer's estimate of the effect of his actions on issue resolution in concrete situations.

3. His reputed influence—the actual influence he exerts in specific issues as reported by group members.

Within each of these areas also there need to be clear specifications of :

(a) the domain of influence, that is, the particular persons over whom control is exercised; and

(b) the range of influence, that is, the particular issues over which the person exerts influence.

These measures then need to be combined in overall estimates of each person's power base and exercise of influence so that group members can be compared in general terms according to their potential and actual ability to affect group action and group decisions.

Methods of measuring power and influence

We will take each of the proposed aspects of power and show how rankings for group members on each can be obtained. However, since some of the measures depend on the existence of a list of "issues," we will deal first with the problem of defining issues which can form the basis for a study of conflict resolution. There are two approaches to be employed which supplement each other. In the first method, the researcher asks group members : "What issues generate most arguments in this group? Over what subjects do the most heated debates or disagreements occur?" From the responses, categories of issues can be devised to obtain a coverage of the conflict areas in group life. In addition, the researcher should follow group discussions carefully and note down conflicts as they occur. This observational material can then be used to check on and extend the "reputed issues" list established through interviews.

Formal authority: Generally speaking, formal organizations clearly specify the domain and range of power of the incumbents of various positions in the organization. Organization charts, for example, show the domain of authority very clearly by indicating through vertical lines who reports to whom and, conversely, who has authority over whom. Similarly the range of authority is usually fairly clear in terms of the number of departments under a person's administration, his membership in committees, the specification of responsibilities in his job description, and so on. Interviewing can usually resolve ambiguities unless these ambiguities are real aspects of the organization.

Informal power: The simplest and most direct measure of informal power is what has been referred to as the "centrality index." In the face-to-face situation, the ratio is

$$\frac{\text{no. acts addressed to individual A}}{\text{no. acts addressed to all individuals in the group}}$$

A similar index can also be constructed for longer term interaction occurring in non face-to-face situations; for instance, where some of the group interaction occurs through correspondence which is filed, the number of letters received by each individual can be compared with the number of letters received by all. This figure is convenient to work with because it can be taken directly from the interaction matrixes discussed in chapter 6. It is a convenient measure of informal power and has been found to relate directly to reputed power in many situations. However, it can be misleading, for centrality has also been shown to result from low-status deviance. Not only those with informal power are accorded undue attention in groups, but also those who break group norms. Another measure which is highly correlated with this but more clearly measures informal power only, is the ratio :

$$\frac{\text{no. submissive acts directed to individual A}}{\text{no. submissive acts addressed to all individuals in the group}}$$

If Bales' interaction process analysis categories are being used the corresponding ratio would be :

$$\frac{\text{no. of questions (categories 7 through 9) asked of X}}{\text{no. of questions asked of all individuals in the group.}}$$

Both of the above variables directly measure deference behavior which closely reflects openness to influence exerted by the person referred to. These latter methods also allow for careful specification of the individual's domain of power, that is, the varying responses of others to any one person in a group can be compared. If rates are compiled separately for the discussion of different issues, the individual's range of power can also be distinguished by determining those specific issues on which others defer to him most.

Reputed power base: The reputed power base consists of the resources for power which group members perceive another fellow member to possess. An individual's reputed power base is determined, therefore, by the researcher asking group members directly how influential they think each person is in the group. The specific questions which are relevant are as follows :

How much influence do you think Mr. A exerts in this group? More than B, C, etc.? Whom does he influence most? Who would not be affected by his opinions? What kinds of group decisions could he affect if he tried? Whom do you think influences him most? On what issues? Who has the most influence over you? On what issues do you think other group members would really listen to what you have to say and be affected by it?

A simple summary measure of the generalized power bases of group members can be compiled by having each group member rank the names or photographs of all group members according to their ability to influence the group. Such a method was used, for example, in a study by Lippitt and others which will be discussed later.[7]

Exercise of authority: The exercise of authority can be studied by searching organizational records and noting the number of authoritative decisions handed down by memoranda or the number of authoritative orders or commands issued in face-to-face situations.

Observed influence: Observed influence can be measured in a number of ways. One common way, which we regard as inadequate, might best be referred to as the measurement of "influence attempts." In this method, an individual's score is based on :

Number of acts initiated by A

1. _____

total acts initiated by all group members

or

number of acts of suggestions, opinion, orientation (categories 3, 4, 5 in IPA) initiated by A

2. _____

total acts of suggestion, opinion, orientation initiated by all group members.

While either one of these methods would be a simple measure of influence, March has shown that these measures are substantially independent of measures of actual opinion change in groups.[8] In other words, a high rate of attempting to influence others does not guarantee that others will be influenced.

A better measure relates influence attempts as measured above to acceptance or rejection of these responses by those to whom the influence is directed. Thus in this method an influential person would be a person with a high rate of accepted influence attempts; conversely an uninfluential person would be either someone who does not attempt to influence others or someone who, while attempting to do so, receives negative responses to his attempts. In IPA, influence attempts would be acts in categories 4, 5, and 6. Agreement would be measured by the categories 1 through 3, "shows agreement," etc., and disagreement by the categories 10 through 12 "shows disagreement," etc. In the interaction scheme outlined earlier, influence attempts would be measured by an act of any intensity on the dominance dimension and acceptance by any submissive or affiliative response. Disagreement would be measured by any hostile or dominant act following the influence attempt.

In studying power relations in three-person groups, Mills measured influence attempts by the individual's relative number of contributions in IPA categories 4 through 9.[9] He then measured the individual's influence by measuring the relative frequency of support (categories 10 through 12) given by others to the author of these influence attempts. Mills' method approximates the one we suggest except that he extends the definition of influence attempts to cover questions as well as attempted answers. He argues that a high rate of participation coupled with a high support intake means that a person is in a relatively strong position, while low participation coupled with a low rate of support means he is in a relatively weak position. But the inclusion of questions in the measure of influence attempts contaminates power-oriented behavior with what is mainly submissive behavior.

Another major study of observed influence was carried out by Lippitt and his associates. The method was somewhat similar to Mills' approach and the study is particularly interesting because the researchers also attempted to measure the reputed power base of group members. Lippitt, Polansky, Redl, and Rosen made a careful study of the dynamics of power among children at the University of Michigan Fresh Air Camp.[10] They defined power as "the number of successful power acts divided by the number of attempts made." They made two attempts to approximate a measure of power. The first was what they called an "index of attributed power" and corresponds to the "reputed power base." This was measured by having children rank all other children in the group on the question, "Who has influence?" Concretely, each child hung pictures of others in the group in rank order on a row of nails on a board. The second measure was one of "direct influence," or "observed influence." In this case a pre-categorized observation schedule was used by a team of field observers to record behavior. The following categories were scored:

contagion initiation
contagion pickup
direct attempt to influence
recipient of influence attempt

(N.B. "behavioral contagion" was defined as "an event in which a person's behavior is changed to resemble that of another person.")

It was found that members with high attributed power were significantly higher than members with low attributed power in inducing behavioral contagion in group members, were more likely to attempt to influence others directly, and were more successful in these attempts.

One of the advantages of these methods is that the domain of an individual's influence can be very clearly defined. The interaction matrix can be used to trace those within the group whom each member attempts to influence, that is, the domain of influence to which he aspires and the relative amount of acceptance or rejection he receives in response from each of these persons. Redl's work is particularly helpful since it suggests that researchers should be sensitive to the fact that persons may be influenced through contagion as well as direct influence attempts, that is, through identification with the other, they may copy his behavior or follow his suggestions even though he has not tried to influence them directly.

Another method of assessing influence can be used where the researcher either knows in advance that an issue is to be debated or can arrange for an issue to be debated. In this case the researcher can measure the position of each member on the issue before it is debated and then compare the final group decision with each person's initial position. The assumption here is that the person whose initial position was closest to that which the group finally reaches has succeeded in influencing the group to accept his position. If possible, this assumption is best tested by a study of the dynamics of influence in the discussion session itself. Nevertheless, the method is a useful one, particularly with smaller groups where there is less likelihood for prior positions to coincide and where positions can be expressed in discrete alternatives or numerical scores.

A very early study of influence using this method was carried out by Simpson.[11] Female college students responded privately to a series of opinion items and later were assembled in groups for the purpose of collectively discussing the same items and arriving at a group decision. Several days after the group decision, the subjects again responded privately to the opinion items. The immediate influence exerted by an individual was measured by the similarity of the group decision to her initial private opinion. Persisting influence of an individual was measured by difference in private judgments pre- and post-discussion and the extent to which others' scores moved toward that individual's. A series of personality, ability, sociometric, and biographical measures were related to the influence indices and it was found that subjects high on both persisting individual influence and immediate group influence were frequently found to exhibit the same characteristics. They had high scholastic aptitude test scores, high scholastic grades, high sociometric likeability, Jewish rather than Catholic affiliation, and were only children.

More widely known today is a variation of this method, called the "revealed difference technique." One study using this technique was undertaken by Strodtbeck using Navaho, Texan, and Mormon families from geographical adjacent territories in the Arizona-New Mexico area.[12] In this case, each husband-wife couple was asked to pick three reference families with whom they were well acquainted. The husband and wife were then separated and asked to designate which of the three reference families most satisfactorily fulfilled a series of 26 conditions such as : Which family has the happiest children? Which family is the most religious? Which family is most ambitious? After the husband and wife had both marked their choices they were asked to reconcile their choices and indicate a final "best" choice from the standpoint of their family. Major cultural differences were found in the extent to which either spouse "won" decisions, and there was a strong tendency for the spouse who talked most to win the decisions, whatever the culture.

An ingenious adaptation of the before and after measure was used by Blanchard in order to recreate influence processes in gangs of boys committed for group rape.[13] Blanchard studied two such groups. He interviewed individual members first and obtained their individual responses to Rorschach tests. He then assembled the boys in their group and had them arrive at group interpretations of the tests. This method allowed Blanchard to : (1) compare the original individual content of the Rorschachs with the final group product and so to estimate who was the most influential member of the group and his characteristic fantasies; and (2) to observe the influence process at work at first hand and so make inferences as to the actual dynamics leading to the rape. Blanchard found that in both groups, the leaders stood out as individuals with clearly defined sadistic impulses, as shown in their Rorschach responses. In addition, the group process revealed that the sexual feeling of the leaders was stimulated by the presence of the group and that the leaders felt they must perform and "exhibit" themselves before the group. It was clear that the leader channeled, crystallized, and directed the attention of the group to sexual-aggressive themes and that this had been of primary importance in provoking the gang into group rape.

A similar approach was used in a very different setting by Torrance.[14] Torrance was interested in the effect of differences in formal status in the air force on participation in decision making. His subjects were all members of B26 bomber crews which consist of a pilot, a navigator, and a gunner. The pilot is the aircraft commander, the navigator is also a commissioned officer, while the gunner is an enlisted man. Thirty-two temporary crews were set up for the experiment. Each crew was shown a projective sketch of a conference group and the individuals were asked to write, in five minutes, a story about the picture. The individual stories were then collected and the group asked to write, in ten minutes, a crew story about the same sketch.

Each crew story was analyzed for the five most salient aspects and then the stories from the individual members were checked for the presence or absence of these characteristics. A score of five was assigned to any individual story containing all five aspects, a score of four to any story containing four aspects and so on. Those stories with four or more aspects were rated as indicating strong influence, those containing three as indicating some influence, and those with two or less as little or no influence. The results showed clearly that pilots exercised significantly more influence than navigators, navigators more than gunners. *None* of the gunners, for example, exercised strong influence on his group's story.

Difficult as the concept of power is, these examples show that it is possible to obtain measures which reliably differentiate between the relative influence of members occupying different positions in a group.

Reputed influence: Reputed influence is best measured in relation to specific issues, and after group sessions where a specific decision has been discussed. The most useful method here is the "post-meeting reaction questionnaire" or PMRQ. This can be a simple questionnaire which can be filled out by each group member in two or three minutes. Slater's study of role differentiation, discussed above, used a PMRQ method, the question relating to influence being phrased: "Who do you think exercised most guidance?" [15] Members were asked to rank all group members using this question as a criterion. If a less formal method is more appropriate, the researcher may simply interview individual members after sessions where issues are hotly debated and ask : "Who, in your opinion, influenced the group (or you) the most when the group was arguing about X subject?"

A rather more elaborate method is illustrated by Herbst's study of husband and wife roles.[16] Herbst was interested in a method of classifying families according to the relative power exercised by the spouses over the range of activities in which they engaged. Herbst used a reputational approach, asking children how their parents decided matters relating to a wide range of activities. A matrix was constructed listing the major kinds of activities and whether or not the decisionmaking for that activity was exercised by the husband alone (Hd), the wife alone (Wd), or decided together (Bd). It was also noted whether the activity was undertaken by the husband alone (Ha), the wife alone (Wa), or jointly (Ba). This yielded a matrix which showed, for each family, the pattern of activity and decision making by the spouses. Herbst estimated the power field for each spouse by adding together those activities in which he or she exercised sole decision, for example the wife's power field is described by the sum (BaWd + HaWd + WaWd). This made possible the description of a number of family types such as the "automatic pattern," where each spouse carried out different activities over which he or she exercised autonomous control (HaHd + WaWd); the "husband dominance pattern," where the husband exercised leadership and autocracy (BaHd + WaHd); and the "syncratic pattern," where there was joint activity and joint decision making (BaBd).

We have elaborated our discussion on power as a source of status to a greater extent than we will do with affiliation or competence. This is because power is a much debated and very complex phenomenon. We have suggested approaching various aspects of power somewhat separately, maintaining what can be important distinctions. The real question in any given situation is, however, whether the distinctions do result in very different rankings. If not, the researcher may well wish to combine these various measures into a single generalized status ranking of group members on power and influence.

Affiliation, attraction, popularity, friendship as a source of status

The measurement of interpersonal sentiments

Part of the status structure of the group must be understood in terms of the patterns of interpersonal sentiment. Even a task-oriented group will disperse into animated cliques over coffee, the cliques forming largely in terms of emotional affinity rather than of power or expert status. Even within a task-oriented group, one of the differentiating factors between task-leaders and socio-emotional leaders is the difference in the extent to which they are liked by group members. Certainly part of the total evaluation of a person by others in almost any social situation relates to their feelings of attraction, liking, and friendship.

Sociometric methods: J. L. Moreno and Helen Jennings together with many others make up the sociometric school of small group analysis and their work is based on the premise that one of the main processes in interpersonal relations has to do with the selection and rejection of individuals in order to satisfy emotional needs. The large volume of sociometric analysis has been partly due to the fundamental significance of this fact and partly because, unlike the analysis of power, the sociometric method is simple to administer and to summarize.

A sociometric test is a method of quantifying the affective relations existing at a particular time between group members. Whichever way the data is summarized, it is essentially designed to reveal patterns of interpersonal choice between group members. What the researcher usually does to assemble data is to have each group member indicate his choices and rejections of other group members for association in some particular activity or social context. Attention then usually centers on plotting some form of structural diagram (or *sociogram*) which identifies the position of the individual in the affective structure of the group. Our concern here will be mainly with using interpersonal affective choices to arrive at a ranking of group members in terms of positive and negative affective choices. This corresponds with a large amount of consideration given in the sociometric literature to "overchosen" (high affective status), "underchosen," and "rejected" (low affective status) persons in groups.

As Secord and Backman point out, sociometric tests have essentially two components : "(1) A prescribed procedure for making choices and (2) a criterion by which choices are made." [17] The prescribed procedure usually instructs the subject as to how many choices he should make. He may be asked to choose the one person whom he most prefers, a number of choices is sometimes specified, or sometimes the person is allowed an unlimited number of choices. If more than one choice is specified, then a ranking of those chosen is usually requested. Each individual group member should be asked to rank all other group members in order to achieve a complete status ranking for the group.

The criterion of choice usually centers around social situations or activities. A child may be asked to choose the person he would like to sit next to at lunch or to rank his classmates in the order he would choose them for his baseball team.

One important distinction is often *not* made in relation to the criterion of choice. This distinction was first made by Jennings in 1947. She distinguished between the psyche-group, "an interpersonal structure where the uniqueness of the individual as a personality is appreciated and allowed for with varying degrees of spontaneous indulgence and affection" and the socio-group which "has psychological structure in relation to a criterion important enough to cause interpersonal choice to arise distinctly in relation to it." [18] In fact, these two groups depend on the use of two kinds of criteria : One for the psyche-group centering around non-task or primarily recreational situations and activities, and one for the socio-group centering around instrumental, goal-oriented activities. The psyche-group criterion should be used in estimating affective status because the other criterion confuses the affective dimension with the task dimension.

Another source of confusion in sociometric studies relates to the difference which can emerge between "public" and "private" popularity. F. Kräupl Taylor has shown that people discriminate between "public" and "private" popularity. As Taylor points out, "There exists, however, another type of popularity which does not have its origin in interpersonal feelings, not—at least—in the narrow sense in which we are using the term "interpersonal" as indicating a person-to-person relationship only. [Public popularity] derives from the feelings a patient invokes in the group audience by his role as a group member." [19]

There can be a real difference, therefore, between persons chosen as "most liked" by individual group members who are making personal choices and persons rated as "the most popular group member" by the same group members. Sometimes those who are most popular have few very good friends, but a large number of more superficial contacts.

F. Kräupl Taylor's work also indicates that group members find it easier to rank each other on a dominance dimension than to rank relative popularity. He assumed in his study that the hierarchical distribution of public variables (such as prestige, popularity, dominance, and leadership) is such a conspicuous phenomenon that group members cannot help noticing it. In order to estimate the structure of these hierarchies, he asked group members to rank their companions with regard to dominance and popularity. The scores obtained on public dominance showed much more consensus than did those obtained on public popularity. Even in the case of self-assessment the rank correlation coefficient was $.76 \pm .05$ in the case of dominance and $.33 \pm .09$ in the case of popularity, with respect to the averages obtained from group member rankings. This seems to be because dominance/power is more clearly defined in members' minds and because emotional ties of friendship bias a person's estimate of overall popularity in a group.

The question may be asked : Why are some people more liked than others? Such a question implies that the sentiment of affection is definitely related to some standard of comparison as well as to some processes of interaction. Those who measure up to certain standards are given affection and acceptance. Those who do not are rejected or ignored. George Homans suggests a number of relationships between certain variables and liking :

(a)   Conformers to group norms tend to be given more sociometric choices than deviates. Deviates tend to be disliked.

(b)   The larger the number of members that like other members the more similar are the activities of the members in conformity to a norm.

(c)   The more a leader controls the activity of others and resorts to negative sanctions, the less liked he will be. (Homans suggests ambivalence is the relation that results. It may indicate a split between the giving of regard and respect or deference to authority and the giving of sentiments of liking to one who is also a group member.)

(d)   Persons of high status are higher in both the number of traits mentioned favorably and disfavorably than those mentioned for low status persons.

(e)   The more a man interacts with another, the more he likes him (unless he is in a punishing situation which he cannot terminate).

(f)   The greater the status congruence in a group, the greater the average friendship.[20]

How, then, shall affiliative status be measured?

First, a distinction should be retained between personal friendship choices and choices on general popularity. The domain of friendship should also be distinguished, that is, the number of group members who choose each individual; and so should the range of friendship, that is, the range of situations and activities in which each individual is chosen. In addition, these *reputed* affiliation choices should be supplemented with the patterns of affiliation the observer can actually see taking place.

Personal attraction: Personal attraction, therefore, can be measured by asking group members to rank all other members according to their preferences for engaging with them in non-instrumental activities or situations, for example, With whom would you most like to eat lunch? play badminton? chat on the phone?

A summary measure which can be used here is to ask for general friendship choices. The appropriate questions being : Who is your best friend here? Who is your next-best friend? Do you have any other friends here? (If "yes," have the person list them and then ask him : Are you more friendly with X than Y, with Y than Z, etc.)

It is also important to elicit rejections of others in the group as well as choices. In the situationally specific choices above, the person should also be asked to designate those members with whom he would *not* like to participate in various activities. In the more personalized friendship question, the researcher should ask : Whom don't you regard as friends? Is there someone or some group members whom you dislike?

General popularity can be estimated by having group members rank all group members according to the criterion : Who is the most popular person in the group in your opinion? Who is the next most popular? etc. Who is the most unpopular group member? Are there any other unpopular group members?

In large groups it may be difficult for group members to rank all group members in a discrete manner. Zeleny uses a five point scale to measure sociometric status.[21] Each group member is asked to express his attitude to each other group member as one of five degrees of intensity, ranging from complete acceptance (a first choice) to complete rejection (a last choice). He calculates a social status index by the use of a formula based on the average intensity of attitudes expressed toward the individual plus or minus the average deviation of individual attitudes from the average attitude. This method obviates the necessity of having every individual ranked and allows the grouping of individuals in a relatively small number of status categories.

Observed affiliation: It is not necessarily valid to assume that reputed friendship and popularity necessarily correspond directly to expressed affiliation. The effect of reputed affiliation scores should be measured by using the positive and negative ends of the affiliation dimension in the interaction scheme suggested, that is, A 1-3 and H 1-3 in the IAA scheme. These are based on direct observation of expressed affection and hostility and individuals can be ranked according to their scores on the ratio

$$\frac{\text{no. affiliation acts directed toward A}}{\text{no. hostile acts directed toward A}}$$

We conclude this section on the measurement by citing a field experiment by Fleming.[22] The experiment was undertaken to improve the ability of secondary school girls to write English compositions. Two class groups of comparable intelligence level were chosen for the study. Group C was used as a control group and Group E as an experimental group. Altogether a series of seven sociometric tests were administered to the two classes and differentiated criteria were used. In the experimental class the results of the sociometric tests were used to form groups of various sizes to undertake group activities related to English compositions—discussion of writing assignments, acting of short plays, writing group compositions. The control group was not involved in group activities of this sort. It was found that in Group E, after a year of group work in English, there was a marked drop in the number of unchosen adolescents, none had fewer than two incoming choices, and long chains of mutual choice relationships existed linking sub-groups with each other. The class as a whole formed a well-integrated unit with relative status differences minimized. Group C, on the other hand, was made up of a number of unrelated cliques with twelve girls excluded from all sub-groups. Another marked difference was that in Group E many pupils exercised some discrimination in choosing companions for different functions. Group E, after a year of group work in English, chose more diversely according to particular criteria than did Group C which had not had this experience. Students were asked to choose three companions for a school lesson and for lunch in the school cafeteria. Comparison of the groups on these two criteria revealed the following differences between the two groups :

> 16 made 3 identical choices on 2 criteria
> 13 made 2 identical choices on 2 criteria
> 4 made 1 identical choice on 2 criteria
> 2 differentiated in all three choices
> 8 made 3 identical choices on 2 criteria
> 19 made 2 identical choices on 2 criteria
> 3 made 1 identical choice on 2 criteria
> 4 differentiated on all three choices.[23]

Thus Fleming's field experiment showed that is is possible to change the affective status structure of groups by introducing certain kinds of subgroup activities and that one may also experimentally induce discrimination on the relation of the domain of friendship choices to the range of group activities.

Competence, responsibility, skill, commitment as a source of status

People often choose partners for reasons other than pure sentiment. In the course of making this point, we have already covered to some extent the topic of competence as a source of status. Where discrimination exists between partners for various kinds of activities, choices of work companions for specific tasks will be based largely on their perceived competence on the task.

All groups have goals of one sort or another, and the achievement of these goals involves the performance of particular activities or tasks. Consequently, the members of a group may be ranked on their skill at these activities or on their relative contribution to goal achievement. In the subsequent discussion of group goals and values it will be shown how valued activities can be related to specific group goals. It is sufficient here to note that the sharing of one's competence, knowledge, and skill can be an important source of reward for others and hence contribute significantly to general status in the group.

Skill, however, is not the only factor. People may be valued because they are dependable, responsible, and committed to the group goals. Competence alone is usually not sufficient in the group to command prestige for an individual's usefulness in promoting goal attainment. An individual may be very competent when performing valued activities, but indifferent and unreliable about performing them. Commitment to the group goals rather than indifference to or rejection of them is the complement of skill.

In fact, extreme superiority in skills can be a threat to the group goals and an expression of rejection of group norms and group status. The "rate buster" of the bank wiring group is an example of a group member with a high level of skill, but contempt for group goals which specify adequate but limited production.

The following methods are suggested for assessing task status:

1. *Perceived task skill:* Ranking of individual members on their relative skill on specific goal-related activities. Appropriate questions here would be: Who has the most expertise at grinding? Who has the best ideas about how to solve math problems? or, with whom would you most like to work to get this job done?

2. *Perceived commitment:* Ranking of individual members on their relative commitment to the group goals. The appropriate question here would be: Who is the member who is most committed to the group and its task? or, who are the most reliable members of this group when it comes to getting things done?

3. *Observed task skill:* This can be ascertained by the ratio of:

$$\frac{\text{no. of attempted task contributions which are accepted}}{\text{no. of attempted task contributions which are rejected.}}$$

4. *Observed task commitment:* This can be ascertained by the ratio of:

$$\frac{\text{no. of task contributions by member A}}{\text{total number of all task contributions.}}$$

Generalized status

Social status is the total evaluation of an individual's position with respect to the three major classes of status. A person who has high social status occupies a position that is highly valued over all these measures of social rank. But, if social status is the resultant of a number of evaluative judgments, then the problem is how these judgments can be combined into a single generalized status ranking and whether it is legitimate to do this. A simple approach to this problem is to average different status rankings. However, the relative importance of popularity, expertise, and dominance varies from group to group, and so this approach may distort results in some cases.

In investigating the various status structures, the investigator should continually inquire why certain choices are made and use this information to determine the relative emphasis placed, in a particular group, on one form of status versus another. In arriving at a summary status evaluation, the researcher can weight each of the three factors in the way that he thinks most realistically represents their value in the minds of group members. He might, for example, decide in a political cabal that power, affiliation, and competence were weighted roughly in the following ratio: 4 : 1 : 3, indicating that affiliative status is regarded as relatively unimportant while power and expertise are much more important. A single generalized status scale is useful in summarizing group relations and performs a function similar to generalized "social class" measures in studies of larger social units. However, the investigator should keep in mind that it *is* a summary measure and as such has limitations in predicting particular kinds of behavior or outcomes. Therefore, two measures which may be made to supplement such a simplified "average" measure are given below: in addition, we shall refer in chapter 9 to a measure of status consensus first introduced in the field by Bales and Slater.[24]

Status congruence:　　This refers to the relation of certain characteristics, such as age, income, education, and so on, to a person's status on any dimension. Zaleznik and Moment give a clear description of how this measure is made and used. They define status congruence as follows, and then go on to clarify its construction, step by step:

The more a member's status position on one status factor occupies the same position on other status factors, the more congruent his status is. According to this definition, for example: Given status factors, A, B, C . . . N and positions 1, 2, 3 . . . n, a member whose position is 1, 2, 3 or n on all status factors from A to N would be 100 percent status congruent; on the other hand, a member whose position is 1 on A, 2 on B, 3 on C, and n on N, would be 0 percent status congruent.

It is important to understand that status congruence is a relative measure. The numerical value of the index indicates a relationship between the status factor scores for one person and the scores for the other members of the particular group. Scores, or the word "positions" in the definition, refer to relative rankings in the group, or to scoring values that award points for the amount of the factor to be ascribed to the individual.

To clarify the construction of the Status Congruence Index we can go through the operations with a simplified sample and procedure, using eight people, four factors, and simple rank positions . . .

. . . In this "group X," we shall assume that the members prize age, seniority, education, and "being American." In interviews with them, and hearing them talking among themselves, it seemed that the older one was, the longer one had been in the work department, the more education one had, and the longer one's family and ancestors had been in the United States, the better. None of these factors refer to actual behavior. The first step in the status congruence (and status) analysis is to arrange the relevant information about each person in tabular form (Table 8.1).

Table 8.1: Group X status factors*

NAME	AGE	SENIORITY	EDUCATION	FAMILY RESIDENCE IN U.S.
John	57	12	18	170
Carl	52	9	10	20
Pat	49	5	15	50
Abe	45	3	13	40
Joe	39	1	11	5
Tom	35	4	9	35
Bill	31	10	16	75
Jeff	26	6	8	100

*All figures indicate years.

The next step is to assign the rank-order number to each person's position on each status factor and to compute status and status congruence scores from these numbers.

Reading across Table 8.2 we see that John ranks first in the group on all four factors. Carl ranks second in age, third in seniority, sixth in education, and seventh in length of time that his family and ancestors had been residing in the United States. The rankings are all relative to the group. If any given member of this group were moved to another group, his status and status congruence indices relative to the new group would be different from those in the old group.

Table 8.2: Group X ranking on status factors

NAME*	AGE*	SENIORITY*	EDUCATION*	FAMILY	STATUS†	CONGRUENCE†
John	1	1	1	1	4	0
Carl	2	3	6	7	18	18
Pat	3	5	3	4	15	7
Abe	4	7	4	5	20	10
Joe	5	8	5	8	26	12
Tom	6	6	7	6	25	3
Bill	7	2	2	3	14	16
Jeff	8	4	8	2	22	22

*Figures are rank-order positions.
†Figures are indices, computed as described below.

In computing the values of the indices, the researcher starts out with the assumption that the four factors are of approximately equal value. If he finds in his preliminary investigation that they do not seem to be of equal value, he can use a technique for weighting the factors differentially in computing the indices. The status index is computed by simply summing up the rank numbers assigned for each factor. This yields an inverted scale in the example: the lower the resulting number, the higher the status.

Status congruence, which is also an inverted scale in this example (the lower the number, the higher the congruence), is computed by adding the differences between the rank number on each factor and the rank number of each other factor. For John, there were no differences, so that his status congruence index is zero, indicating perfect congruence. For Carl, the computation of status congruence was made as follows:

From the table of rank orders: Carl

Computation of differences:

(a) The difference between 2 and 3 is 1
(b) The difference between 2 and 6 is 4
(c) The difference between 2 and 7 is 5
(d) The difference between 3 and 6 is 3
(e) The difference between 3 and 7 is 4
(f) The difference between 6 and 7 is 1

The sum of the difference is   18, which becomes Carl's status congruence index.

Going one step further with the example, the eight men can now be ranked in relation to each other on their status and status congruence index numbers (*see* Table 8.3).

Table 8.3: Group X rankings on status and status congruence indices

	STATUS		STATUS CONGRUENCE	
NAME	INDEX	RANK	INDEX	RANK
John	4	1	0	1
Bill	14	2	16	6
Pat	15	3	7	3
Carl	18	4	18	7
Abe	20	5	10	4
Jeff	22	6	22	8
Tom	25	7	3	2
Joe	26	8	12	5

The measurement methods and assumptions are known to be rough approximations, at best, of the group's consensus about its values, which in reality could be quite ambiguous. Further simplification will help summarize the data, compensate for some of the error, and provide for easier analysis at later stages. This is accomplished by assigning the top four ranks to the category "high" and the bottom four ranks to the category "low," on both status and status congruence. This division in two areas will yield a fourfold classification scheme.

		STATUS CONGRUENCE	
		Low	*High*
	High	Bill	John
		Carl	Pat
Status			
	Low	Jeff	Abe
		Joe	Tom

An important idea contained in this analysis is that status level and congruence are theoretically independent of each other. Persons high in status, when status is conceived of as an aggregate of several factors, can be either high or low in congruence. Similarly, a low-status person could be high in congruence.[25]

Status discrepancy: This refers to the fact that a person has status in more groups than one and that he may be given high status in one group and low in another. So long as these groups are effectively segregated, the different evaluations may have no effect on one another. When there is some cross-contact, then the evaluation in one group may have a significant impact on the evaluation in another. Status discrepancy occurs when someone is given high status in one group which may be considered a salient source for the evaluation of the person, and that person is being accorded low status in the second group which is doing the evaluating. Status discrepancy relates status within the group to status outside the group, and so is an important element in predicting the relative value any individual will place on his participation in the group under study.

Having set out, in some detail, the useful approaches for estimating status in groups, we move on now to a consideration of the processes of valuation which underly the status structure of groups.

PART B: GOALS AND VALUES *

The nature of values

Everyone seems to know what values are, or at least everyone has his own idea of what they are. Social scientists are no exception, but even a cursory perusal of the literature quickly unveils a wide range of definitions and approaches. Because of the multiplicity of definitions we will try to outline clearly what a "value" is and how it is related to similar concepts. Although the study of values has been neglected in primary group analysis, it could and should be given central importance.

Value has been used to refer to any number of things—from an object in which an individual has invested a significant degree of affect, to utility in the economists' sense, to broad, thematic cultural patterns. But the idea of evaluation and preference has been central to all definitions. No individual places an equal amount of importance or interest on all the things that impinge on his life. Certain objects, certain ways of adjusting to the experience of life, certain relations to the past, present, and future are selected from the vast range of possibilities.

Given this general point, there are a number of issues which must

* David Frazer made a major contribution to the material on group values and goals.

be faced when specifying and elaborating a definition of values. Allen Barton has singled out five recurrent crossroads confronted by every value-analyst.[26] They are listed here in the form of questions and we will try to clarify our viewpoint by providing answers.

Are values attributes of people or aspects of objects?

When social scientists speak of people "having values," they often mean that people act as though they have standards or tendencies of choice. This is reflected particularly in the massive research done on attitudes. Hence, one may "have" this value: "Aesthetic appreciation is an important component of being authentically human." Some scientists speak of the objects, or desired states which people seek, as values. Any desideratum is a value and, therefore, "Large Vase of Flowers" by Pierre Renoir may be a value to an art collector. Whatever is valued in this sense *is* a value.

Emile Durkheim faced this problem in his analysis of the sacred.[27] His solution in that context can be extended to value-analysis in general. Durkheim found the sacred to be a symbol, for sacredness has no intrinsic causal connection with its multifarious objects. Things varying from the sublime to the ridiculous have been considered sacred. The same is true of valued objects. There is no end of things which have been "valued," nor of things that have been simultaneously considered valuable by some and rubbish by others. For this reason, Durkheim was driven to consider the individuals or groups who maintained a ritual relation with sacra, and he chose to look at the sacred as an aspect of humans rather than as a distinguishable quality inhering in certain objects or states. For somewhat similar reasons, we choose to speak of values as standards of evaluation or tendencies of choice held by particular people. Desideratum will be clearly distinguished as "valued objects or states." However, this conclusion does *not* mean that there are no basic regularities in what has been valued. Men have always found it easier to value some particular things or ways of life than others.

Are values individual or collective phenomena?

The problems that arise at this point are among the more significant in small group research. An adequate answer to this question implies the conceptualization of the relationships between personality and the group with its cultural aspects, the knowledge of how personal and group elements can be separated in a meaningful manner, and the ordering into a theoretical system of the concepts of needs, motives, goals, attitudes, norms, and values. Part of the difficulty in providing such a comprehensive answer is that these relationships are still elements of the unfinished agenda of research. A contributing factor to these difficulties is that it has not always been clear just what is meant by "group values." Allen Barton points out that the "values of an organization" can mean: (1) the values held by a majority of individuals; (2) the values actually rewarded by the system; or (3) the failure of the investigator to think through social processes involved in the interaction of individuals within collective units.[28]

Our primary focus in studying the group is on the collective, shared aspects of life, and so we will consider those values which are collective phenomena. This does not exclude the individual, but highlights those aspects of personality that are more centrally affected by and involved in group processes. Isolating values shared by the majority of members also involves isolating individually held values. Interpreting the significance of the group for the individual involves a delineation of the impact of group norms and values, group activities and rewards on idiosyncratic attributes.

Are values explicit, subject-formulated standards, or are
they implicit, inferential constructions of the analyst?
Thousands of books have been written on the values a particular author holds to be best for this world. Many articulate people find no difficulty in explicating their values to an analyst. Anthropologists have found certain informants to have a rather detailed and comparatively accurate knowledge of the values of their people. But not all persons are equally thoughtful or clear as to their own "philosophy of life." Even when people are articulate about values, social scientists are often reluctant to accept all such statements at their face-value. Psychologists of different persuasions have demonstrated that the repressed elements in the personality can strongly affect behavior, particularly in group situations.

This split between explicit-implicit is important in value analysis. The problem with explicit, verbalized statements of values by an informant is that they may reflect more about his personality's defensive system than about his operative values. A verbalized version is not to be depreciated for this reason. The idealized image a person has of himself and his group is an important part of group life. But for the very reason that the subject may not be sensitive to certain processes of shared values, the scientist finds it essential to go beyond explicit value statements. Part of the problem in building a coherent picture of the group is the integrating of the verbalized values of group members with the more inferential value-constructs posited to explain certain regularities. There are no easy formulae available for this integration. Content analysis of verbatim records supplies some of the more explicit elements. The perceptual acuity and interpretive skill of the scientist must provide the integrative and inferential factors. The resulting formulation is a *combination* of both explicit and implicit elements.

Objections have often been raised that value analysis is circular. The researcher studies a given body of explicit statements, combines inferences with those statements, and derives certain values. He then uses the derived values to explain the same data from which they were derived. (F. Kluckholn [29] treats this problem in detail.) This charge is not really devastating. The derived values do not have to be used to explain the same body of data. It is quite possible to deduce hypotheses from the formulated values about other behavior and situations, thus providing some kind of independent test. Values are also one of the simplest forms of shorthand available to the reporter. Viewing a particular group's processes in terms of values is one of the simplest ways to communicate its basic features to others who cannot observe it. The combination of explicit and implicit values results in a picture of the group values which may be in no *one* member's mind but which is a useful analytical tool for the researcher.

It is important to distinguish between : (1) the explicit values of a group; (2) the implicit values that may be recognized by only a few group members or totally inferred by an investigator; and (3) the interpretive account relating and structuring explicit/implicit values relative to group processes. We are concerned here to explain as clearly as possible both the methods by which the explicit group values can be coded and the methods by which the interpretive account can be formulated.

Are values desires or obligations?

The distinctions which were made in discussing roles and norms also apply here. Catton considers values as any and all preferences [30] while C. Kluckhohn limits values to concepts of the desirable which are held to be justified for one reason or another.[31] There is no reason to eliminate either from consideration. Allen Barton's distinction between preferential values and normative values seems to be useful. It recognizes that matters of taste and matters of obligation differ in their effect on group processes, in their openness to change, and in part in their relations to the sanction system. Preferential values have a tendency to become legitimate by reference to normative values rather than vice versa. Preferential values seem to be more open to change. Normative values appear to group members to be intrinsic to the conduct of group affairs and, therefore, as right or moral.

Are values a few basic standards or do they include all specific preferences and standards?

Level is perhaps one of the more difficult problems with which value-analysts wrestle, and we have faced it before in the general discussion of levels of content categories in content analysis. Ethel Albert's classification illustrates the various levels that have been investigated (*see* fig. 8.1).[32]

Premises and value-orientations are the most general conceptions of desirable and undesirable modes, means, and ends of action. "Value premises, as rationale of a value system, are existential statements defining the nature and locus of the valuable, and postulating 'ultimate' values. Premises also include value-orientations, that is, statements in which existential and normative functions are combined." [33] Focal values are

Figure 8.1: Albert's classification of values

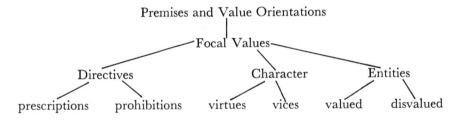

Adapted from: Ethel Albert, "The Classification of Values, Method and Illustration," *American Anthropologist,* vol. 58 (1956): 225. Reproduced by permission of the American Anthropological Association.

those around which detailed, numerous, specific values cluster. They form a matrix which has the characteristics of *not* being organized in a hierarchy and of being circularly self-justifying. Such focal values as work, health, personal success, knowledge, family, possession, and community progress are examples of this level. Character refers to the qualities of personality that are approved or disapproved, rewarded or punished. "Directives are phrased in terms of action to be done or avoided, virtues and vices specify the characteristics of persons as moral agents." [34] These are predicated by *ought, good,* and *bad,* previously listed in the content categories. Valued and disvalued entities are the lowest level of generality of the value system. They comprise the numerous specific objects, feeling states, situations, and activities. These focal values and personal qualities are the qualities previously listed as ideal values in the content analysis scheme.

While recognizing the necessity of investigating all forms of normative culture, Talcott Parson's solution in differentiating values from lower level normative elements seems preferable.

When differentiation of roles is present, it becomes necessary to distinguish between two components of the normative culture of the system: that of values, which are shared by the members over and above their particular roles, and that of role-expectations, which are differentiated by role and therefore define rights and obligations applicable to one role but not to the other. I propose to use the term *values* for the shared normative component, and the term (differentiated) *norm* for the component that is specific to a given role or, in more complex systems, to other empirical units of the system, i.e., various collectivities such as families, churches, business firms, governmental agencies, universities.

The universalistic aspect of values implies that, at the relevant level of reference, they are neither situation-specific nor function-specific. . . . When values are said not to be situation-specific it is implied that their normative validity is not a function of the particular categories of personalities available for membership, nor, for example, of the particular levels of technological knowledge available for implementing these values. When situation-specificity is introduced, we speak analytically not of values, but of goals.

Similarly, values are independent of the internal differentiation of the systems in which they are institutionalized; they are relevant on a level of generality which "transcends" functional differentiation.[35]

While this formulation does not solve the problem of ordering the various levels of *value,* it does give a clear differentiating rule : Values are normative culture applicable to the whole system under consideration. Norms are lower level, function-specific standards. Values are basic, generalized standards. In terms of the small group, the membership role specifications are values. So are the more generalized preferences and obligations for men and women provided they are applicable to all of the specified sex. Normative culture applicable only to the leader, for example, is on the level of norms rather than values.

Therefore, values are a few, basic standards or tendencies of choice rather than the more specific preferences or norms. Later in this chapter, the problems involved in deciding on appropriate levels and mapping the organization of values and lower-level norms will be discussed.

We now have the basic elements for a typological statement of values. Values are generalized, basic standards or tendencies of choice which are at varying levels of explicitness and which are constituted by both preferential and obligatory components. A value system is an organized set of normative cultures specifying both the desirable and desired aspects of reality. In terms of the primary group, values are those shared aspects of its normative culture that are meaningfully related to its behavior as a group.

The emphasis on the "shared" aspect points not to the holding in common of certain orientations about specific objects, but to the application of that orientation to all members. While all members may share the value "leaders must be persuasive," such an orientation applies only to one or two persons in the group. As such it is not a value but a norm. All members may also share the orientation "tactful honesty must be adhered to at all times." Because it is *applicable* to the behavior of all members, it is considered a value. The emphasis on meaningfulness points to the fact that the only evaluation tendencies that are relevant are those that are salient to the group's behavior. A commonly held orientation to hippies is not a group value, unless it has some meaningful significance to *group* processes. Such an orientation may be commonly held but never communicated in any manner from one member to another and may therefore remain on a personal level. Commonly held, implicit values which may never be explicitly communicated are meaningfully related to the group's behavior if there is *implicit communication.*

There are three important dimensions that distinguish various kinds of normative culture : (1) the generality of the standard; (2) the rationalized nature of the standard; and (3) the severity and kind of sanction associated with the standard. Thus, the first dimension runs from specific matters of taste and norms to generalized preferential and obligatory values. The second dimension runs from the most implicit, uninstitutionalized values to the highly institutionalized, explicit values. The third dimension runs from matters that are recognized as legitimately subject to some degree of difference, considered as preferences, to matters that are relatively closed in regard to debate and change, and with which rather strong sanctions are associated.

Looked at from the perspective of the group members, values order and integrate their personal preferences and legitimize the common concerns and activities of group members. From the perspective of the value-analyst, who is often working with a plethora of the lower level attitudes and preferences, values are abstract evaluative components common to a large number of lower level orientations.

Values and the primary group

Theories of the social functions of the primary group have always stressed the importance of the primary group in mediating social values to the individual, yet there is probably no area of primary group analysis which has been so neglected in empirical studies. Cooley's original formulation of the nature of the primary group stressed the fact that the primary group was the key factor in the integration of society because the central values of the greater society were instilled in the individual by his participation in primary groups.[36] More recently this view has been sharply challenged by Shils. He points out that Cooley's formulation assumes a substantial harmony between value orientations in primary groups and in the greater society, but that Mayo's research on primary groups in industry and Shil's own research on primary groups in the military do not support this proposition.[37] Shils, for instance, noted in his studies that the ordinary soldier was largely indifferent to the central social values for which he was supposed to be fighting and that his willingness to fight effectively was based largely on affective bonds in the group rather than on values derived from society.

The relation of group values to the social environment
Shils also points out that some primary groups are strongly integrated around particular values, which sometimes take the form of ideologies :

I found that persons with an intense preoccupation, continuous and fervent, with the symbols associated with authority in the corporate organization, within which the primary groups were formed, seemed to be different kinds of people from those who had a looser, more intermittent and less zealous attachment to the symbols. Conversely, those with strong personal attachments to the personal dispositions of their associates seemed relatively unresponsive to the symbols of the larger society which were incorporated in the authorities of the society and its major organization.[38]

In support of the view that there are great differences in the extent to which primary groups orient themselves to central social values, Shils quotes Berelson's study of voting behavior in the U.S. which indicated that the members of some primary groups (the "fervents") were strongly and actively concerned with voting issues, others were completely apathetic, while other groups again were intermittently concerned or unconcerned depending on the issues.[39]

Values are always a central element in a primary group. No primary group can exist without a value system to guide behavior, but the extent to which the values of a group are derived directly from its social context is always an empirical question. The location of a primary group in terms of its larger social context is an important element in developing an understanding of its internal processes. This includes, of course, understanding those shared elements of culture which the group holds with the broader social system as well as the more differentiating aspects.

A concrete example of a situation where the immediate social system is a major determinant of group values exists in the value systems of some delinquent gangs. Miller, for example, distinguished a number of "focal concerns" of lower class culture which carry across to lower-class delinquent gangs and affect their value structures.[40] For example, one value which is directly taken over from the lower class value system is that of "toughness." Miller makes the point that the high percentage of female-dominated households in the lower class creates a youth culture in which males are highly concerned with proving their masculinity and hence emphasizing "toughness" as a central value.

Short and Strodtbeck took up the ideas of Miller and others and made a rare and thoughtful empirical analysis of the relationship of the value systems of a number of lower-class gangs to the value systems of the middle-class and lower-class conflict, criminal, and retreatist subcultures.[41] Short and Strodtbeck's description of their method is quoted in some detail. Their method is a rare example of an empirical study of primary group values and is interesting because of its use of Osgood's semantic differential [42] as a method of approaching value analysis.

The data were gathered by means of a semantic differential, which consists of a number of seven-point, bipolar, adjectival scales against which any set of concepts or descriptive images may be rated. This instrument measures what Osgood terms "connotative meaning" which, for a variety of populations, has been found to have two main orthogonal dimensions when a large number of scales and concepts are administered and the scales then intercorrelated and factor-analyzed. To obtain adequate measures of these dimensions, only a small number of scales, found to have high correlations with the appropriate dimensions, are required. A score for a dimension is obtained by averaging the appropriate scale values, which ranged from one to seven. These dimensions and the corresponding scales used in this study are:

EVALUATION	POTENCY
clean–dirty	hard–soft
good–bad	large–small
kind–cruel	strong–weak
fair–unfair	brave–cowardly
pleasant–unpleasant	rugged–delicate

Table 8.4: Semantic-differentiation images

SUB-CULTURE	LABEL	IMAGES: SOMEONE WHO . . .
Middle-class:		
Dominant goal activity	GRAD	works for good grades at school
Leisure activity	READ	likes to read good books
Ethical orientation	SAVE	saves his money
Lower-class:		
Dominant goal activity	SJOB	has a steady job washing and greasing cars
Leisure activity	HANG	likes to spend his spare time hanging out on the corner with his friends
Ethical orientation	SHAR	shares his money with his friends
Conflict:		
Dominant goal activity	TUFF	is a good fighter with a tough reputation
Leisure activity	HANG	(*see* lower-class)
Ethical orientation	STIK	sticks by his friends in a fight
Criminal:		
Dominant goal activity	FENC	knows where to sell what he steals
Leisure activity	HANG	(*see* lower-class)
Ethical orientation	CONN	has good connections to avoid trouble with the law
Retreatist:		
Dominant goal activity	PIMP	makes easy money by pimping and other illegal hustling
Leisure activity	DRUG	gets his kicks by using drugs
Ethical orientation	COOL	stays cool and keeps to himself
Additional images:	GIRL	makes out with every girl he wants
	SELF	myself as I usually am
	I EGO	myself as I would like to be
	GANG	is a member of (enter group name or, if none, "your friendship group")

Three additional scales, derived from Miller's "focal concerns" of lower-class culture, were also included. These were "smart–sucker," "lucky–unlucky," and "exciting life–boring life." The images (*see* Table 8.4) to be rated were chosen to represent salient examples of instrumental or dominant goal activity, leisure-time activity, and ethical orientation for each of five theoretically significant subcultures—middle-class, lower-class, conflict, criminal, and retreatist. Leisure activity appeared to be essentially the same for three of the subcultures, and is therefore represented for all three by a single image. Although they do not figure prominently in this analysis, the three aspects of subcultural roles did provide a basis for sampling widely within each domain. Of four additional images included because of their theoretical interest, only the one identified by the label "GIRL" requires comment. This image was included to furnish responses relevant to sexual demonstrations of masculinity. Hopefully, images were phrased so as to be as concrete as possible and yet personify the values hypothesized to distinguish the subculture.

Administration of sematic differential to small numbers of subjects at a time took place in an old, rather shabby one-time apartment building, where the subjects were fed hot dogs and soft drinks. The tester was quite permissive toward all departures from normally decorous behavior that did not jeopardize the validity of measures. Considerable care was taken to explain directions and check the boys' responses. A few boys, unable to read, had the semantic differential read to them as they responded.[43]

Strodtbeck and Short conclude a detailed discussion of the results of applying this procedure with the following summary :

(1) For all six populations, the endorsement "in principle" of middle-class prescriptive norms is uniformly high. (2) Gang lower-class, and middle-class boys differ most in their attitudes toward behaviors proscribed by the middle-class, and they tend to be ordered as listed with respect to their tolerance toward these behaviors. (3) Legitimacy or practicality, as measured by a "smart-sucker" scale, seems to be a meaningful basis for distinguishing behavior. There is some evidence that gang boys, more than other boys, may be led by this distinction to a choice of criminal behavior over legitimately gainful behavior. (4) The hypothesis of a sex-identity problem for lower-class and gang boys appears worth pursuing further.[44]

Short and Strodtbeck present behavioral evidence that, despite the general assent given at the individual level to middle-class values, certain group situations arise for the gang where immediate action brings other values into play in determining concrete behavior. In particular, the high status members of the group are often forced to engage in conflict and other risk-taking actions, which conflict with middle-class norms, in order to maintain their status within the gang. This illustrates the point that values enter the social situation most forcefully through the actions and opinions of central figures who set the "value atmosphere" of a group. Individuals possessing status in the group disproportionately affect evolving group values, and the values they express may be ones which will support their status or the status of their membership group rather than the central values of the larger society.

The concern with deviance of lower-class delinquent gangs has meant that studies of these particular groups are the most fruitful source of systematic methods of group value analysis. Spergel used a different approach to that of Short and Strodtbeck by devising a "value norm index" to measure the degree of illegitimate orientation in various gangs.[45] In all he listed nineteen items, some of which were direct value statements (for example, are racketeers good or bad?), while others were designed to establish the likelihood of participation in various kinds of illegitimate activities such as gang fighting, car stealing, and rape. The responses of gang members were added over the items and a criminal value score obtained by computing the percentage of the total responses of each group, which indicated an illegitimate orientation. These scores indicated that the predicted differences in criminal value orientation for different areas were largely correct.

In cases where groups resist in whole or in part the pressures to conform to the values of larger or more powerful groups, they develop specific contra-values of their own to cope with the threatening environment. This is clearly shown in a study by Orth of classes at the Graduate School of Business Administration at Harvard University.[46] Orth points out that "coping values" emerge to develop and enforce the solidarity of the group in the face of outside pressures. In this case, the threat lies in the emphasis of the faculty on competition among students and the search for those of outstanding excellence among them. This could have led to a spiral of frenetic effort on the part of students as they strove to outdo the others. Consequently, two norms developed in the classes studied by Orth : "Don't try to be too much of a "star" and show up the rest of us, and, don't dominate the discussion by talking too often or too long." These values were enforced by such measures as communal hissing in the class and ostracism outside class.

Sherif and Sherif also give examples of coping values in delinquent gangs.[47] These values perform the essentially similar functions of protecting and maintaining group solidarity. The values described by these authors relate particularly to "ratting," "squealing," and being "yellow." Ostracism and physical punishment are normally meted out to offenders for these group crimes. Lombard also describes coping values in his study of a sales girls' clique.[48] Here the threat to the group was that, in response to proffered rewards by management, one or more girls might compete too successfully for sales with her peers and thus reduce the income of some. The girls therefore developed the following values : "We should have locations of our own; we should have merchandise of our own; we should not sell more than $100 per day." Thus an important part of the value structure of any group is the values which are developed to cope with the group's external environment and which define the interests of the group and its members differently from those of surrounding groups or the larger society.

Methods of the kinds discussed have the limitation of pre-specifying the range of value orientations which are to be examined. This leaves the researcher open to the possibility of overlooking central values which he has not anticipated. Consequently, the content analysis of freely expressed value statements should be collected from one or more of three sources : (1) What members say to each other, their openly expressed values; (2) what members indicate are their values by their actions, particularly their value expression when conflicts emerge in the group; (3) what members say to the field researcher in the course of open-ended interviews and conversations.

Charting group values by content analysis

An example of a method of content analysis of values will be presented which was used to map the value system of the trust department of a bank and to study the "deviant" values of sub-groups within it. Although the method is applied to interviews, it is also applicable to interaction transcripts or recordings.

In the study, I was interested in testing the hypothesis, developed in chapter 2, concerning the differentiation of primary groups within secondary structures. The trust department of a large city bank was chosen, and it was found that primary groups developed corresponding to the "organizer" (vice-president), "cabal" (investment officers), strategic (trust officers), and apathetic (research analysts) types. Open-ended, non-directive interviews were conducted with most of the members of these groups, but with only a sample of the trust officers, who were more numerous. From these interviews all value statements were selected by using the content categories shown in table 8.5, which specify the linguistic signs by which the process of evaluation is conveyed in communication.

Two obvious categories are synonyms for "good" and "bad" which may be simple words like "attractive" or phrases such as "not . . . (fast or efficient or capable) . . . enough." Another obvious category is a short list of synonyms for "ought." The words "ought" and "should" indicate preferences, while the words "must," "have to," "has to," "had to" indicate obligations. Words implying purpose (both nouns and verbs) usually indicate the rationale behind some state which has been instituted. The category *need* signals the presence of a basic premise of some kind, i.e., it marks a statement of some existential factor perceived by the speaker. The three final value signals (*ideal values, goals,* and *negative goals*) are end states to be desired or avoided. Ideal values relate to behavior,

personal characteristics, and entities which are valued, and the list consists
of verbs, modifiers, and abstract nouns. All three of these categories demand a knowledge of the situation, for what is assumed to be a basic
value in a bank (profit, for example) may be a negative goal in another
social group (Communist Russia, for example).

Following Albert's basic model of a value hierarchy (*see* fig. 8.1,
page 239), we suggest that the top of the hierarchy will consist of goals
and premises which will be signalled by the categories *goals* and *need*
respectively. Focal values are logically derived from these for, given certain
goals *and* a set of basic assumptions about the nature of reality, then
particular focal values are needed to guide action alternatives. Prescriptions,

Table 8.5: Value categories used in coding interviews

Note: The words listed under category headings are examples of words coded into
the categories. The lists are not intended to be comprehensive.

GOOD	BAD	GOALS
good	useless	performance
better	worthless	yield
best	bad	income
well	awful	capital gains
attractive	absurd	security
optimum	ridiculous	economies
essential	not——enough	safety of principal
perfect	too——(big, etc.)	handling of aggressive accounts

NEGATIVE GOALS
risk
losses
cost
speculation

IDEAL VALUES
valued behaviors:
  verbs: expedite
  verb modifiers: fast (-er, -est)
valued personal characteristics:
  nouns: creativity, judgment
  noun modifiers: flexible
valued situational characteristics:
  nouns: balance
  noun modifiers: progressive
valued entities:
  nouns: quality

NEED (premises)	OUGHT	PURPOSE
need	preferences:	purpose
demand	should	purposely
want	ought	designed to
require	prescriptions:	policy
emphasis on	must	reason
pressure for	have to	meant to
prefer	has to	the theory is that . . .

proscriptions, and preferences (*ought*) are the next level of specificity below focal values, and these, in turn, are finally articulated in specific norms relating to behavior, personal characteristics, and situational qualities.

The above scheme was applied to the interviews with bank officers. First, all value statements were identified by reading each sentence to see whether it contained one or more words or phrases which could be coded in one or more of the eight value categories. These sentences were then retrieved from the general text of the interviews after having been marked to identify the speaker and interview number. The remaining sentences were re-read and checked to see that they were, in fact, value neutral. The eight value categories correctly discriminated evaluative from non-evaluative statements, so that the categories can be regarded as exhaustive.

The evaluative sentences were then sorted out, coded, and arranged by the following procedure :

Sentences tagged *goal* were inspected for the extent to which the goal specified could be regarded as "ultimate" in character for the trust department. Any goal which could be regarded as contributing to any other was regarded as a sub-goal. Conversely, any goal which could not be regarded as contributing to another (department) goal was considered an ultimate goal for the department. Thus the ultimate goal for the department clearly emerged as "the effective management of trust accounts." But two kinds of accounts were distinguished constantly by those interviewed—these were usually termed "regular" and "aggressive" accounts respectively. . . . The two basic sub-goals for the department were then : (1) The effective management of regular accounts, and (2) the effective management of aggressive accounts. In explaining the differences between these two kinds of accounts, sentences stating the corresponding basic premises were reiterated again and again. Linguistically these were stated in thematic form, i.e., in subject-verb-object relationships. The themes were summarized in their most general form as follows :

    1.   Regular clients need security.
    2.   Corporate clients need performance.

Examples of theme two illustrate some of the varied forms in which this theme was expressed :

These clients are making *demands* for more *aggressive results.*
CORPORATE CLIENTS   NEED   GOAL=PERFORMANCE

Large corporations demand a *high investment return.*
CORPORATE CLIENTS NEED GOAL=PERFORMANCE

So now there's a tremendous *pressure* (by *corporations*) on the trustee for
                 NEED CORPORATE CLIENTS
performance.
GOAL=PERFORMANCE

From the goals and premises, it was appropriate to move on to those sentences tagged "purpose," for these sentences specified the more concrete policies or prescriptions for the implementation of these goals of security and performance (*see* fig. 8.2 for a schematic rendering of the value structure of the trust department). Part of the policy consisted in setting up specific committees (T.C.=Trust Committee; T.I.C.=Trust Investment Committee; T.A.C.=Trust Administration Committee; S.I.G.=Special Investment Group) to carry out or supervise the carrying out of these policies. Prescriptions and proscriptions for these committees were also outlined in value statements. Generalized values could also be associated with these committees, in that these values were frequently, although not always, mentioned in relation to the purpose of the committees (for example, "S.I.G. will act *faster* when necessary"—here the value of speed is connected with the purpose of S.I.G.).

The valued personal characteristics and required behaviors for various differentiated roles could also be related to these values. The value structure of the trust department, then, can be schematically represented as in figure 8.2, and consists of a hierarchy with ultimate goals at the top and specific differentiated role requirements at the bottom.

The fact that these consist of spontaneously expressed sentiments indicates that the formal structure has been well internalized by the members of the organization and is now strongly supported by their expectations about organizational objectives and action. However, it is also clear that there is a built-in conflict between value structures related to the respective goals of performance and security. As this analysis is extended below, we shall see that the respective importance attributed to these goals varies from one functional group to another within the division, so that the value conflict takes on political dimensions.

Non-functional values and primary group interests

The majority of value statements from interviews are summarized in figure 8.2. However, there were some value statements which could not be reviewed as logically deriving from organizational goals and which, therefore, must be considered from the point of view of those goals as *non-functional*. The majority of these remaining statements related directly to the primary groups which had evolved out of the functional differentiation of positions in the division. These non-functional values were of particular interest because of the light they shed on the relation of primary groups to the environing organization.

Figure 8.3 summarizes the distinctive primary group values expressed by members of these functionally differentiated groups within the department. While certain organizational goals and values are widely held by

Figure 8.2: Value structure of the trust division (functional values only)
Ultimate Goal: The Effective Management of Trust Accounts

Sub-goal: The effective management of regular accounts (90% of all accounts).

Premises: (1) Massachusetts law—needs—a "prudent man" policy for personal trust accounts.
(2) Regular clients—need—security (safety of principal   FOCAL VALUE = SECURITY
(conservation of wealth
(economies in account operation.

Prescriptions for T.C. (1) Set overall policy for the division.
(2) Minimize risks, losses, excessive costs, speculation.
(3) Maximize reasonable income, capital security, modest growth of capital to cover inflation, i.e., "appreciation."

Hence T.C. policy for the division:
Prescriptions: (1) Money must be invested only in "safe" stocks on the approved Common Stock List.
(2) Incoming money must be invested over a period of months.

Prescriptions: (1) No more than 70% of funds in an account to be in common stocks (balance to be in tax exempt and corporate stocks).
(2) Diversification by no more than 5% in any individual stock.

Hence Prescriptions for T.I.C. (1) Review stocks suitable for regular accounts and recommend to T.C. for inclusion on, or removal from, C.S.L.
(2) Allow committee members to express opinions on these stocks to ensure they are "safe."
(3) Discuss overall investment policy and recommend changes.
(4) Ensure, through subcommittees, that investment policy is actually carried out in individual accounts.
(5) Maintain a membership balance between investment and account officers.

Hence investment officers—need—personal characteristics of: experience, knowledge, judgment, caution.
—behaviors: to communicate their expertise to accounts officers.

Hence investment analysts—need—behaviors: to review and report regularly on common stocks on list, to suggest new stocks when appropriate on basis of security, price, yield.

Hence Prescriptions for T.A.C. (1) Advise account officers, particularly by reviewing discretionary payments.
(2) Make hard decisions and take responsibility for them.
(3) Deal with possible legal issues and avoid costly mistakes.
(4) Approve guardian ad litum and ensure equitable treatment.
(5) Supervise account administration to ensure policy is carried out.
(6) Advise account officers of current policy.
(7) Protect the bank's financial interests.

Hence T.A.C. members and account officers—need—personal characteristics: experience, judgment.
But (premise) the number of regular accounts has expanded rapidly.
And (premise) the number of junior account officers has expanded rapidly.
Hence account supervision meetings' purpose: to pass down policy to account officers.

250

Hence account teams' goal: to handle any kind of (a wide variety of) accounts.
  sub-goals: to give everyone a general familiarity with all accounts supervised by team in order to broaden experience (valued personal characteristic).
    to ensure coverage of accounts and cover officer absences (value = coverage).
    to continue the in-service training of young officers (value = education).

But these measures are not enough.
Hence the division needs: increased service personnel, more specialized assistance, a more formalized training program.

Sub-goal: The effective management of aggressive accounts (10% of accounts).

Premises: **Corporate clients—need—performance.**

Mgts. of pension/profit-sharing funds—need—cost of funds cut.   FOCAL VALUE = PERFORMANCE
Large corporations   —demand—increased capital gains.
New, aggressive accounts   —require—higher investment return.

Hence specific policy changes are needed: (1) Larger % of funds in common stock.
                                          (2) More investment in aggressive individual stocks, less diversified accounts.
                                          (3) Prompter, more frequent action and better timing, of sales and buys.

Hence S.I.G. purpose: to gather together the best investment people in a small group to handle aggressive and special accounts by **specializing** in "performance" stocks.

Hence prescriptions for S.I.G.: (1) Maximize speed and timing of purchases and sales.
                                (2) Disseminate current investment ideas throughout the division.
                                (3) Minimize cumbersome, time-consuming decision-making procedures.

Hence investment officers—need: changed personal characteristics: openness to new ideas, current awareness, flexibility in approach, creativity.

                              : changed behaviors to seek expert advice from S.I.G.
                                                     to investigate tips on shares.
                                                     to identify buy/sell signals.
                                                     to accept risk and responsibility for personal decisionmaking.

                              : changed situational characteristics:—changed situation:
                                                     higher salaries, expanded research facilities, more and better-trained analysts.

Hence investment analysis department—needs—changed situation:—increase supporting staff works, more outside technical information.

251

all members of the division, figure 8.3 shows that the relative importance of particular values varies systematically through the structure of the organization—primary reference groups based mainly on job classification tend to stress those organizational values which enhance the status and activities of their group. In addition, each group develops distinctive values which are not related to the instrumental goals for which the division is organized. These distinctive "non-functional" values separate the groups and relate to position in the organizational hierarchy and to job technology in a way predictable from the theory advanced in chapter 2.

Figure 8.3: Distinctive primary group values of banking sub-groups

Administrators:
1. Stability and balance.
2. Planned, controlled change to improve the effectiveness of the division.
3. Maintenance of differences of opinion among investment officers, i.e., "fluidity."
4. Expansion of business, reduced administrative costs, increased earnings.
5. A larger part in the formation of policy, i.e., more policy decisions made at levels lower than the Trust Committee.

Summary: Maintenance of control over means of goal implementation and extension of influence over policy making (goal setting).

Trust officers:
1. Desire for variety in types of work.
2. Emphasis on use of team to preserve and enhance independence of action.
3. Personal relationships with customers as chief source of satisfaction.
4. A strong emphasis on the values of regular accounts.

Summary: Support of account teams and satisfaction of customer needs.

Investment officers:
1. Individual initiative.
2. Individual responsibility for decision-making, especially freedom from bureaucratic procedures.
3. A strong emphasis on values of the aggressive accounts.

Summary: Increased control over means by avoiding direct administrative controls; upgrading status of investment skills and providing for the informal, interpersonal exchange of information and influence.

Investment analysts:
1. A frustrated desire for leadership, social interaction, and teamwork to cope with the system.
2. Rejection of the system as "bad."

Summary: Rejection and withdrawal; frustration at low status and isolation.

Thus far, methods have been presented for mapping the status hierarchy and the value hierarchy in a primary group. The final section of this chapter deals with the ways in which the flow of resources within the group, and from and to the environment, can be studied in relation to the structures which set the basic priorities for resource processing and distributing.

Group resources and resource processing

The nature of resources

The term "resources" will be used for all those objects, behaviors, skills, and personal attributes relevant to group values and goals and/or the values and goals of individual group members. Resources are not values or goals themselves, but rather the means of actualizing values and of achieving goals. For instance, if making money is a group goal, then investments may be a group resource and so may crucial information related to the current state of the stock market.

But an object is only a resource if it is relatively scarce and if it is valued by group members. Thus air is not generally a group resource because, while it certainly affects the attainment of group goals, it is not scarce. Conversely, a scarce item is not a group resource if members do not value it. Resource processing occurs only when members seek actively to exchange something valued in the group generally, or valued by some individuals in the group, for something they value themselves. Exchange occurs when the group offers the individual something he could not gain in isolation or could only gain with greater difficulty or cost outside the group. In a sense, the study of group resources, of their distribution and use, is the "economics" of small group life. However, because of the communal nature of primary group ties, much of the exchange in the group is not in monetary terms.

The idea of studying resource processing in small groups is fairly recent and is usually written about under the heading of "social exchange." Some systematic approaches to the subject have been made by Homans, Blau, Thibaut and Kelley and, in relation to parent-child relationships, by Whiting.[49] These approaches have in common the idea that human interaction is more likely to be sustained if it is mutually rewarding to those involved, and that to be mutually rewarding, those involved must "get something out of it." The "something" received can be regarded as resources. Economic principles have been extrapolated to explain noneconomic exchange behavior and its results. Blau, for instance, quotes the economic principle of eventually diminishing marginal utility : "as a consumer increases the consumption of any commodity, keeping constant the consumption of all other commodities, the marginal utility of the variable

commodity must eventually decline." [50] He found that this principle applied in the case of the federal agency with which he was concerned; the
more an agent was asked for advice by his colleagues the more the value
(utility) of the respect that this implied declined. Put another way, the cost
to the consultant of the consultation time increased because he had less
time left for other activities. Similarly, the questioner finds expert advice
becoming increasingly costly for him the more he seeks it, for in seeking
it he diminishes the expert's respect for him. Such cases have led Homans,
among others, to conclude that "no exchange continues unless both parties
are making a profit," [51] where profit is conceived of as reward less cost.

The study of the exchange of social resources is much more difficult
than would be the study of economic exchange processes in such a small
collectivity. Social resources are often ephemeral as compared with raw
materials, economic goods, or even "services" as economists define them.
Longbaugh has stated that "they can be as specific as 'my mother's smile'
or as general as 'information'." [52] The vagueness and variety of their
definition makes the analysis of resource processing difficult, and the problem is added to by the fact that they cannot be expressed in a generalized
medium of exchange such as money. Social exchange proceeds by a process
that is closest to a system of barter. If, for instance, you provide me with
some important information and I have no information which you need,
I may invite you home to dinner to discharge my obligation. In this case
a dinner has been exchanged for a particular piece of information on the
old principle that "one good deed deserves another." In other words, the
"price" of the information was the dinner, including both the cost of
the food and the time involved. Some exchanges are simpler than this.
Gossip is a case of simple information exchange. But many exchanges are
a good deal more complicated as in the case, for example, of the average
friendship where there is constant and complex interchange of many
different kinds of resources and where the process of accounting may be
anything but exact. Where there is constant interchange, it becomes more
difficult to specify the "value" of the multiple ideas, information services,
and objects passed back and forth among the participants.

Nevertheless, the usefulness of the concept of exchange outweighs the
difficulties involved, and progress has been made in studying the exchange
of resources in a systematic way. We will carry through the threefold
scheme for understanding interpersonal behavior over into this area and
distinguish between affective resources, work resources, and power resources.

Types of resource processing

Affective exchange is, by definition, the basic process in primary groups.
Affective resources are, therefore, extremely important to the development
and continuance of primary relationships. Affective resources are directly

"consumable" and are valued for their own sake rather than as means to other ends. Affection, support, love, and sex are typical affective resources, and they have in common the fact that they cannot be "stockpiled" for the future or transformed into some other commodity. They are relatively scarce in that continual demand for them soon dries up the source.

Primary groups exist, at least in part, for the emotional satisfaction that group members can achieve through interpersonal relationships. The ability to provide such emotional satisfaction to others through the possession of desired attributes, the dispensing of love and support, and the manipulation of affective symbols is an important source of status in primary groups. The adolescent girl who has an attractive figure has an important affective resource for enhancing her relative status in the peer group. If she can also dance well, she possesses another resource—a skill—which further enhances her status. If she can afford attractive clothes, she has even more affective resources—objects. And, if in addition, she can effectively use the current romantic conceptual images—cultural objects—her success is assured. But the dispensing of affection, support, or prestige is not necessarily the only or even the central affective resource. Particular groups, and most groups at some time, place value on other kinds of affective satisfaction. A group may value the expression of hostility over the receipt of affection and, in this case, the skill of effectively and appropriately focusing group hostility may be an important resource. A resource is not defined by some intrinsic characteristic but by the group's values and goals.

In this section we are concerned mainly with the *processing* of group resources. In chapter 2 we provided a theoretical background for a study of this in the affective sphere by outlining the importance of the psychological mechanism of projective identification with role specialists. These role specialists are responsible for directing the main currents of group emotion; they are the nodal points for the main affective interchanges underlying group solidarity. Different individuals bring differing emotional needs to the group and look for different kinds of emotional satisfaction. In a group where roles are differentiated, all members do not have to receive the same emotional rewards or make identical emotional contributions to maintain a similar level of emotional satisfaction. In fact, the greater the variety of emotional returns a group can offer, the more likely it is to retain and increase the emotional investment of group members. These emotional returns not only include the receipt of affection or support from others, but also the discharge of undesirable emotional tensions or the elimination of "negative resources," that is, undesired or undesirable personal characteristics.

The processing of affective resources in the group is often most clearly focused in the interchanges between affective specialists. A beginning in understanding the role of affective specialists was made by Freud in his

Group Psychology and the Analysis of the Ego,[53] but Freud did not progress beyond the idea of a single group "leader" as the focus of affective relations in the group. A major advance was made by Redl,[54] who wrote of the "central person," rather than the leader, and indicated that by this term he meant the person around whom group formative processes take place, who crystallizes group formation through his ability to focus the emotional drives of group members. Redl distinguished ten role types, each of which could act as a catalyst for group formation. These were roles such as the seducer, the tyrant, or the organizer. Redl's most valuable contribution lies in his analysis of the reciprocity in the relations between the central person and the other group members. In each case, the central person provides affective resources valued by the group members and the group members provide him with another affective reward. The "central person as love object" may be used as an example : "There is a group of sixteen-year-old girls in a class of a girls' high school. In charge of them is a male teacher—young, attractive but narcissistic enough so that they are not too frightened sexually from the outset. It is known that in such cases 'the whole class falls in love with him'." [55]

Here the affective resource possessed by the teacher is a personal characteristic—his sexual masculinity; the resource exchanged his sexualized feminine affection. The personal needs of the incumbents of the counter positions are so complementary that they interlock in an exchange that sets the tone of the group.

In his analysis of this and other cases of affective exchange, Redl focused on the patterns which are always of this kind, that is, all group members relating uniformly to one central person. In doing this, Redl elaborated on Freud's earlier work. But such a notion does not help explain a situation where the interpersonal needs of group members vary from one member to another, or where there is a marked shift in member needs.

Mann did much to remedy these defects.[56] He studied changes in the relationships between the members and formal leaders of four self-analytic groups. He distinguished six major changes in the predominant mode of relating to the leader and designated these phases as : initial complaining, premature enactment, confrontation, internalization, separation, and terminal review. But Mann made a very close and detailed analysis of differences between members in the way each behaved toward the leader and showed how modes of relating change at these major points of group development. For instance :

During the initial complaining phase tension develops between those who are urging the group to see the new situation in terms of nurturance and control themes and those who are pressing for the centrality of the competence theme. Furthermore, sub-groups and antipathies develop over the appropriate strategy to employ, even holding constant thematic construction of the member-leader relationship.[57]

There are times when a strong coincidence of intense and similar inter-personal needs creates the simple kinds of exchange relationships described by Redl. However, the more usual situation is one of variant needs and a struggle to establish and consolidate more than one kind of affective exchange. Mann's study traces the history of this struggle over the life of four self-analytic groups and gives a new, but appropriate emphasis to the parts played by cliques and individuals in establishing predominant types of exchange.

My own study of self-analytic groups complicates the analysis of exchange relationships in another way.[58] I have described the central affective exchanges as occurring between a number of central persons rather than a single group leader or focal person. In self-analytic groups, the pattern of relationships between these projective specialists seems to remain relatively constant over time, but the emphasis on particular relationships among the total set may vary considerably from one time to another. Consequently, affective interchange is studied through an analysis of the central sets of reciprocal, affective relationships between these role specialists. However, as the resources exchanged are not concrete objects but are symbolic in nature, the meaning of these symbols to those involved has to be taken into account.

Power resources can be regarded as those objects—items of information, personal characteristics, and skills—which are relevant to the "managerial" sub-system of the group. Formally designated authority can also be a power resource. Possession of a power resource contributes to a member's ability to control and coordinate group action. As noted earlier in this chapter, a person's total power resources define his power base but do not necessarily reflect his effective power in the group. Exchanges which involve influence, dominance, and submission are those which carry power resources. Influence processes are often mutual, with A influencing B and B influencing A. In this regard, an interesting case of exchange occurs where power resources of different kinds are traded in order to enhance the power potential of both trading parties. This kind of behavior is most characteristic of the cabal where, for instance, A may give B information while B may give A the benefit of his skill. The result is that the power of both is enhanced. Thus the trading of different power resources leads to a coalition which can form a new center of power in the group.

A work resource is valued by group members because of its contribution to task achievement. For instance, the skill of carpentry is a work resource in a building team. Work resources contribute to the production system of the group, and their exchange and transformation contributes to the central "secondary" functions of the system. In the case of a peer group, these secondary functions may be the socialization of members into the class structure; in the case of the cabal they may be the increase in political power of the cabal and its members; or in the case of the industrial work group, they may be the earning of a regular minimum wage plus bonuses. Work resources are defined by the secondary goals of the group and may vary from such concrete commodities as tools and physical energy to intangibles such as ideas and creative imagination.

The analysis of resource processing

As with most other areas of group life, what people do and what people say are the two basic sources of information about the kinds of resources which are valued in the group. We shall concentrate first on methods of analyzing the resource-oriented behavior of group members.

A simple, but effective, method of tracing exchange relationships in an industrial work group has been employed by Zaleznik.[59] Zaleznik noticed that, during work hours, the men called upon one another for help or for the loan of tools. These requests were relatively infrequent so that Zaleznik did not attempt to collect quantitative data. He simply recorded

Figure 8.4: Pattern of interactions helping and lending tools

Requested help or borrowed tools

	Axel	Ron	Steve	George	Jim	Charlie	Marc	Vito	Bruce	Larry	Luke	Paul	Nick	Hal
Axel			×											
Ron					×		×	×	×	×	×	×	×	×
Steve										×				×
George														
Jim														
Charlie														
Marc					×						×			
Vito														
Bruce														
Larry													×	×
Luke														
Paul														
Nick														×
Hal													×	

(row label at left: **Gave help or loaned tools**)

Reprinted from A. Zaleznik, *Worker Satisfaction and Development* (Boston: Harvard Univ. Div. of Research, Grad. School of Bus. Admin, 1956), p. 32.

whether or not such exchanges occurred. Figure 8.4 is a matrix reproduced from Zaleznik's account. The names of all men in the shop are listed
on both axes in order of formal job classification and pay.

Zaleznik makes the following analysis of this matrix :

Ron gave help and loaned tools to more people than anyone else in the
shop. Ron was one of the top machinists in the shop, rating behind only
Axel in rate of pay, but on a par with Steve, George, and Jim. He was also
a Negro, one of four in the shop. We can observe also that not everyone
asked Ron for help or tools and that those who did were mainly operators.
In fact, all the operators turned to Ron for help or tools at one time or another.
Only a few machinists did so, however, Axel, George, and Charlie never asked
any one of the workers for help or tools, and Steve sought help only occasionally.
When Steve did seek help, he turned to Axel. . . .[60]

We can see that in this situation the pattern of resource processing
complements and reinforces the status structure of the group. Seeking help
or tools from another lowers or reinforces a relatively low status *vis a vis*
the person from whom help is sought. The offer of help, when accepted,
has the effect of raising one's status or reinforcing a superior status. In
the case of many interactions in this setting, the task resource sought by
group members was a superior skill possessed by Ron. As Zaleznik notes :

Almost all requests for help or tools directed toward Ron and toward Steve came
with the implication of a teacher-learner relationship. To illustrate, Larry had
difficulty honing the bore of a cylindrical piece; the piece would not move freely.
He called Ron over and showed him the work. Ron took over the machine, made
some adjustments and corrected the difficulty. He explained what he thought was
wrong and why he had made the particular adjustments. Ron stayed with Larry
for a few minutes after he had made the adjustments to see if Larry could carry
on alone.[61]

Zaleznik concludes, after reviewing many such incidents, that Ron's
position as informal leader was established and reinforced by the frequent
requests for help addressed to him. This is clear case of resource exchange
despite the fact that Ron appears to be "giving" away advice and help.
He receives, in fact, an important power resource that he can use if he
wishes, on future occasions. That the exchange is sensed by those in the
group is indicated by the fact that those members of the group nearest
to Ron in status are the most reluctant to seek his help. In at least one case,
one high status member found it necessary to do this but attempted to
disguise the consultation as a joke.

Zaleznik's use of this simple measure of exchange relationships has
some limitations, as he himself points out. The data in the matrix does not
show the frequencies with which the tools were borrowed and does not
indicate cases where help was sought but not given. More importantly, it

does not indicate the kind of resource sought, whether tool, physical labor, or machining skill. In discussing the matrix, Zaleznik supplies the reader with much of this information, but one would like a more systematic way to score and record these other important components of the exchange relationship.

In a recent contribution, Longabaugh has developed a category system for coding interpersonal behavior as social exchange.[62] The scheme is designed to record just those kinds of data we have discussed. A distinction is made between "resources" and "modalities." Resources are defined as "things which people value in one another and attempt to secure from one another." Modalities are defined as interaction modes peculiar to the exchange relationship; more concretely they are seeking, offering, and depriving by taking away or withholding, and accepting or not accepting by ignoring or rejection. The coding scheme categorizes interpersonal behavior in terms of its salient mode(s) and resource(s). In defining his basic unit, Longabaugh opts for what we would call an "organic" rather than a "mechanical" unit of exchange.

Tracing the fate of resources becomes possible when the sequence of acts in which the resource remains salient is categorized in terms of modes. If a resource is offered it must either be accepted or not accepted. If a resource is taken away, this loss must be either accepted or not accepted. Offerings and deprivations may occur without prior seekings. A resource may be offered spontaneously (without being previously salient). A resource deprivation can occur spontaneously when a resource is taken from another person without first being offered by that person. Acceptance or non-acceptance can only occur in response to prior offerings or deprivations.

By tracing the initial saliency of the resource and its fate we record who is perceived to possess the resource (to possess a resource is to have it within one's control); under what circumstances it passes to someone else; whether resources pass in the other direction as well; and under what circumstances these events occur.[63]

It is interesting to note that Longabaugh classifies resources into three categories : control, support, and information. These seem to be closely related to our three dimensions of power, affect, and task resources, respectively. In his original contribution to the development of this method, Longabaugh explains how scores on this system can be used to construct indices first of the rate of exchange between pairs of members and, second of the relative amount of the salient resources possessed by each member. The operational measure of exchange is "the rate resource acceptance of both of the members (of the interchange) for the time observed," [64] where resource acceptance equals the sum of resources offered by A to B, plus the sum of resources offered by B to A, minus the sum of ignorings and rejections or resources offered by B to A and A to B. A measure of the relative deprivation of resources is suggested as the best measure of actual resource distribution.

Longabaugh's scheme provides us with ways to study resource processing at first hand and to classify resources systematically in a way compatible with our basic three dimensional typology. It allows us to make a description of the dynamics of resource distribution; to see more clearly who gets what from whom, and then to raise the question "why?" The method is applicable also to the interrelationship of the group with its environment. The same kind of analysis can be used to describe the relationships between key mediating roles and the most significant people and groups in the social environment of the target group. In this way, the flow of resources from the environment to the group and from the group to its environment can be charted. The relative value placed by the larger system on the target group's "exports" will be a major factor in determining the prestige of the target group. Conversely, to the extent that the target group is dependent on the larger system for the resources it considers vital, its autonomy will be substantially reduced.

We have discussed two methods of observing processes of exchange in the primary group. But such observational methods are only one general approach to understanding the nature and value of resources. The other main approach is supplied by content analysis. We have already indicated that resources are defined by the values of the group. They are the objects of valuation. In our discussion of values, we indicated how the researcher can go about charting the value structures of groups. We outlined a method for determining the value hierarchy in a group and noted that, at the levels of greatest specificity, in value statements, there is an identification of resources. These are, of course, resources which are consciously perceived by the group members themselves. This will be a narrower range of resources than those identified through observational procedures, for a great deal of resource processing in informal groups goes on automatically and unconsciously. In particular, where there is a formal and explicit task for the group, task resources are usually explicitly defined and known. A reference to the data provided on the value structure of a bank will show that those resources which are mentioned by officers in interviews are almost solely task-related resources. The identification by content analysis of valued objects, types of information, personal characteristics, and skills is an important part of understanding resource processing, but it provides only partial information.

Notes

1 Karl Deutsch, *The Nerves of Government* (New York: Free Press, 1963).
2 Robert Dahl, *Modern Political Analysis* (Englewood Cliffs, N.J.: Prentice-Hall, 1963), p. 47.

[3] Dorwin Cartwright, "Influence, Leadership, Control," in *Handbook of Organizations,* ed., James March (Chicago: Rand McNally, 1965), p. 22.

[4] Talcott Parsons, *Sociological Theory and Modern Society* (New York: Free Press, 1967), chap. 11, pp. 297–354.

[5] Dahl, *Modern Political Analysis,* pp. 53–4.

[6] Cartwright, "Influence, Leadership, Control," pp. 4–5.

[7] Ronald Lippitt, Norman Polansky, Fritz Redl, and Sidney Rosen, "The Dynamics of Power: A Field Study of Social Influence in Groups of Children," *Human Relations,* vol. 5, no. 2 (1952): 37–64.

[8] James G. March, "Influence Measurement in Experimental and Semi-Experimental Groups," *Sociometry,* vol. 19 (1956): 260–71.

[9] Theodore Mills, "Power Relations in Three Person Groups," *American Sociological Review,* vol. 18 (August 1953): 351–57.

[10] Ronald Lippitt, et al., "The Dynamics of Power."

[11] R. H. Simpson, "A Study of Those Who Influence and Those Who are Influenced in Discussion" (New York: Contributions to Education, no. 748, Teachers College, Columbia University, 1938).

[12] Fred L. Strodtbeck, "Husband–Wife Interaction Over Revealed Differences," *American Sociological Review,* vol. 16 (August 1951): 468–73.

[13] Walter Blanchard, "The Group Process in Gang Rape," *Journal of Social Psychology,* vol. 49 (May 1959): 259–66. .

[14] E. P. Torrance, "Some Consequences of Power Differences on Decisionmaking in Permanent and Temporary 3-man groups" (Wash.: Research Studies, vol. 22, Washington State College, 1954): 130–40.

[15] Robert F. Bales and Philip Slater, "Role Differentiation in Small Decisionmaking Groups," in *Family Socialization and Interaction Process,* Talcott Parsons and Robert Bales (Glencoe, Ill.: Free Press, 1955).

[16] P. G. Herbst, "Task Differentiation of Husband and Wife in Family Activities," in *A Modern Introduction to the Family,* Norman W. Bell and Ezra F. Vogel (Glencoe, Ill.: Free Press, 1960), p.341.

[17] Paul F. Secord and Carl W. Backman, *Social Psychology* (New York: McGraw Hill, 1964), p. 239.

[18] Helen Jennings, "Differentiation of the Psyche-group and the Socio-group," *Sociometry,* vol. 10, no. 1 (1947): 71–9.

[19] F. Käupl Taylor, "Quantitative Evaluation of Psychosocial Phenomena in Small Groups," *Journal of Mental Science,* vol. 98 (October 1951): 698.

[20] George Homans, *Social Behavior: Its Elementary Forms* (New York: Harcourt Brace, 1961), pp. 120–307.

[21] Leslie D. Zeleny, "Status: Its Measurement and Control in Education," *Sociometry,* vol. 4 (May 1941): 193–204.

[22] Charlotte M. Fleming, ed., *Studies in the Social Psychology of Adolescence* (Routledge and Kegan Paul, London, 1957).

[23] Ibid., p. 110.

[24] Bales and Slater, "Role Differentiation in Small Decisionmaking Groups."

[25] Abraham Zaleznik and David Moment, *The Dynamics of Interpersonal Behavior* (New York: John Wiley, 1964), pp. 331–34.

[26] Allen Barton, "Measuring the Values of Individuals," in *Religious Education,* vol. 57 (1962): S–62—S–97.

[27] Emile Durkheim, *The Elementary Forms of the Religious Life* (New York: Free Press, 1965).

[28] Ibid.

[29] Florence Kluckholn, *Variations in Value Orientations* (Evanstown, Ill.: Row, Peterson and Co., 1961), pp. 96–102.

[30] William J. Catton, "A Theory of Value," *American Sociological Review,* vol. 24 (June 1959): 310–17.

[31] Clyde Kluckhohn, "Values and Value Orientations in the Theory of Action," in *Toward a General Theory of Action,* eds. Talcott Parsons and Edward Shils (Cambridge, Mass.: Harvard University Press, 1951).

32 Ethel Albert, "The Classification of Values," *American Anthropologist*, vol. 58 (1956): 221 ff.

33 Ibid., p. 225.

34 Ibid., p. 226.

35 Talcott Parsons, ed., *Theories of Society* (Glencoe, Ill.: Free Press, 1960), pp. 42–3.

36 Charles H. Cooley, *Social Organization* (New York: Charles Scribner's Sons, 1909).

37 Edward Shils, "Primordial, Personal, Sacred and Civil Ties," in *The Study of Society*, Peter Rose (New York: Random House, 1967), pp. 178–92.

38 Ibid., p. 190.

39 Bernard Berelson, Paul Lazarsfeld, and William McPhee, *Voting—A Study of Opinion Formation in a Presidential Campaign* (Chicago: University of Chicago Press, 1954).

40 Walter B. Miller, "Lower Class Culture as a Generating Milieu of Gang Delinquency," *Journal of Social Issues*, vol. 14, no. 3 (1958): 5–19.

41 James Short and Fred Strodtbeck, *Group Process and Gang Delinquency* (Chicago: University of Chicago Press, 1965).

42 *See* Charles E. Osgood, George G. Suci, and Percy H. Tannenbaum, *The Measurement of Meaning* (Urbana, Ill.: University of Illinois Press, 1957).

43 Short and Strodtbeck, *Group Process*, pp. 50–1.

44 Ibid., p. 76.

45 Irving Spergel, *Racketville, Slumtown, Haulberg* (Chicago: University of Chicago Press, 1964).

46 Charles Orth, *Social Structure and Learning Climate* (Boston, Mass.: Division of Research, Graduate School of Business Administration, Harvard University, 1963).

47 Muzafer and Carolyn Sherif, *Reference Groups* (New York: Harper and Row, 1964).

48 George Lombard, *Behavior in a Selling Group* (Boston, Mass.: Division of Research, Graduate School of Business Administration, Harvard University, 1955).

49 George Homans, "Social Behavior as Exchange," *American Journal of Sociology*, vol. 53 (1958): 597–606; George Homans, *Social Behavior: Its Elementary Forms* (New York: Harcourt, Brace, 1961); Peter Blau, *Exchange and Power in Social Life* (New York: John Wiley, 1964); John W. Thibaut and Harold H. Kelley, *The Social Psychology of Groups* (New York: John Wiley, 1959); John Whiting, "Resource Mediation and Learning by Identification," in *Personality Development in Children*, eds. Ira Iscoe and Harold Stevenson (Austin, Tex.: University of Texas Press, 1960).

50 Blau, "Exchange and Power," p. 137.

51 George Homans, *Social Behavior*, p. 61.

52 Richard Longabaugh, "A Category System for Coding Interpersonal Behavior as Social Exchange," *Sociometry*, vol. 26 (September 1963): 322.

53 Sigmund Freud, *Group Psychology and the Analysis of the Ego*, trans. J. Strachy (London: Hogarth Press, 1922).

54 Fritz Redl, "Group Emotion and Leadership," *Psychiatry*, vol. 5 (1942): 573–96.

55 Fritz Redl, in "Group Emotion and Leadership," in *Small Groups: Studies in Social Interaction*, eds., A. Paul Hare, Edward Borgatta, and Robert F. Bales (New York: Knopf, 1955), p. 79.

56 Richard Mann, *Interpersonal Styles and Group Development* (New York: John Wiley, 1967).

57 Ibid., p.154.

58 Dexter C. Dunphy, "Social Change In Self-Analytic Groups," in *The General Inquirer*, Philip Stone, Dexter C. Dunphy, Marshall Smith, and Daniel Ogilvie (Cambridge, Mass.: M.I.T. Press, 1966), pp. 287–340.

59 Abraham Zaleznik, *Worker Satisfaction and Development* (Boston, Mass.: Division of Research, Graduate School of Business Administration, Harvard University, 1956).

60 Ibid., p. 33.
61 Ibid., p. 34.
62 Longabaugh, "A Category System for Coding Interpersonal Behavior."
63 Ibid., p. 323.
64 Ibid., p. 334.

chapter 9

Group integration and disintegration

We have discussed how the researcher can distinguish differentiated structures and processes within the primary group. There remains the final task of identifying how the various parts or units of a small social system are linked together into a coordinated whole. The term integration refers to the articulation of the various units with each other so that they form the kind of organized and interdependent whole which can be legitimately regarded as a system. As a process, integration also refers to the series of events which lead to the development of a unified system. Thus integration refers both to the process of units assuming a regularized and coordinated set of relationships with each other and to the resultant state. Integration implies that the whole which is formed from these units is one that functions with minimal interference and conflict between units. The degree to which this is true is the measure of the kind and amount of integration of a particular group.

In order to avoid the most frequent fallacy of functionalism, it should be remembered that disintegration is also a feature of groups. Disintegration as a process has been neglected in most studies, but all primary groups eventually disintegrate completely and in most groups there are periods of major distintegration followed by reintegration. For example, adolescent peer groups undergo major structural and cultural metamorphoses over the course of their member's adolescent years. It is important to realize that conflict, disharmony, and the loss of integral parts of the system are as important as their opposites.

Internal integration

Integration can result from the explicit rational techniques of formal organization. Since formal integration is a conscious contrivance, constant effort is required to maintain it. Integration of this kind is a result of the setting of official goals, the delegation of formal authority, and coordination through explicit procedural rules backed by visible sanctions. But integration in a primary group more usually results from unplanned processes growing out of uncontrived interaction. Informal integration of this kind can be observed in the emotional affinity between group members, in an informal status consensus, in the sharing of goals and values, and in the emergence of symbols and myths which interpret the meaning of group action.

Traditional approaches to group integration

A primary group is characterized by spontaneous emotional relationships. We have pointed out that such relationships are sustained and valued mainly because of intrinsic rewards gained from interaction. A primary relation is an end in itself, whereas a secondary relation is dominated by utility. Not surprisingly, therefore, small group studies have generally equated integration with either the level of personal attraction between group members or to the group as a whole, or with the level of satisfaction with the group expressed by individual members.

The term "cohesiveness" is frequently used rather than "integration," and there is certainly a general appeal in the idea of comparing tightly knit groups with loosely knit groups. There has been a persistent feeling among researchers that some measure of cohesiveness can be used to predict a variety of other group characteristics. For instance, studies have indicated that the activities of highly cohesive groups are generally regarded as more rewarding, that participation in cohesive groups is more equal and intense, and that rates of voluntary absenteeism and turnover are less in such groups.

Festinger originally defined cohesiveness as "the total field of forces which acts on the members to remain in the group." [1] However, problems appear as soon as attempts are made to express this formula in operational terms. How does one measure "the total field of forces?" Unfortunately, there is no TFF instrument to tap this phenomenon, although a number of attempts have been made to approximate a reasonable measure of cohesiveness.

The earliest instruments employed were sociometric in character. The measure of cohesion was the ratio of the number of friendship choices made within a particular group to the number of friendship choices made outside a group. A high ratio was interpreted as indicating high cohesiveness, a low ratio as indicating low cohesiveness. [2] Obviously such a measure takes into account the centrality of personal ties in primary groups.

Another general approach has been to define cohesiveness as an aggregate, or average, of the attraction to the group expressed by members. Schachter devised a questionnaire that emphasized this approach. After experimental situations, his subjects were asked :

1. Do you want to remain a member of this group?
2. How often do you think this group should meet?
3. If enough members decide not to stay so that it seems the group may discontinue, would you like the chance to persuade others to stay?[3]

A similar approach was employed by Seashore in studying the cohesiveness of work groups in a factory.[4] The three sets of questions used to measure cohesiveness were designed to show the extent to which members felt they "belonged" to their groups, their desire to remain in them, and their general estimation of their own work group in relation to others. Specifically the questions were :

1. Do you feel that you are really a part of your work group?
——— Really a part of my work group.
——— Included in most ways.
——— Included in some ways, but not in others.
——— Don't feel I really belong.
——— Don't work with any one group of people.
——— Not ascertained.
2. If you had a chance to do the same kind of work for the same pay, in another work group, how would you feel about moving?
——— Would want very much to move.
——— Would rather move than stay where I am.
——— Would make no difference to me.
——— Would rather stay than move.
——— Would want very much to stay where I am.
——— Not ascertained.
3. How does your work group compare with other work groups at Midwest on each of the following points?

	Better than most	About the same as most	Not as good as most	Not ascertained
The way men get along together	———	———	———	———
The way men stick together	———	———	———	———
The way men help each other on the job	———	———	———	———

Gross studied informal groups of from two to four enlisted men at an air force base, and used as measures of cohesiveness, the degree of liking between the men and the extent to which they expressed a wish to correspond with each other after leaving the air force.[5] He added, however, a direct measure of association—frequency of association during thirty-five meals—to supplement the more subjective responses. This method included the real as well as the perceived and desired association as criteria for cohesiveness.

The proliferation of different measures of the same concept raises the question of validity : do all these methods really measure the same thing? Bernice Eisman attempted to test this by interrelating five operational measures of cohesiveness.[6] The measures were :

1. Sociometric index based on friendship.
2. Direct rating of group attractiveness.
3. Average number of reasons given by members for belonging to the group.
4. Number of same reasons for belonging given by a majority of members.
5. Degree of similarity among members' values.

The results were disheartening. The rank correlation coefficients among the five measures revealed no significant relationships and Eisman interpreted the results as supporting growing criticism of the usefulness of the concept. (Ramuz-Nienhuis and Van Bergen's research subsequently corroborated Eisman's findings.)[7] Obviously cohesiveness is an attractive concept, but it is equally obvious that social scientists are unclear about exactly what it refers to. Can anything be done to clarify the issue?

A redefinition of group integration
A major problem with all these approaches to studying group integration lies in their failure to distinguish *what* is being integrated. The integration of the individual into the group is not the same thing as the integration of the component parts of the group itself. The group is not made up of individuals alone—it has structures and substructures and distinctive cultural patterns. Group integration properly refers to the interrelation of these structures and patterns, and by contrast the problem of integrating people into the group is a boundary problem, as indicated in chapter 2. Personal attraction to the group and personal satisfaction with it are important, but they are not as central to understanding *group processes* as are other measures such as affective consensus and status and goal consensus. We shall consider these measures first, and then turn to the integration of the group with its external environment, that is, with other social groups, and last integration with the individual personalities of members will be discussed.

Structural integration or status consensus

Since affective ties are the central feature of the primary group, they should have the most influence on the integration of such groups. But a group may be considered well integrated even if there are strong expressions of hostility within it. Integration does not imply that all or most members express high levels of attraction to all or most other members, but simply that there exists a basic agreement on who is highly regarded, who is liked, who is ignored, and who is rejected. This is the affective consensus of a group.

Integration on the power dimension similarly results from the shared recognition of who has the most to who has the least power in the group. Such a consensus reduces conflict and maximizes coordination and conformity. Once again, integration is not affected by the relative distribution of power. Power does not need to be equally distributed for a group to be well integrated on this dimension, nor does a tendency for the equalization of power imply that the group is becoming "more integrated."

Integration on the task dimension stems from sharing a common view of what the task is and how the group can be best organized for it. The term "task" here is, of course, used in the widest sense to imply those instrumental activities engaged in by the group to fulfill its goals, whatever they may be. Maximized cooperation and minimized conflict in the pursuit of goals results from a situation where the various group goals are given a similar emphasis by the group members and where there is a similar estimate of the relative contribution of each member to the pursuit of these goals. These measures are termed "goal consensus" and "task contribution consensus," respectively. In the case of the task dimension, therefore, the relative agreement on the emphasis to be given to various goals as well as the relative rank of *members* on the dimension will be measured.

But how can the consensus be measured? The most generally used measure is Kendall's coefficient of concordance which measures the degree to which there is agreement between peers in their ranking of group members on one or more dimensions. This consensus can be investigated at any of the levels, that is, at the level of the evaluation of components —the amount to which group members agree on how an individual ranks on power-rank, affiliation-rank, etc.—or at the total evaluation level—the amount to which group members agree on an individual's overall importance and value. There are many reasons for a lack of consensus. In terms of the scheme set forth it might be any of the following :

a. Lack of consensus on comparison standards, that is, on norms and values.

b. Lack of consensus on which standards are primary or which components being used in a total evaluation are primary.

c. Lack of status congruence of people rated on standards.

d. Lack of agreement in judging individuals even though the same standards are being applied.

e. The group has not been active long enough to crystallize judgments.

Bales and Slater provide a succinct description of how status consensus is measured using Kendall's coefficient of concordance (W):

It is obtained from a matrix of rankings, each individual (placed in vertical order on a series of rows) ranking each individual (placed in horizontal order in a series of columns). The formula follows:

$$W = \frac{12S}{M(n^3 - n)}$$

S equals the sum of squares of the deviation of the column totals from the grand mean, and n equals the number of individuals ranked by M observers. In our rankings n = M, since everyone in the group ranks everyone including himself. When agreement is perfect, W is equal to one; when there is no agreement, W is equal to zero.[8]

Bales and Slater obtain the measure W from rankings on the questions, "Who had the best ideas?" and "Who did the most to guide discussion?" The two W's are averaged for each group and when the average index is .500 or above, the group is regarded as high on status consensus.

This particular measure gives a member's general *rank* in the group and the extent of agreement on it. But nothing is revealed about the extent to which group members share common expectations about the role performance of the occupant. It is possible for group members to agree on a particular member's social standing in the group, but to disagree wildly on what he should *do*. This can be an important source of conflict in a group as anyone knows who has heard children arguing, for example, about parental behavior. Confused or contradictory normative expectations are a key factor in disrupting the smooth functioning of groups and in creating opportunities for change in group patterns. Appropriate methods for measuring the degree of normative consensus have been presented by Gross in connection with his study of school superintendent and board groups.

The particular statistical measure favored by Gross uses the variance as a measure of the amount of agreement among the members in a group. The formula for computing the variance is:

$$V' = \frac{\sum_{i=1}^{N} (x_i^2)}{N - 1}$$

where x_i is the score assigned the response of individual i, x_i is this score in deviation form, and N is the number in the group.[9]

Gross goes on to apply this measure of role consensus to school boards and traces the relationship of this variable to other variables which might be expected to affect it. He tests, for example, the hypothesis that "the greater the homogeneity among or between position incumbents, the more consensus they will have on the expectations for their own and others' positions." [10] He finds that similarity in the educational attitudes of board members has no demonstrable relationship to consensus on role definition, but that similarity in political-economic attitudes does have a significant relationship to role consensus in this situation.

To conclude, a group structure can be characterized as highly integrated *internally* when the group is high on both status and role consensus. Conversely, its structure will be poorly integrated *internally* when it is low on these factors. However, a consideration of the *external* factors which can strongly affect the structural integration of a group will show that the effects of the factors we have just discussed can sometimes be nullified.

External integration

External integration centers around three issues similar to those around which internal integration centers, i.e., the integration of affective bonds, the problem of achieving environmental control, and the commonality of important goal-directed activities. These issues will be discussed in order under the headings of reference group commonality, autonomy, and enclosure.

Reference group commonality

Reference group commonality means similarity in the patterns of the external identifications of group members. Two rather well known facts highlight the investigation of external identifications : (1) a person need not be a member of a group in order for that group to influence him; (2) membership in a group does not necessarily mean that a person will be greatly influenced by the group. The study of the influence of non-membership groups has been called reference group theory. The study of the influence of membership groups has been included in reference group theory (though largely neglected by it) and has also been approached through the investigation of cohesiveness. The study of external identifications is concerned with the influence of external membership and nonmembership groups on the formation of the individual's attitudes and standards of judgment.

The investigation of reference groups has proved important in understanding subjective status, work satisfaction, the acquisition of new attitudes, and voting behavior. In studies of these issues, the psychological identification of the person with particular groups, roles, social categories, and individuals has been found to exercise a crucial influence on his behavior.

A reference group is any social unit which an individual takes as a frame of reference for self-evaluation and attitude formation. The term was coined by Hyman during an investigation of subjective socio-economic status.[11] Hyman discovered that the status which a person thinks of himself as having could not be predicted directly from such factors as education or income. To some degree subjective status was dependent on what social groups were used as a frame of judgment; frequently people used groups of which they were not members. For these reasons, Hyman found it helpful to distinguish between "membership groups" (groups in which a person is actually a member) and "reference groups" (groups which a person uses as a basis of comparison for self-appraisal). While a membership group might also be a reference group, not all reference groups are membership groups.

The term "reference group" is used to include more things than just what is usually thought of as a group. Merton has distinguished three types of social units that serve as reference "groups :"

1. The group proper: a number of people who interact with one another on the basis of established patterns, who define themselves as group members, and who are in turn defined by others (both fellow members and non-members) as members of the group.
2. Collectivities: people who have a sense of solidarity by virtue of sharing common values, and who have acquired an attendent sense of moral obligation to fulfill role expectation.
3. Social categories: aggregates of social statuses, the occupants of which are not in social interaction.[12]

One additional note should be added : Reference group, as originally applied, was used for both groups and individuals. Reference individuals have also been referred to as opinion leaders and models. Opinion leaders are specialized role performers in particular content areas. Depending on the area, both the opinion leaders and the persons they influence have different characteristics. In the area of fashion, younger women are usually leaders, whereas in the area of religion, older men with a great deal of education or charismatically endowed lay persons usually fulfill leadership roles. Opinion leaders have also been found :

1. To personify the values and attitudes of their group more closely than others.
2. To be more competent, that is, have more expert knowledge than others.
3. To be more centrally located in the communication hierarchy (Katz, 1957).

Models are generally of two kinds : personal and positional. At this level the reference individual is one with whom the person has "identified" in the classic psychological sense. Identification is the more or less lasting influence of one person on another, so that the identifier takes another person's attributes (perceived behavior, attitudes, traits, views) as a model for his own attributes. A personal model is one which the individual uses as a reference for particular kinds of personal qualities, be they undesirable or strongly desirable. Such qualities transcend any particular role context. A positional model is one which the individual uses as a reference for particular role attributes. Merton makes a very similar distinction. He limits the term reference individual to the personal model and calls the positional model a role model. A person identifying with Merton's reference individual attempts to approximate the behavior and values of that individual in several roles.

Kelly has pointed out that reference groups can serve two functions: the normative and the comparative.[13] The normative function is centered in the setting and enforcing of standards of conduct and belief. In this fashion, a reference group serves as a source of values and norms which the individual assimilates. The comparative function centers in the provision of a standard by which the individual evaluates himself and others. In this fashion a reference group serves as a means by which the individual can evaluate his position relative to that of others. It is this comparative functional type of reference group that has been stressed in the study of relative deprivation and distributive justice.

The reference group does not necessarily have to be a group to which the individual aspires to be a member. Newcomb has observed that adolescent rebellion may be regarded as a form of reference group behavior in which the parents serve as a *negative* reference group.[14] A negative reference group is one whose norms are rejected in favor of counternorms, whereas a positive reference group is one whose norms and standards are adopted as a frame of reference.

The primary tasks in the investigation of the influence of identifications on the cohesion of the group are to identify (1) the extent to which the group itself contains the significant figures or groups with whom members identify, and (2) the extent to which members *share* attitudes to those figures and groups with whom they identify.

Obviously a membership group which is itself the main reference group of members is more likely to be cohesive than one where all members aspire to belong to other groups. On the other hand, if members identify with others outside the group, but share the same pattern of external identification, this can be a source of affective unity in the group. The measure of the extent to which the membership group coincides with the reference groups of individuals can be ascertained by calculating the ratio of ingroup choices to outgroup choices, where choices can be of particular persons, classes of persons, or of groups.

The commonality of outgroup choices can be determined by examining outgroup choices to see whether they are focused on a small number of social objects or scattered over a wide range of external social objects. Consider the outgroup choices, for example, in Groups A and B illustrated in figure 9.1. Group A exhibits little uniformity in external choices while

Figure 9.1: Reference group commonality

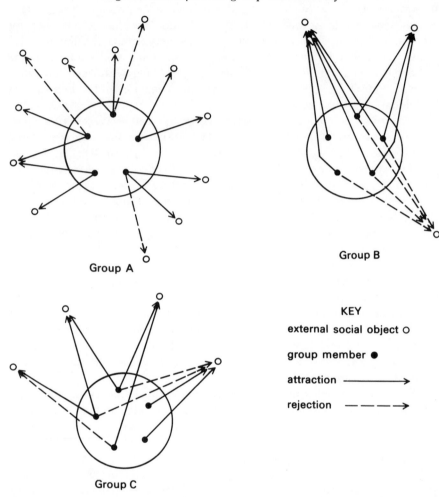

Group A

Group B

Group C

KEY

external social object ○

group member ●

attraction ——————→

rejection — — — —→

Group B exhibits a high degree of uniformity or commonality of choice. Another possibility is marked disagreement between members on the suitability of external social objects as reference figures. The reference figures chosen by some might be actually rejected by others in the group as illustrated in figure 9.1 by Group C. This is obviously a case where major conflict in the group is likely to occur.

An appropriate measure of reference group commonality which takes all these factors into account is as follows : Consider each external social object separately at first. For each, add the number of positive choices made, subtract from the sum the total number of rejections of that object, then multiply the resultant figure by itself. Then add across all persons chosen and rejected. The resultant score is an index of reference group commonality.

For the three groups illustrated in figure 9.1, this would give the following calculations and scores:

Group A : $8(1 \times 1) + 1(2 \times 2) + 3(1 \times 1) = 15$
Group B : $1(5 \times 5) + 1(3 \times 3) + 1(4 \times 4) = 50$
Group C : $1(0 \times 0) + 2(2 \times 2) + 1(0 \times 0) = 8$

Thus, although in Group C there are three external figures who are each chosen by two group members as against only one so chosen in Group A, the conflicting choices in Group C substantially reduce its integrative index.

Despite the amount of writing about reference groups, remarkably little systematic empirical work has been done on external reference groups. Very little systematic comparison of different groups has been made and, when it has been attempted, results have usually been presented in an impressionistic way. Spergel, for example, in his study of delinquent gangs in different areas asked the question of the gang members : "what is the occupation of the adult in your neighborhood whom you would most want to be like ten years from now?" [15] He found that in Racketville "most" of the delinquents identified with the role of racketeer whereas only one did in Haulberg. More precise measures might have allowed other researchers to make exact comparisons with gangs in entirely different neighborhoods.

Autonomy

"Autonomy" refers to the amount of control members perceive themselves as possessing over issues significantly affecting group activities and group life.

Autonomy refers to the ability of a system to make decisions and to respond independently of the decisions and will of other surrounding systems. This implies some degree of self-determination. The critical issue in autonomy is whether the location of control is centered inside the system, or whether outside groups control certain processes essential to the decisions and response patterns. Autonomy must be considered when demonstrating how the primary group under study is integrated with surrounding groups. To what extent do external persons or groups have to be taken into account by group members in their decision making? The limits of an autonomous group should be coterminous with a basic communication differential :

. . . The limits of an autonomous organization can be described in terms of a *communication differential*: among members or parts of an organization there should be more rapid and effective communication than with outsiders. This differential between internal and external communications may serve in turn as a means of identifying membership in borderline cases. A high differential between inner and outer communication may let an organization appear relatively cohesive vis-a-vis its social environment; whether such an organization will also be functionally or operationally cohesive, however, will depend far more on the effectiveness of inner communications measured against the tasks imposed on them, rather than upon the mere difference between inner and outer communications. If the former are poor, the fact that the latter are still poorer may serve as a test of separateness rather than of viability. Attempts to increase the distinctive identity of an organization, group, party, or people by reducing their communications to non-members, instead of increasing the communications among their members, may thus lead to superficial success but may eventually reveal themselves as attacks at the wrong end of the problem.

Within the organization, lesser communication differentials might provide a measurable test for the difference between "insiders" and ordinary members, and permit a study of cliques, influence, and corruption from this aspect.[16]

The following scale can be used to assess the extent to which group members perceive their group as being autonomous.

Q: How much freedom do you think your group has to make its own decisions about important matters affecting the group?

+2	+1	0	—1	—2
We are completely free to make our own decisions.	We have considerable freedom to make our own decisions.	We are free to make some decisions, but not others.	We have very little freedom to make our own decisions.	We must defer to others and obtain authorization.

Enclosure

External integration is affected also by the extent to which members are dependent on the group to pursue activities which they value. If the group possesses a near monopoly on important activities, then this is a strong lever to produce conformity. Of course, different groups preempt different activities; some religious groups, for example, preempt all religious activities, but no political ones. Therefore, group members should be asked to rank group activities according to how important the activities are to them, and then to indicate whether or not they carry on the activity elsewhere.

ACTIVITIES

Rank	Reverse rank	Carried on elsewhere?	Never (2)	Seldom (1)	Often (0)
1	6				
2	5				
3	4				
4	3				
5	2				
6	1				

The enclosure of the group is then the sum of the scores for all members of the reverse rank multiplied by the frequency weighting. Thus the group with the highest score is the most enclosed. A group with a score of zero would be the most open.

We have outlined a scheme for measuring the internal integration of a group through measures of status and role consensus, and its external integration through measures of reference group commonality, autonomy, and enclosure. This provides an approach to the analysis of structural integration. But well-integrated groups develop cultural products which reflect their integration and at the same time reinforce it.

The products of group integration: rituals, themes, and myths

The more time a group spends together, working and playing at various activities, the more likely it is that the members will come to share a common definition of their social situation. This common definition allows members to replicate, independently, the rankings of each other on various criteria suggested by the investigator. But this common definition of the situation also reveals itself more directly in the cultural life of the group. A commonly held definition results in repetitive, routine interaction patterns which reduce ambiguity and express group solidarity. Such patterns are called "rituals" because they perform functions similar to religious rituals, although they may not be so highly formalized.

Rituals

Ritual is the repetitive enactment or dramatization of certain aspects of group life. While the ritual is in some ways routinized behavior, it differs radically in character from the merely routine. The primary dimension in which ritual is distinguished is that of meaning. The meaning to members of a group all gathering at a regularly set time in a church for a service is quite different from what it would be if they were assembling on a railway station to catch the same train. Similarly, the act of eating a meal at regular times is usually routine, but the act of eating the wafer at holy communion is ritual. Both routine and ritual are regularized and repetitive to some degree. However, routine acts have been routinized for the sake of releasing attention for other occupations, while ritual acts have been routinized for the sake of fixing attention on certain central meanings of group life Ritual is a visual-verbal dramatization of central group sentiments; the researcher needs to identify which behavior patterns are ritualized and also to decipher the meaning of the rituals for group members. Typical rituals in small groups include initiation rites (fraternities), the annual office party (business), grace before meals and other elaborations of eating etiquette (families). Not much attention has been paid to rituals in small groups, and, even in anthropological field studies, ritual has generally been analyzed intuitively rather than in some systematic quantitative manner. Probably the most extensive and systematic study of primary group rituals has been made by Bossard and Boll.[17] These authors gathered accounts of rituals in 400 families and attempted to relate the observance of family rituals to the degree of family integration. After studying their data, the authors concluded that rituals served a number of functions in this regard. First, the observance of rituals implies a like-mindedness among family members and so ritual observance is an indication of a positive desire for the continuation of the family group. The development of rituals is usually a cooperative process and it develops a sense of group participation and family pride. Ritual also makes for predictability in behavior and so it also reduces strain and disorder. The authors conclude that "ritual is a relatively reliable index of family integration." [18] Some family rituals are daily affairs (grace before dinner), others may be observed annually (birthday parties), or irregularly (picnics). They have in common fixed sequences of patterned behavior, known to all group members, and they often have associated objects or symbols whose full meaning is known only to the group members. In my own family, for example, decorating the Christmas tree is an annual ritual which involves the whole family. Various treasured decorations are produced and unwrapped and each decoration has its own peculiar history which is reviewed as it is placed on the tree. Such a procedure recalls other Christmasses, the enjoyment associated with them, and the treasured relationships with close family friends. In such a case, to review is to renew, as Durkheim pointed out in his analysis of religious rituals.[19]

Blau shows the importance of the annual office Christmas party in the agencies which he studied.[20] These parties enhanced a sense of belonging among agency officials by bringing all of them together into one room in congenial circumstances; this was particularly important because some of them had little opportunity to interact in the normal course of duty. The social activities, particularly dancing, forced the officials to cross status lines and so de-emphasized status differentials. In addition, the group acts and songs, which were presented, vented stored up feelings about common frustrations and the underlying hostility of lower status groups to higher status groups was given expression in a jocular, legitimate way.

Initiation rituals are frequently used to form an initial bond of solidarity when new members are introduced into a group. This is particularly the case for exclusive, secretive, and deviant groups where the distinction between ingroup and outgroup is clearly defined and of crucial importance. Spergel observed one initiation ceremony in a slum gang which was said by the members themselves to be designed to instruct new recruits in the importance of taking punishment without "ratting" to the police. The ceremony marked the graduation of a "Vulture Tot" to the status of a "Vulture Junior :"

I saw a large number of fellows in the park. Louie, a Senior, was administering a certain rite referred to as "pink belly." He selected one of the Tots. The fellow lifted his shirt from his trousers, exposing his belly. Two other Seniors, Jackie and Ally, held the fellow on either side. Louie administered the slaps—at first slow and easy, then faster and harder. The skin turned light red, then purple. The fellow writhed in pain. Louie kept urging the boy, "Don't cry, control yourself." Louie stopped several times to give the boy a breather and encouraged him to maintain control.[21]

Spergel reports other ceremonies where members had to observe more extreme rituals—to fight other gang members, to join in a gang fight, to knife or shoot someone to prove their toughness and unflinching loyalty to the gang.

Because rituals express and enhance group solidarity, they present important and central aspects of the group in a dramatic and vivid manner. The analysis of ritual involves noting the central symbolic roles, the proto-typical actions, and the dominant emotions expressed. As the analysis of ritual is in these respects similar to the analysis of group themes and myths, we will proceed to discuss these first before elaborating a systematic method of analysis.

Group themes

Berelson defines a theme as "an assertion about a subject matter." [22] A theme is an existential statement about reality which is reiterated again and again in slightly variant forms. In the introduction to the method of content analysis, we gave an example of a typical small group theme (p. 129). Recently a number of studies of self-analytic groups have analyzed successive content themes taken up by groups in the course of the group development. Slater, for example, describes several of these and speculates on the reasons for their emergence at various stages of group evolution.[23] The first predominant theme described by Slater is expressed in various forms but may be summarized as :

Authority figure—manipulates/experiments on—group.

This is followed after some time by the emergence of a theme which may be summarized as :

Group—will exclude/destroy—authority figure.

Other themes follow as the groups evolve. Such themes are sometimes expressed directly in relation to the self-analytic group itself ("the group leader was using us for his books as a live experiment" [24]) and sometimes in displaced form through "irrelevant" stories introduced into group discussion ("Every time the rat presses a bar the experimenter drops in a piece of food, and the rat goes over and presses this bar when he's hungry . . ."[25]).

Group myths

A similar integrative function is performed by group myths. We dealt at some length in chapter 2 with the integrative role of group mythology. Group myths are most likely to arise in situations of conflict and tension, to represent the conflict and tension in symbolic terms and to embody a "solution." Like rituals, group myths express proto-typical images of the group, its social structure, and key social processes. Because myths are built up out of symbols with powerful emotional resonance for group members, they exert a controlling force on group action when re-expressed in full or partial form.

A myth is basically a story that allows people to exercise imaginative control (prediction) and understanding over part or all of their existence. Slater points to this in his discussion of the part played by myths in self-analytic groups :

For play, religion, and indeed all of culture may be seen as an attempt to create an improved little world, ordered and manageable, intellectually imaginable, with fixed rules and a finite set of outcomes, as an escape from and an insulation against the accidental, uncertain, infinite, chaotic, ambiguous, and inexorably indifferent and insensitive character of nature. Choice seems to frighten humans and when religious fantasies decay men employ clocks and other machines to regulate their movements.

Training groups have similar difficulty in accepting the idea of an un-programmed existence. They react with dread to the realization that nothing will happen unless they make it happen—that they are literally being left to their own devices, that there are no rules, no plan, no restraints, no explicit goals. They, too, construct myths which serve to deny the frightening responsibility and alone-ness which this state of affairs confers upon them.[26]

Group integration rests ultimately in cultural consensus. Until there is a degree of conscious or unconscious acceptance of some idea of what the group is, what its purpose or task is, and what kind of environment it has to work in, a great deal of energy and attention will have to be in-vested in the resolution of conflicts that occur. Members will feel uncertain and anxious about what is acceptable behavior and what is not because they have no idea of what the group is.

In the primary groups of modern society, myths often display much less scope than the myths of primitive cultures. The primitive myth has not had the competition of historical religion with its theology, or of em-pirical science with its rationalism. The primitive myth encompasses most of existence in a sweeping cosmology; its historical breadth begins at the dawn of all time and ends in the mystery of future life. The small group myth is usually more specific and more limited. Slater discusses a number of myths, arising in self-analytic groups, that reveal this limited quality.

The myth of the "scientific experiment" for example explains group events as all part of the manipulation of the situation by some experimenter. The reference of this myth is clearly less limited in what it is meant to explain than were the Babylonian myths of the origin of the universe. This is quite understandable. If myth helps to reduce anxiety in the face of unpredictable elements of life, the reduction of the limits of what is unpredictable will also reduce the limits myth need encompass in order to be satisfying. Basically, however, despite differences in scope, a myth is an idealized, universalized plot in which symbolic persons are portrayed as involved in some kind of personal or interpersonal conflict. The myth typically presents some kind of ideal resolution to the conflict.

In studying and comparing the myths that arise in primary groups, the researcher will want, therefore, to answer questions such as the following :

1. What social relationships are pictured—actors, action, relationship, conflict, emotion, conflict resolution? How are points of stress in the social structure expressed and imaginatively resolved in myth?
2. What stereotypic pictures are given of important actors in the group life and experience?
3. What forms of wish-fulfillment are expressed in the myths? How do the myths seem to tie into the personalities of group members?
4. How are the myths related to espoused value and normative systems? Are there conflicts? Do activities denied in group life get acted out in myths?
5. What aspects of reality are focused on by myth? Why are not the other aspects of reality expressed in myth?

The collection and analysis of group myths has generally been neglected in primary group studies, but brief descriptions of such myths occur here and there in the literature. In our introduction to content analysis in chapter 4, we gave an example of a myth prevalent among the members of a boys' gang in Sydney. Blau gives an instance of another myth, developed in a federal enforcement agency, which also functioned to reinforce group solidarity and exercise normative control. The myth he outlines centers around the group norm by which enforcement agents ignored the department regulation stipulating that bribe offers should be reported. One version of this myth was as follows :

I'll tell you of one case. . . . He did exactly what you say. He went into a bar with a guy who had promised him money. He was supposed to give it to him in the bar. Then the F.B.I. came in, and they actually came in just like in the movies. The sirens were blasting. They happened to be late, and could only get there on time by using their sirens. And they came in with their guns, asking "Who is offering a bribe here?" By that time, the client had said, "Excuse me, I have to go to the washroom," and left the place. You know what happened?

The F.B.I. didn't say it had made a mistake. It wrote to the Commissioner telling him that the agent had handled the case badly. So you can get into all kinds of trouble if you turn a man in.[27]

This example illustrates the moral imperative frequently contained within myths. They serve to define, rationalize, and reinforce the boundaries of action relevant to group interests. In the bank study described earlier, a number of members of the Trust Administration Committee reported a myth concerned with the early disbursement of funds in the estate of a deceased person. The committee was constantly under pressure to release funds to the family of the deceased as quickly as possible. But the bank was liable to pay outstanding bills presented for up to six months after the decease. Whenever there seemed to be some danger of officers over-identifying with the family involved and risking the security of the bank, a senior member would recall the occasion, years earlier, when funds were disbursed only days before the six month period expired and, on the day before the expiry date, a bill for half a million dollars was presented. The result had been a long and costly lawsuit.

Coding group myths
Because myths are stories, they require a complex form of content analysis. A simple tag-type analysis is insufficient because, for one thing, transitive relationships must be considered. Consequently, a contingency analysis is necessary—complex co-occurrences must be systematically examined.

A myth involves *actors,* with particular *personal qualities,* involved in a sequence of *actions* and *interactions* in situations of various kinds. The first step in myth analysis is, therefore, to make an image analysis of the main actors. First the individual actors are enumerated or, if there are quite a number of these, categories of actors may be examined (for example, male, female; young, old; hero/heroine, villain). The image of each actor is then examined by listing and classifying all the qualifiers applied to the particular actor. We will illustrate what we mean by analyzing a well-known set of myths—the Arthurian legends. We have chosen these to illustrate the method because of the lack of any systematic collection of myths from particular kinds of small groups. (We shall use for our analysis a short version of these legends written for children.[28] No doubt these are presented in a simplified form for children. However our aim here is not really to present a detailed analysis of the Arthurian legends but simply to show how the analysis of myth could proceed if we had a suitable corpus of myths from particular small groups.)

In these myths, central males are of two kinds, either heroes or villains, while central females are always presented as heroines. In addition either sex may be presented as innocents. The modifiers attached to these central types reveal that each has a consistent image of essential characteristics always present which may be embroidered with other optional characteristics that provide interest and variation. Figure 9.2 shows characteristics of both these kinds.

Figure 9.2: Characteristics of the arthurian central figures

Males		Females	
Heroes	Villains	Innocents	Heroines
virtuous (essential)	*evil* (essential)	*innocent* (essential)	*virtuous* (essential)
honest	cruel	innocent	pure
trustworthy	treacherous	good	chaste
faithful	wicked		good
honorable			
brave (essential)	*fierce* (essential)		*kind* (essential)
valiant	bloodthirsty		loving
daring	violent		gentle
courageous	terrible		tender
fearless			gracious
powerful (essential)	*powerful* (essential)	*weak* (essential)	
strong	strong	old	
mighty	powerful	poor	
powerful		young	
noble (optional)	*emotionally labile* (optional)		
princely	angry		
royal	ashamed		
exalted	enraged		
famous			
good-looking (optional)	*ugly* (optional)	*unprotected* (essential)	*beautiful* (essential)
handsome	ugly	alone	lovely
fair	deformed	traveller	fair
		pilgrim	beautiful

Thus we see that in these myths as presented for children there are good and bad men but only good women; that powerful men may be either virtuous or evil, but if they are evil they will not be good-looking and if virtuous they will not be ugly. While men such as old knights and pilgrims may be innocent and weak, these characteristics are more closely allied to ʾhe feminine image. A woman can be *both* heroine and an innocent, whereas a man must be a hero, or a villain, *or* an innocent.

But an image analysis of this kind omits the vital element of action, and action is central to the moving power of a myth. Having identified the character of the main *dramatis personae* in the myth, we must look next at the characteristic actions attributed to them. Table 9.1 lists the characteristic actions in the role types discussed, and also the transitive relationships between actors where these exist.

Table 9.1: Characteristic actions in the Arthurian legends

heroes—	help	king
heroes—	challenge, fight, conquer, kill or spare	villains
heroes—	save	innocents, heroines
heroes—	marry	heroines
heroes—	seek adventure, perform deeds of valor, move actively (ride, leap, hurry, rush), bleed, die bring peace	
villians—	deceive	innocents
villians—	rob, imprison, maltreat, hold for ransom, kill	innocents
villians—	fight, wound, kill	heroes
villians—	rebel, try to seize kingdom	
heroines—	recognize, encourage, succor, marry	heroes
heroines—	despise	villains
heroines—	move passively (sit, rise, walk)	
heroines—	express emotion (laugh, sing, hope)	

Innocents are not seen as active or as initiating action except for references to *travel*. Where actions are transitive they describe prototypical role relationships such as those between heroes and villains. These transitive relationships may be referred to as themes and the chief themes in these myths are : villains maltreat innocents; heroes rescue innocents; heroes conquer villains; heroes marry heroines.

An analysis of myth must also deal with a third major component— the situations within which action takes place between actors. Here again we can employ an image analysis similar to that employed for actors. We will not present this in detail here but simply note that the main situations are London Town. In London, the King's Court, The Cathedral and environs, and the tournament field receive considerable emphasis. Against London with its regulated and ordered life are contrasted Camelot and The Wilds. The Wilds are forested and mountainous areas in outlying parts of the kingdom frequented by robber barons, evil knights, and rebellious lords. Camelot represents a romantic outpost, sharing the danger of The Wilds but upholding the central authority of Church and State. One can go beyond this to analyze even such small features as the colors which are linked to these symbols to show how even these are selected systematically to reinforce the basic environmental images.

While the kinds of analysis suggested capture much of the "flavor" of the myths, they provide no way of examining the plot structure of the myths. It is this which links actors, actions, and situations together and gives them a fuller meaning. Plot structure depends on a sequential analysis which places these basic elements in order. Figure 9.3 provides the basic plot structure for the Arthurian myths. It will be seen that, like most myths, there is a tripartite plot structure consisting of : a prologue which gives the basic premises for action, the main action itself, and then a limited number of outcomes of which some can be used as alternatives.

Figure 9.3: Plot structure—Arthurian myths

PROLOGUE:

   A. Knight seeks adventure   optional

   B. Villain mistreats (robs, imprisons, etc.) innocents   essential

MAIN ACTION:

   C. Hero challenges villain   essential

   D. Hero and villain fight   essential

OUTCOME:

   E. Villain wounds hero

   F. Villain kills hero (if so, repeat to E with another hero)

        or   essential

   G. Hero, heroine rescues hero (if so, repeat to E with   essential

      same hero)   essential

        or

   H. Hero conquers villain

   I. Hero kills villain

        or   essential

   J. Hero spares villain

   K. Hero rescues innocents   optional

   L. Hero marries heroine   optional

Myth is the cornerstone of group cultural life. It takes the main symbols and themes of group culture and assembles them into a dramatic form which has a compelling emotional power for group members. We may speculate, for example, on the role of the Arthurian legends for the social situations out of which they emerged. It must have been tempting for a knight, in the absence of a powerful centralized authority, to set up an independent sphere of influence and to live by waylaying travelers and ravaging the countryside. Such action widely pursued would, and at times did, reduce the country to strife and chaos. It is not surprising, therefore, that stories of this kind emerged, emphasizing the morality of inner control, loyalty to the king, and to principles of elementary social justice. One wonders what part such stories played in the evolution of a centralized monarchy with legitimized control over the weapons of war.

We have chosen a literary example because of the absence of a corpus of myths gathered from contemporary primary groups. We hope, however, that our analysis will draw attention to the existence of myths in contemporary small group settings and to the important functions they play in group integration. They are certainly a source of insight to the researcher who can discern in them a simplified picture in miniature of the central social forces and tensions of the group.

Processes of socialization and disaffection

In groups which are fairly stable over extended periods, an important contribution to stability is made by regularized processes of socialization. Socialization processes operate not only to induct newcomers into a group, but also to promote individual members from one level of the status hierarchy to another. The case of the newcomer is, of course, the most obvious case of the operation of informal processes of training. The newcomer to a group is soon apprised of the fact that some of his customary patterns of behavior are regarded as inappropriate in this new setting, and group members take action to see that his behavior is appropriately modified. This is well illustrated in an incident I observed where a peer group leader (Brian) deliberately "remodeled" a friend (Clive) whom he was introducing into the group.

One evening before a party in Brian's home, I was present when Clive arrived. The party was informal and Clive had worn a sports suit, sports shirt and tie. When he walked in Brian remarked: "What are you all dressed up for? Hang your coat up in my cupboard." A little later he followed this with: "You've got a blue sports shirt on and your tie's blue too. Here, give me your tie and wear this red one." Having re-dressed him according to the acceptable pattern, Brian remarked: "That looks better; you should pass now."[29]

The most systematic analysis of the stages in the socialization of individuals into primary groups has been made by Parsons and Bales for the family.[30] In the family the child is not only a newcomer at the time of his birth but, in a sense, he is also a newcomer at each major stage of his personal development. At each level of maturation, he is expected to learn new roles so that he can be admitted into successively wider systems of social relationships within the family group. According to Parsons and Bales, the first stage of any socialization cycle is introduced by the socializing agent—for example, the mother—creating a crisis in the relationship by making new and unexpected demands on the child. The child responds with frustration and acts to correct the situation by reasserting the old behavior. When this is again not rewarded, the child reacts with aggression, anxiety, and regressive fantasies. These are essentially mechanisms designed to defend himself against change. The reaction of the socializing agent at this stage is most important. If socialization is to be effective, the socializer must tolerate, but not reward, such behavior, and at the same time increase the amount of emotional support for behavior in the range demanded. This allows the child to perceive more clearly what is demanded of him and to control his dependency and aggression in the interests of receiving more rewards. In this way he gradually internalizes the new role behaviors and integrates them into his evolving personality structure. As this occurs it is important that the socializing agent denies reciprocity to overtures based on the old form of the relationship. In the final phase, the socializing agent actively manipulates rewards and punishments to strengthen the child's growing identification and to extinguish the old responses. As time goes on, however, the child is increasingly able to do without these external props for they have become incorporated into his superego.

The above analysis was designed primarily to examine socialization in the family, but it seems capable of extending to other kinds of primary groups. It probably overemphasizes the resistance of the newcomer to socialization, for one of the outcomes of successful socialization experiences in childhood is an openness to personal growth, even a conscious seeking of it. In addition, in many primary groups there is not the same demand as in the family for a total restructuring of the personality. The description offered by Parsons and Bales also seems to play down the role of punishment in the socialization process, but in many primary groups, including the family, physical punishment plays quite an important part in the total system of punishments. In most groups and societies, when other methods of control fail, force is the ultimate deterrent and it has a way of clarifying issues.

Detailed studies of socialization into and through the systems of primary groups are not numerous. But some attention has been devoted to this, as our own earlier references to initiation rituals indicate quite clearly. But almost totally neglected both theoretically and practically is the process by which individuals become alienated and detached from primary groups. We refer to this process as "disaffection." One might imagine, for example, that with the current concern over the high divorce rate in our society there would be an analysis, comparable to that given the socialization of the child, of the processes of disaffection between spouses. Similarly, the current social emphasis on the control of deviant groups might be expected to lead to studies of the factors and phases underlying the breakup and dissolution of gangs, or of the disaffection of particular gang members. Standing almost alone, in treating the process of members withdrawing psychologically from membership groups, is Mills' study of a self-analytic group.[31] In this particular study, he emphasizes the importance of the fact that the group ends at a certain time of the year and he

studies the ways in which group members detach themselves psychologically from the group as it nears its end. It seems that we need more
descriptive studies of this kind, made both from direct observation of the
behavior of members as they become disaffected and from an analysis of
their views of their own changing relationship to the target group.

Conclusion

This book has proposed a model of the primary group, which is first a
working model, that is, it is designed to model the sequence of activities
performed by researchers as well as the intellectual constructs to be employed in analysis. In suggesting an operational sequence of research
activities for the field worker, we have drawn on our own experience and
have combed accounts written by other social scientists. The resulting
sequence of phases for field study makes good sense, but the extent of its
usefulness will be fully known only when other researchers have employed
the methods and techniques suggested in a variety of situations.

The model is also a *descriptive* model; that is, when the researcher
has carried through the sequence of activities suggested here, he will have a
thorough description of the central constants and the key processes in the
groups he is observing. Because we have not presented an *ad hoc* collection
of research techniques, the resulting picture will be a unified view of the
group. While admitting to incurable eclecticism, we have tried to systematize the concepts and methods we have gathered and developed so that
they are supplementary rather than unrelated or contradictory. One
method of achieving this end has been to keep before us the idea that a
small group is a microcosm of the larger society. We have tried, therefore,
to use variables basic to general social theory rather than employ only those
already familiar in the small group field. We have also included in the
book a substantial review of previous research on primary groups. Both
these features of the book should help the researcher to orient his work to
the prior research undertaken in this specific tradition and also to contemporary social theory as a whole.

The model is intended to be *comparative*. In our initial review of
primary group research we covered literature relating to primary groups of
all kinds. The model we have presented draws from the full range of
group types studied in prior research and it is meant to be useful in
studying the whole range of group types. The model is designed to facilitate
exact comparisons of one group with another. To employ the model in
this way is to advance the pace of systematic research into the character
of primary groups in a manner comparable to the advance achieved
in the analysis of secondary organizations when a comparative approach
was adopted. So far the study of primary groups has been characterized

by the sensitive, intuitive case study. This kind of approach can suggest hypotheses, but to fashion a viable theory, systematic comparisons of carefully designed variables observed in numbers of groups are needed. We will be satisfied if this book stimulates work along these lines.

This book represents an early step in the formation of a comprehensive methodology and theory for primary group analysis. It proposes a conceptual model but the model is unevenly developed. It is strongest on the side of structural analysis and weakest in those areas which relate to group culture. The weakness is unavoidable at this stage because most of the research methods and tested constructs derive from laboratory studies of transitory groups. Such groups have little chance to develop distinct subcultural variation. Nevertheless, the methods and concepts presented for the analysis of group culture show considerable promise for increasing the range of cultural variables that can be studied in a systematic fashion. Use of the proposed methods should lead to significant advances in our knowledge of the nature and power of such cultural phenomena as themes, images, and myths.

Finally, we hope that this book will stimulate numbers of social scientists to get out of their offices and airconditioned laboratories and into the field to confront the confusing and variable patterns of human relationships in continuing groups. Natural scientists have increasingly realized the limitations of animal studies carried out under laboratory conditions. The field of ethology is the latest expression of discontent with a simple-minded devotion to such studies and is a declaration of the value of close and careful observation of the social behavior of animals in their natural habitat. George Homans has observed that "some social scientists will do any mad thing rather that study men at first hand in their natural surroundings!" We hope that this book will help restore the legitimacy and increase the effectiveness of first-hand observation of the social behavior of humans in that most natural of human surroundings—the primary group. For we now have methods that make this possible, and are developing concepts to handle the complexity and variety of human behavior in groups. In due time, therefore, a theory of the primary group will assume its rightful place as part of general sociological theory.

Notes

[1] Leon Festinger, Stanley Schachter, and Kurt Back, *Social Pressures in Informal Groups* (Stanford, Calif.: Stanford University Press, 1950), p. 164.

[2] Ibid., and *see* William E. Martin, John G. Darley, and Neal Gross, "Studies in Group Behavior," *Educational and Psychological Measurement,* vol. 12 (1952): 533–53; Seth A. Fessenden, "An Index of Cohesiveness—Morale," *Sociometry,* vol. 16 (November 1953): 321–26.

[3] Stanley Schachter, "Deviation, Rejection and Communication," *Journal of Abnormal and Social Psychology,* vol. 46 (1951): 190–207.

4 Stanley Seashore, *Group Cohesiveness in the Industrial Work Group* (Ann Arbor, Mich.: University of Michigan Press, 1954).

5 Edward Gross, "Primary Functions of the Small Group," *American Journal of Sociology,* vol. 60 (July 1954): 24–30.

6 Bernice Eisman, "Some Operational Measures of Cohesiveness and Their Interrelations," *Human Relations,* vol. 12, no. 2 (1959): 183–89.

7 Wilhelmina Ramuz-Nienhuis and Annie Van Bergen, "Relations Between Some Components of Attraction-to-Group," *Human Relations,* vol. 13, no. 3 (August 1960): 271–77.

8 Robert F. Bales and Philip Slater, "Role Differentiation in Small Decision-making Groups," in *Family, Socialization and Interaction Process,* Talcott Parsons and Robert Bales (Glencoe, Ill.: Free Press, 1955).

9 Neal Gross, Ward S. Mason, and Alexander W. McEachern, *Explorations in Role Analysis* (New York: John Wiley, 1958), p. 168.

10 Ibid., p. 183.

11 Herbert H. Hyman, "The Psychology of Status," *Archives of Psychology* (Columbia University), vol. 38, no. 269 (1942).

12 Robert Merton, *Social Theory and Social Structure* (Glencoe, Ill.: Free Press, 1957).

13 Harold Kelly, "Two Functions of Reference Groups" in *Readings in Social Psychology,* Guy Swanson, Theodore Newcomb, and Eugene Hartley, eds., rev. ed., (New York: Holt, Rinehart and Winston, 1952).

14 Theodore Newcomb, *Personality and Social Change: Attitude Formation in a Student Community* (New York: Holt, Rinehart and Winston, 1943).

15 Irving Spergel, *Racketville, Slumtown, Haulburg* (Chicago: University of Chicago Press, 1964), p. 36.

16 Karl Deutsch, *The Nerves of Government* (Glencoe, Ill.: Free Press, 1963), pp. 205–06.

17 James H. Bossard and Eleanor S. Boll, *Ritual in Family Living* (Philadelphia: University of Pennsylvania Press, 1950).

18 Ibid., p. 203.

19 Emile Durkheim, *The Elementary Forms of the Religious Life* (New York: Free Press, 1965).

20 Peter Blau, *Dynamics of Bureaucracy* (Chicago: University of Chicago Press, 1963), pp. 166–67.

21 Ibid., p. 75.

22 Bernard Berelson, "Content Analysis," in *Handbook of Social Psychology,* ed., Gardner Lindzey, vol. 1 (Reading, Mass.: Addison-Wesley, 1954), p. 489.

23 Philip Slater, *Microcosm* (New York: John Wiley, 1966).

24 Ibid., p. 24.

25 Ibid., p. 13.

26 Ibid., pp. 12–3.

27 Peter Blau, *Dynamics of Bureaucracy,* p. 19.

28 *King Arthur and the Knights of the Round Table* (New York: Random House, 1954).

29 Dexter C. Dunphy, *Cliques, Crowds and Gangs* (Melbourne: Cheshire Publishing Pty., 1969), p. 142.

30 Ibid.

31 Theodore Mills, *Group Transformation: An Analysis of a Learning Group* (Englewood Cliffs, N.J.: Prentice Hall, 1964).

Name Index

Albert, Ethel, 238, 239, 247
Allport, Gordon, W., *90*
Angell, Robert C., 4
Arensberg, Conrad M., 180
Arsenian, John, 199

Backman, Carl, 226
Bain, Robert K., *156-157*
Baldwin, Alfred L., *127*
Bales, Robert F., 84, *85-86*, 87, 88, 105, 106, 107, 109, *171-172*, 220, 232, 270, *286-287*
Barker, Roger C., 30
Barton, Allen, *236-237*, 238
Bates, Alan P., 200
Benne, Kenneth, 199
Bennis, Warren G., *56-57*
Berelson, Bernard, 242, 279
Berrien, F. K., *91, 94*
Blanchard, Walter, *223-224*
Blau, Peter, *155, 157, 178,* 181, 253-254, 278, *281-282*
Blood, Robert O., *209-210*
Boll, Eleanor, 5, *278*
Bossard, James H., *278*
Bott, Elizabeth, *183-184*
Burns, Tom, 74

Cannon, W., 93
Carr, Lowell J., 4
Carter, L. F., *109*
Cartwright, Dorwin, *215-216*
Catton, William J., 238
Caudill, William, 22, 144
Chapanis, Alphonse, *81-83*
Chein, Isador, 90

Christensen, C. R., 21
Cloward, Richard A., 14, *60-61,* 62-72, *passim*
Cloyd, Jerry S., 200
Cohen, Albert K., *14-15*
Collier, R. M., *92*
Cooley, Charles Horton, *3-5,* 6, 7, 12, 47, 241
Cormie, Mary, 187
Couch, Arthur S., *109*

Dahl, Robert, 215, 216
Dalton, Melville, 74, *148*
Davis, Allison 17,
Decarie, Theeese G., *41-42*
Deutsch, Karl, *213-214*
Dewey, John, 11, 29
Dickson, William, 20
Dunphy, Dexter C., 16, 30-31, *109-110,* 117, 120, *130,* 153, *180-181,* 184, *203-204,* 206-207, 257, 286
Durkheim, Emile, *9-10,* 14, 20, *236,* 278

Eisman, Bernice, *268*
Erikson, Erik H., 40
Ezriel, Henry, *46*

Festinger, Leon, 144, *187,* 266
Flanders, Nell A., 105
Fleming, Charlotte M., *229-230*
Frazer, David 235n
Freud, Anna, 46
Freud, Sigmund, *10-11,* 16, 41, 53, 255-256; on projection, *46,* 47

Subject Index

Achievement: conflicts resolved by group role specialists, 55. *See also* Aspiration, Goal achievement

Adaptive problem. *See* Environment

Adolescence: social theories of, 15; socialization in, 17; studies of, 17; adolescent rebellion, 273. *See also* Youth culture

Adult peer groups, cliques, *17–19*, 34

Affectivity: stressed in "human relations" school, 22; in military units, *24–25*, 241; development among group members, *40–52;* influence of projective specialists on, *52–53;* in developmental group phases, 56, 120; effect of environment on, 59; as motivator, 63, 77; and group cohesion, 67, 269; in erratic groups, 69; in organizer groups, 75; as major dimension of interpersonal behavior, *110–112;* affective differentiation, 215; measurement of, 226; affective resources, 254–255; the affective specialist role, *255–256;* affective exchange, *256. See also* Affiliation, Approval, Emotional involvement, Emotional relationships, Loyalty

Affiliation: as category for scoring interpersonal behavior, *110–111;* measurement of observed affiliation, *229–230. See also* Approval, Affectivity, Emotional involvement, Emotional relationships, Loyalty

Age: gang, 14; clique, 15. *See also* Adolescence, Adult peer groups

Aggression. *See* Hostility

"Aggressor" role, *57–58,* 65, 69, *129,* 201

Alienation. *See* Control of secondary system, Frustration

Ambivalence, 57

American Sociological Society, 15

Anomie, 14

Apathetic groups, 61–62, 65, 66–68, 246

Approval, need for, 27, 42

"Arrivists," in upper class cliques, 18–19

Aspiration, success aspirations, 14, 62, 70. *See also* Achievement, Goal Achievement

Associations: voluntary, 7; formal, 18

Attention, distribution in group, 51, 57

Attitude: of workers to job, 21; of individuals in classroom group, 29; measurement, *127*

Authority: and youth revolt, 15; as problem in groups, *57;* as institutionalized power, *216–217;* formal authority, *219;* exercize of, 220; as a power resource, 257. *See also* Status

Authority figure, 26, 28, 31, *45,* 49, *56,* 57–58, 279–280

Automation: effects on organization, 23

Autonomy. *See* Group

Behavioral sequences, 44

Behavior setting analysis, 30

"Best-liked" man, role of, 197–198

Boundary: ego, *47–48;* group, *89–91,* 94, 96, *159–160*

Cabal, groups, 5, *65,* 73–74, 77, 153, 232, 246, 258

Category construction: need for generalized category system, *103–104;* common problems in, *104–109;* in content analysis, 120–126 *passim;* specific content categories, *131–137*

Centrality index, measure of power, 219–220

Charisma, *53,* 55, *68*